The Seeking

A Contemplative Approach to Mission and Pioneering

Ian J. Mobsby

scm press

Published in 2025 by SCM Press

Editorial office
3rd Floor, Invicta House,
110 Golden Lane,
London EC1Y OTG, UK

www.scmpress.co.uk

SCM Press is an imprint of Hymns Ancient & Modern Ltd
(a registered charity)

Hymns Ancient & Modern® is a registered trademark of
Hymns Ancient & Modern Ltd
13A Hellesdon Park Road, Norwich,
Norfolk NR6 5DR, UK

British Library Cataloguing in Publication data

A catalogue record for this book is available
from the British Library

ISBN: 978-0-334-06585-2

Typeset by Regent Typesetting
Printed and bound in Great Britain by
CPI Group (UK) Ltd

Contents

Acknowledgements   v

Introduction   1

**Part One: Why Do We Need a More Contemplative Model
and Approach to Christian Mission?**   5

  1 The Challenge of Living in a Post-Secular Market Society
    Context   7

  2 The Crisis of Personal Identity and the Rise of Spiritual Seeking
    and the 'Spiritual But Not Religious'   22

  3 How the 'Spiritual But Not Religious' Seek for Spirituality   45

Part Two: A Contemplative Theology and Model of Mission   71

  4 Developing a Missional Contemplative Theology   73

  5 Developing a Contemplative Model of Mission: 'God's
    Kenosis, Our Theosis'   106

Part Three: The Christian Contemplative Missional Journey   141

  6 Awakening: The Beginning of the Spiritual Journey   143

  7 Purgation: The Crisis Stage   163

  8 Illumination: The Insight Stage   177

  9 Union: The Transformation Stage   188

 10 Afterword   202

*Appendix 1 Script for the meditation group using an
adapted John Main Approach*   206

*Appendix 2 Contemplative Worship Service Liturgy
(adapted Anglican Version of the Service of the Word)*   210

References   214

In grateful memory of my mum, Jacqueline Mobsby, and my friend and fellow contemplative Christian, Simeon Barnes. Both have gifted me with much love, and both remain greatly missed by many.

Acknowledgements

My early exposure to the importance of the contemplative tradition and of mission with the 'Spiritual But Not Religious' (SBNR) goes right back to the 1990s and the writings and practices of Mike Riddell and Mark Pierson in the Alternative Worship Community 'Parallel Universe' in New Zealand. More recently, my interest was kindled and formed through my experiences of working with the Moot Community and the dynamic staff team of Vanessa Elston, Aaron Kennedy, Peter Johnson, Tim Dendy and Jonathan Spoor. These challenging times were the beginning of a particular focus to mission drawing on contemplative theology and spiritual practice. I am extremely grateful for the lessons learnt and the beginning of the research questions of the PhD thesis as a basis to this book. I am also grateful for the support of Bishop Jonathan Clark and Sandra Schloss as I wrestled with these same research questions when engaging with the SBNR in Peckham, south London in the context of the Parish of St Luke's Peckham and the Wellspring New Monastic Community.

Regarding the PhD thesis and research project on which this book is based: my thanks go to my current Diocesan Bishop, Susan Bell of the Diocese of Niagara in the Anglican Church of Canada, Canon Will Cookson, the previous Dean of Fresh Expressions and Pioneer Ministry, Jane Steen, formerly Archdeacon of Southwark and now Bishop, and Dean Mandy Ford, the former Director of the Diocesan Training Department, who all formerly worked for the Anglican Diocese of Southwark. I am grateful for the encouragement to research and develop the concept of a contemplative approach to mission. I am extremely grateful for my colleagues who helped form and co-facilitate the dialogue groups in the research, including Andrea Campanale, Aaron Kennedy, Simon Bubbs, Sheridan James and Vanessa Elston. Thanks also go to the 32 participants who were prepared to take part in the PhD study fieldwork and be so willing to share their lives and experiences.

I am particularly grateful for the support, guidance and wisdom of my long-suffering research supervisors, Dr Cathy Ross and Dr Nick Shepherd. Thanks also go to my recent colleagues at Christchurch

Blackfriars and the Blackfriars New Monastic Community as we continued to explore contemplative approaches to mission, particularly my friend and colleague the Revd John Henry, and Jenny O'Neill for proof reading the PhD thesis. Thanks also to my good friend the Revd Louis Darrant for his reading feedback for this book.

My thanks are also due to the following organizations and Trusts for the various funding needs of the PhD research study that informs this book: to the Diocese of Southwark for the costs of PhD study fees and the costs of publicity and the trialling of five of the dialogue groups; to St Luke's College Foundation for the support towards the costs of studying, books, computer equipment, library membership and the NVIVO software; to the Sion College Trust for the costs of library membership; and to the Lady Peel Legacy Trust for help with publishing costs and resources to help develop the dialogue groups further.

I also want to say a very big thanks to Micah Hayns for his beautiful illustrations, and for the 30 people who contributed to the crowdfunding to cover costs.

Finally, my particular thanks go to my partner Didier and family, who have coped with giving me the time, space and emotional support required to complete the PhD research study and this book.

Introduction

Our Challenging Context and the Need for the Christian Contemplative Traditions

It is not enough simply to confront external violence. We must also dig out the roots of violence in our own hearts, in our personal agendas, and in our life projects.[1]

If ever there was an urgent need for a contemplative approach to Christian mission, it is now. It is not an underestimation to say that the twenty-first century has moved the world from the serious problems of the twentieth century to various critical crises now. Global warming has become climate breakdown; societal disintegration has led to geopolitical fragmentation and conflict between the minority super-rich (who now own 98 per cent of the world's resources) and everyone else of the 2 per cent who are increasingly desperately fighting for survival and change.

In the last four centuries many have sought to bring systemic liberation and change, but these attempts have mostly failed. Political revolutions and war sought to birth new societies of equality and shared stewardship of the world's resources and commodities, but these just created new tyrannies. The marketization of nations was supposed to birth a meritocracy with equal opportunities not driven by privilege and wealth, but these proved only to enslave people through economics and enrich the privileged even further. New political movements fought battles through democracy, seeking the empowerment of the oppressed and voiceless, but these never broke through the ceilings of racism, homophobia, classism, misogyny and tribalism. The turn to nationalism and localism, which sought to empower neighbourhoods and local people, just led to xenophobia, demonization of the 'other' and, in my own experience, the joys of Brexit and political populism driven by atomized selfish individualism. This scourge has not left the churches unaffected. For some, church is completely disconnected through fear of the real world, becoming a form of asylum; elsewhere, reform was recognized but translated into a new managerialism that has sought to make churches forms of programme-driven businesses. The dominance of what some have named the 'immanent cultural frame' deeply impoverishes the church, leaving it stuck in a mindset of modernity (when most of the world has shifted to a more post-secular cultural context), and thus disconnected from its vocation. Mission then becomes distorted to be the 'dumbed-down' function of conforming new converts to be sucked into the church as 'bums on seats', rather than the transformation of the whole universe in the restoration and healing of all things through the interior life of each person as they follow the way of Jesus Christ.

What is common to all these happenings is that the instigators in good faith sought ecological, economical and societal transformation via the external and the egoic through an attempt to challenge power, violence and adversarial political change. But at the same time, such approaches underappreciated the darker side of our common human nature regarding greed, fear, anger and the other deadly sins, with an added dose of delusional avoidance. What most miss, but which the Christian mystics and contemplatives have voiced throughout millennia, is that true personal and societal transformation, including mission, starts with change in the interior life of every human being, and therefore we must attend to the heart. Indeed, the mystics and contemplatives have been oppressed and some burnt at the stake for using such challenging words to those in power who were resistant to this message and instead sought to maintain the bondage of the status quo. All change begins with the transformation of the inner life of each human being. Indeed, I believe societal change can only begin when significant numbers of people have made the contemplative interior journey towards God to be able to face the critical crises of our time.

Yet I believe, paradoxically, that there is a profound hope for our age. Increasingly it is being recognized that it is the inner wounding of people that leads to the externalization of systems of violence, oppression and new tyrannies. Indeed, hurting people hurt people. Instead, a contemplative and mystical focus echoes the words of Christ and the essence of Christianity about the orientation of the heart of the 'true self' and of faith as a process of restorative healing. This can help establish a deeper spiritual identity than the distortions of the rational, 'egoic' or 'false' self driven by need for external power. Jesus said, 'It is what comes out of a person that defiles. For it is from within, from the human heart, that evil intentions come' (Mark 7.20–21).

At the same time, we are seeing the rise of new social groupings including spiritual seekers, some calling themselves 'Spiritual But Not Religious' (SBNR) and some who spiritually seek using different languages and terms as part of a spiritual quest of the heart to live a better way that does not harm themselves, other people or the planet.

So the transformation of each human being is centred on an internal journey of discovery of God and discipleship. However, in my experience, Christian mission, discipleship, contemplative prayer and spirituality have not usually been deeply connected in this way. Contemplative prayer has been seen as the preserve of nutters, eccentrics and the over-emotional. Yet now more than ever the place of the Christian contemplative traditions and their connection to mission is badly needed in the context of a palpable cultural spiritual hunger and yearning of those interested in forms of spiritual exploration.

This book seeks to address this need for a more contemplative approach and path to the essence of the Christian faith. It will look quite practically at what a more contemplative approach to mission as a transformational pilgrimage of the heart looks like. I hope this will bring the reader greater well-being, integration and clarity about the Christian spiritual prayer traditions and practices. In turn I hope it will inspire a greater appreciation for a more contemplative approach to mission to engage the many who are hungry and spiritually seeking but who do not trust church or Christians.

Over the last six years I have completed a research PhD exploring the stories of people taking part in missional dialogue groups aimed at spiritual seekers. Out of listening to these stories I have had a growing sense of the vital importance of contemplative Christian spirituality and practice to resource contemporary mission in post-secular cultural contexts.

I hope this book will encourage confidence in church communities within my own Anglican tradition and beyond, many struggling with the complexities of contemporary life, to consider a sustainable and deeper sense of mission drawing on the ancient contemplative Christian paths.

This book is in three parts. Part One (Chapters 1 to 3) explores research to understand our current cultural context and resultant spiritual seeking. Part Two (Chapters 4 to 5) seeks to explore a distinctively contemplative approach and model of mission. Part Three (Chapters 6 to 9) explores the application of the model in practice through the stages of awakening, purgation, illumination and union, with resources to support spiritual learning. In Chapter 10, I explore some final thoughts about this approach to mission.

In Chapter 1, I look at what has been named as post-secular contemporary culture as a norm for most post-industrialized Western nations in the early twenty-first century and why this has wounded people, creating so many dechurched and unchurched spiritual seek-ers. In Chapter 2, I address the crisis of personal identity and spiritual seeking, with the rise of those who are interested in spirituality and not religion. In Chapter 3, I draw on research to understand how the 'Spiritual But Not Religious' seek for spirituality and what this involves. Chapter 4 digs deeper to articulate a contemplative theology drawing on contemporary accounts of the contemplative Christian path and experience. Chapter 5 explores a Christian theological understanding of 'God's Kenosis, our Theosis', which lies at the heart of such an approach to mission through awakening, purgation and 'dark nights of the soul', illumination and union. Chapter 6 explores the important first step of awakening to the Christian spiritual journey. In Chapter 7, I explore the difficult and painful stages of purgation and 'dark nights of the soul' in the contemplative path. Chapter 8 explores the conse-quences of illumination and the growing awareness and hope for the mysterious love of God. In Chapter 9, I explore the process of becoming 'in Christ' and the realities of sustaining a state of growing mystical union with God through Jesus Christ. In Chapter 10, the afterword, I share some thoughts about sustaining the contemplative Christian life into resilience and maturity. Chapters 6 to 9 will include content for a contemplative and immersive approach to Christian formation drawing on this new model of mission.

Each of the chapters will also include the stories of those who took part in the PhD research, where the names and some of the details are changed to ensure that those involved are kept anonymous.

I hope that by the end of this book the reader will not only have a greater appreciation of contemplative practice and spirituality, but will also be encouraged to see that mission does not require confron-tative speech based on a sales pitch. Rather, let us have confidence to be hospitable, generous and encouraging of spiritual seekers to experience forms of the love of God as Christian spirituality, and, when asked ques-tions, to share wisdom for the pilgrimage journey towards the mysteries of our Trinitarian God.

Revd Canon Dr Ian Mobsby

Note

1 Leonardo Boff and Frei Betto, *Mistica y Espiritualidad* (Madrid: Trotta, 1996).

PART ONE

Why Do We Need a More Contemplative Model and Approach to Christian Mission?

The Challenge of Living in a
Post-Secular Market Society Context

Graffiti Art, Lower Marsh, Waterloo, London 2022

One of our great challenges as Christians living in the twenty-first century is to be fully embodied and to live well, guided and enabled by the love of God. To do this we need to understand what is going on in cultural change. It is my contention that the church has not woken up to our post-secular world and the oppressive reality of the church's 'immanent cultural frame', which colludes with the global market society defined by capitalism. I do believe we have shifted from a modern, to a post-modern, to a post-secular society. It is the consequences of our market society that have caused many to become seekers of spirituality in a post-secular context.

The term 'post-secular' appears to have first been used by Jürgen Habermas, a German philosopher and sociologist, to describe the loss of confidence in modernist culture and its assertion that religion would diminish in importance and eventually die out.[1] At the same time, post-secularization also denotes the evolution and shift from a modern culture driven by secularization and the dominance of scientific rationalism through to the rise of individualism and distrust in objectifying meta-narratives of modern culture. The Canadian philosopher and sociologist

Charles Taylor's classic work, *A Secular Age*, explores the implications of the history and development of the secularization of culture, climaxing in the late twentieth century and inevitably leading to the creation of new forms of cultural pluralism.[2] Taylor, alongside others, was critical of the effect of the immanent cultural frame that remains prevalent in the church, reflecting modernist culture even though contemporary culture was increasingly post-secular. This cultural frame includes such features as the following:[3]

- Local church overdefined by doing rather than being.
- Emphasis on rational knowing focused on head knowledge rather than heart knowing, and so dumbing down on discipleship, experience of God and prayer.
- Focus on 'having' and resources – concern with buildings and money more than with depth of faith and the health of the spiritual community.
- Sacraments ending up transactional and overly individualistic rather than building up the body of Christ.
- Collusion with the separation of the sacred from the secular and with the forces that diminish real, relational and apostolic mission.
- Focus on control, 'church as business' in a market society.
- Overfocus on stability and risk avoidance rather than being open to the discernment of the Holy Spirit regarding risk taking for the gospel.
- Unconscious focus on being religious rather than following the way of Jesus Christ; and hence disconnection from a God who is interventionist and requires trustful waiting, openness, transformation, relationship and obedience.

Some like David Lyon and James Smith have identified Charles Taylor's argument as part of the stream of post-secularism although he never used this term in his work.[4] For Lieven Boeve, a Belgian Catholic systematic theologian, this shift from post-modernity through to a post-secular culture is marked by a new pluralistic context that includes the renewed place of the spiritual and religion in public discourses.[5]

Barry Taylor, a British writer on contemporary theology, the arts and culture and a former adjunct professor, identifies the post-secular as highly technological and scientific: it is marked by modernism but at the same time people are seeking the impossible over the possible. He describes this aspect of post-secularism as the result of a re-enchantment and resacralization:

What we have seen then, is the emergence of a new environment in which the religious now functions. It is the product of the reenchant-ment, the resacralization, of society. This resacralization is itself the product of a number of interrelated issues: the imposition of modern-ity via the postmodern; the world's continuing globalization result-ing in an emerging global culture, connected by media technology and global flows of information, entertainment, and peoples; and the resultant role of the imagination as a major force, for the production of social meaning.[6]

The language of re-enchantment denotes a sense of the renewed presence of the spiritual in the whole of life, in nature and the planet. Resacraliza-tion names not only the return of religion back into the public discourse of a post-secular context, but also the sense of the sacred in the ordin-ary. The key spiritual development of a more post-secular culture is this reconnection of the sacred in the ordinary. As Barry Taylor has said, 'The postsecular age represents the collapse of the old order and a new permeability; thus, the return to God is signaled in art, literature, and movies … This process is about exploring spirituality in the postsecular as a lived experience.'[7]

This new permeability, as Taylor calls it, has brought together a greater appreciation of subjective spiritual experience renewed by post-modernist sensibilities, alongside the rationalism established through the scientific endeavour birthed in modernity and the Enlightenment. For some, this new subjective experiential knowing has been called 'hyper-rationalism'[8] or 'trans-rationalism' – forms of knowing through art, wisdom, experience, intuition and spiritual encounter.[9] Some, includ-ing B. S. Turner, a British and Australian sociologist, have determined that our current post-secular culture has been created as a consequence of individualistic consumerism and an unrestrained capitalist society where every aspect of life is now driven by the market.[10] For Habermas, post-secular cultures are only to be found in affluent societies in Europe, USA, Canada, Australia and New Zealand.[11] For Turner, the connec-tion between the consumerism of market societies and post-secularism has led to the exponential rise in globalized mass consumerism affect-ing every locality on the planet.[12] By implication of Turner's thinking, post-secularism is therefore the resultant effect of global consumptive capitalism and the rise in individualism combined with new technolo-gies that make this globalization of the market possible. For Habermas, there are three constituent factors to a culture of post-secularization:[13]

1. The rise of religious fundamentalism and religious violence in response to the effects of globalization and consumerist post-secular culture affecting many regions in the world.
2. The rise of new forms of social pluralism, where religion is once again included at the table of public discourses in the world and in national contexts where previously it was excluded in more secularized societies.
3. The rise of low-paid immigrant populations with people coming with traditional or conservative religious views and values into a post-colonial context.[14] This creates the tensions of intolerant co-existence within the resident cultural context. Cheap labour is needed to sustain the machinery of a market society based on consumption.

It is into this complex context, formed out of the effects of a culture driven by consumerism, post-colonialism and post-secularism, that a new form of pluralism has emerged. Unfortunately, this pluralism does not mean that the secularizing principle has ended; quite the contrary, as Boeve states: 'Christianity has not been replaced by a secular culture, but a plurality of life views and religions have moved in to occupy the vacant space it left behind as result of its diminished impact.'[15]

This form of continuing secularization and pluralism is subject to a new cultural force within post-secularization, which has been termed 'de-traditionalization'. This de-traditionalization is part of the ongoing process of secularization as institutional erosion, 'individualization' and 'subjectivization' of religion result in the transformation of religion in Europe. Further, this post-secular de-traditionalization and subjectivization is expressed in how seekers, including the 'Spiritual But Not Religious', explore spirituality using multimedia and consumerist individualistic ways:

> A growing number of people are increasingly unwilling simply to accept the pronouncements of institutions, whether they be religious, political, or otherwise, and are instead looking to themselves, to their peers, and particularly to alternative resource centers, such as internet web sites and contemporary media, in order to create new means for grappling with questions of ultimate reality.[16]

It is in this context that new forms of religious plurality lie, and it is a complex picture to say the least:

> [The] combination [of] detraditionalization [and] pluralization of religion [has led to] a dynamic multi-religious society, full of complexity

and ambiguity … this also implies that the rather classic analysis of the religious situation in European societies in terms of a continuum between 'churched Christians' and 'professing atheist humanists' is far too simplistic.[17]

It seems that choice, or more specifically a freedom to choose, is a defining feature of those who are religious or spiritual in this post-secular pluralistic society. Individuals who seek for religion or spirituality are self-defining or aligning themselves with forms of choice, which is associated with the freedom to 'buy into' whatever form of religion or spirituality they so choose. As Colin Campbell, a British professor of sociology writing on cultural change, consumerism and religion, has said, people are using consumerism as a way to associate themselves with self-defined expressions of spirituality and religion; or, as he puts it, 'I shop therefore I am'.[18] The language of how someone relates to a particular religion, therefore, is increasingly self-defined in relation to different consumerist positions. This is a big shift away from the previous cultural form (in pre-modern and modern cultures) where a religion often had the privileged power to define who was 'in or out' of a particular religious community.[19] An individual's relationship with a religion was therefore defined by either being allowed to participate in a form of religious community or being excluded from it, and rarely by consumer choice. As Anne-Christine Hornborg, a Swedish professor of the history of religions writing about market societies, has stated, this form of spiritual or religious consumerism is therefore the consequence of the connection between post-secularism and the creation of a 'market society'.[20]

It is in this more pluralistic consumerist market society that we find the language of 'dechurched', 'unchurched', 'Christian', and 'post-Christian', where individuals self-define their spiritual sensibilities regarding the Christian faith through personal choice.[21] In this context social and spiritual identity are less about something to 'join in with' as about 'buying into' something out of personal choice. As David Lyon, a Scottish sociologist, has said:

Where once Westerners might have found their identity, their social togetherness and the ongoing life of their society in the area of production, these are today increasingly found through consumption … We are what we buy. We relate to others who consume the same way that we do.[22]

Grace Davie, a British sociologist of religion, has coined the phrase 'believing without belonging', to name the separating out of belief from participation in forms of spiritual community.[23] Being Christian is therefore a consumerist choice with no sense of having to belong to a church or participate in a spiritual community in this self-defining process.

For Boeve, this pluralistic context is dynamic and fragmented, as shown in Figure 1 below.[24]

Figure 1: The Pluralism of Post-Secular Culture

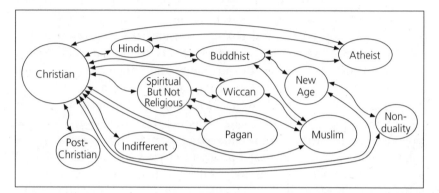

Tom Greggs, a British systematic theologian, stated that one of the consequences of this de-traditionalization is an increasingly 'religion-less' or 'religion-light' Christianity where the church shifts from being authoritative to being advisory.[25] In effect this makes forms of mission and evangelism harder to initiate, because of the lack of depth of discipleship in many forms of church, when it is spiritual depth that the Spiritual But Not Religious are seeking.

This pluralistic, complicated and increasingly consumerist context means that people not only define themselves in relationship to Christianity through forms of individualistic consumerist choice, but possibly are involved in different forms of religion and spirituality all at the same time. Boeve notes that many people have a more 'pick'n'mix' approach to religion and spirituality in our post-secular context:

> The importance of meditation and contemplation; belief in a higher power, spirit or force, rather than a personal God; belief in life after death (including reincarnation); an interest in different religious traditions rather than in one particular tradition. In general, this group claims to be in search of spirituality.[26]

In 2007 Tearfund UK completed national church attendance research and defined eight different categories relating to attending church.[27] Drawing on these statistics, it is clear that the non-churched and dechurched together amount to 66 per cent of the population, and that the Spiritual But Not Religious (SBNR) are contained within this 66 per cent with a pick'n'mix approach to their spiritual lives.[28]

What seems missing from the literature concerning church and churchgoing is the rise in religious fundamentalism as outlined by Habermas. The effects of de-traditionalization and pluralization (as part of the post-secular continuation of secularization) have provoked anxiety and concern among those coming from a more conservative religious background.[29] In the pluralistic context of post-secularization, religious fundamentalism is a specific, chosen spiritual pathway among others, and this is a very different path from that of those who define themselves as SBNR. Religious fundamentalism is the antithesis of the SBNR; it can be understood as a reaction against consumerism and taking part in a market society, or as the reaction of those who are excluded from participation through economic poverty.

Depressingly, the process of 'unchurching' people continues, with an ongoing trend of less participation in religious communities.[30]

However, in a European context, Yves Lambert, a French sociologist of religion, found that younger people who were unchurched seemed to attach renewed importance to traditional values of faithfulness, social order and being part of community.[31] He concluded that there seemed to be a reactivation of traditions and openness to religion. Some of this appeared to be driven by a greater belief in life after death and the desire to seek wisdom from non-authoritarian forms of religion that aid the spiritual seeker to find sources of meaning-making, ethics, sociability and personal identity. This is consistent with the post-secular context we have outlined, with a renewed place for spirituality and religion as sources for inspiration and wisdom. Boeve, reflecting on Lambert's work, suggests that religion and spirituality will only be used in a post-secular situation when they are not controlling and allow individual seekers to be individualistic, autonomous spiritual questers.[32] Religion is therefore relativized through the filter of individual subjectivity. Boeve notes a new craving among younger unchurched people of the middle classes across Europe for forms of 'far-eastern spiritualities', which are in essence more mystical and contemplative.[33]

It is in this context that we hear the language of the SBNR as a self-determination of spiritual identity. Clearly there is a rejection of participating in any form of religion, whereas spirituality is seen in a different way – as an individualistic consumerist choice to follow a certain path.

However, this perceived freedom of spiritual choice is an illusion. An important element of a market society is advertising and marketing in different forms to promote various products and services. In 2016 in the UK alone, £21.4 billion were spent on TV, newspaper and online advertising, the fourth largest in the world.[34] In 2014, an adult in the USA was exposed to a daily average of at least 5,000 advertisements and marketing messages.[35] These factors are important when we look at the underlying psychology of a market society and the effect this has on spiritual seekers. At its heart, consumerism and consumption are a way of life. As Zygmunt Bauman, a Polish and British sociologist, has said: 'While consumer society rests its case on the promise to gratify human desires to an extent which no other society in the past could reach or even dream of reaching, the promise of satisfaction remains seductive only as long as the desire stays ungratified.'[36]

Ongoing consumption is dependent on maintaining a subtle 'dissatisfaction', otherwise nothing would be bought or sold. This is the subtle message of advertising, that we need this or that to make us satisfied. These subtle messages say that we are not good enough or that we need some form of product or service to bring satisfaction, which will never fully happen. Advertising therefore must be deceitful:

> Each single promise must be deceitful, or at least exaggerated, lest the search grind to a halt or its zeal (and so also its intensity) fall below the level needed to keep the circulation of commodities going ... Without the repetitive frustration of desires, consumer demand would quickly run dry and the consumer-targeted economy would run out of steam.[37]

In our post-secular consumerist society, we are therefore bombarded by messages that promote dissatisfaction with the psychological aim of creating enough dissatisfaction to make people unhappy.[38] There is therefore a direct link between unhappiness and the dissatisfaction promoted by consumerist post-secular cultures that unsettles people. Further, in a consumer culture not only do people buy commodities, but the process of commodification turns every participant into a commodity. As Bauman has said: 'Consumers are themselves consumer commodities, and it is the quality of being a consumer commodity that makes them bona fide members of that society. Becoming and remaining a sellable commodity is the most potent motive of consumer concerns.'[39]

Even more concerning is the reality that many are using forms of consumerist commodification to define themselves through materialism by the types of cars they drive, the computer models they work from, the clothing labels they wear and the bars and networks they associate with.

As Bauman has stated: 'Consumerist culture is marked by a constant pressure to be someone else ... they cultivate constant dissatisfaction with the acquired identity and the set of needs by which such an identity is defined.'[40]

This creates the frightening reality of the promotion of unhappiness with an undermined self-knowing determined by consumerist material-ism. This combination is toxic regarding health and well-being. It is this connection between commodification as 'making yourself up' and the promotion of dissatisfaction as unhappiness that creates the conditions for people to seek for well-being and happiness through the search for spirituality. This seems to be why some people call themselves SBNR. Many people are seeking for meaning and identity through the pathway of individualistic consumerist gratification.

This strategy would also help to explain why so many seek spiritual identity through the strategy of shopping through social media and web-site resources. Bauman calls such people 'addicts of identity alteration'.[41]

Building on the work of B. Taylor, Bauman, Boeve and Lambert, the literature suggests that this post-secular consumerist reality of unhappi-ness and commodification lies at the heart of the increasing spiritual searching of the SBNR in our new pluralistic and multi-choice culture where the emphasis is on individualistic consumerist gratification. It is this context that leads not only to new approaches to spirituality, but also to the reappearance of religion in public debate and discourse. But at the same time, the process of 'de-and-un-churching' people continues. There remains a paradox: in a consumer culture there may be increasing numbers of spiritual seekers but at the same time there is a reluctance to face the deep existential questions of life, because this requires you to face who you really are rather than buying something to 'make yourself up' or help you to feel better. As Oliver James has said:

> Consumerism has found it easy to offer distractions and false individu-alism, supplied by possessions. People differentiate one another by what they own, not who they are, by Having rather than Being. The self of this Homo Consumens is experienced as a thing, to be bought and sold just like a car or house.[42]

This all being so suggests that this post-secular desire to seek out the spiritual is the result of a crisis in well-being, physical and mental health. Some, including Christopher Lasch, an American academic historian, and Graham Cray, a retired bishop and writer on Fresh Expressions and mission, have questioned whether this is really a time of renewed exploration of spirituality, or rather a time of mental illness and the need for therapy or psychiatric treatment. As Lasch has said: 'People today hunger not for personal salvation, let alone for the restoration of an earlier golden age, but for the feeling, the momentary illusion, of personal well-being, health, and psychic security.'[43]

For many who have tried to avoid facing the existential question of what life is for, this can in time lead to issues of deepening mental illness and forms of addiction.[44] When people are literally brought to their knees psychologically, they are forced to face who they really are and the deep religious and philosophical questions of existence. This, I think, is why Nancy Ammerman makes the observation that most 'Extra-The-istic' spiritual seekers seem to begin seeking after a crisis, normally involving illness. It also explains why the outcome of addiction 12-step groups for those coming to terms with various forms of addiction, as a result of our consumerist post-secular culture, often reconnects people's health and well-being with the spiritual questions of life.[45]

It is this market function of post-secular culture that creates the condition of instability to maintain consumption, and hence why so many people are struggling with addiction, mental health and a healthy sense of self-identity.[46] Cray noted: 'There are a larger number of "seekers", on a therapeutic quest, looking for healing more than spirituality. The contemporary climate is therapeutic not religious.'[47]

Central to this book are the insights of the Christian contemplative traditions and mystical theology, which I will draw on later. For the Christian mystics and contemplatives, spirituality and therapy are deeply connected. They teach us that the spiritual search can often take us to the ends of ourselves, and indeed touches on mental ill health as God, or the consequences of life, seem to force us to have to let go and surrender our lives to God.[48] The spiritual path may need therapy as well as spirituality, possibly even more so in situations where our lives are defined by materialism. In a post-secular culture those who are SBNR are seeking in a culture that covertly promotes dissatisfaction and unhappiness, questing for well-being through individualistic consumerism.[49]

Turning to the consequences of the connection between post-secularism, consumerism and market societies, attention needs to be drawn to the social requirement to spend money to be able to participate, whether or not this is affordable.

One of the greatest fears for individuals living in consumerist societies is to not be able to consume through having insufficient financial resources to participate. The poor cannot define themselves through materialism, or fully contribute to a culture defined by 'consumerist participation'. The poor are therefore seen as 'failed consumers'.[50] To not be able to consume is a modern-day form of social exclusion; it is to be part of a new 'underclass' where there is no way back unless they become again able to consume.[51]

Ultimately very few people can afford financially to sustain a life driven by post-secular consumerism to maintain consumerist gratification. This is a profoundly unhealthy way of life. Thinking of the UK context, Bauman states that he believes that only 30 per cent of people can afford to live this way to sustain such a lifestyle.[52]

Stories of wounding by the market society of post-secular culture

In my PhD research most of those who considered themselves Spiritual But Not Religious were extremely negative about the market society and had found it dehumanizing and harmful. In fact the damaging effects of the consequences of a market society were the catalyst for most of those involved in the study to become spiritual seekers. These were particularly pronounced in the stories of Anton, Calum, Trevor and Cathy.

Anton was ethnically Caribbean. He came to London for education and to escape family trauma, poverty and an unhealthy culture of drugs and alcohol. Anton had begun postgraduate training but his studies had been disrupted by continuing issues with drugs and alcohol and the trauma of childhood experiences:

> The situation at home was unsafe, and I remember as a child getting down on my knees and begging God to help ... seeking escape from a bad social situation ... helping me in a time of crisis ... spirituality felt an important place for me to express my heart and seek a better life ... I turned to the spiritual to help me through. (Anton, Life History Interview)

For Anton, there was the awareness that much of contemporary culture promotes the egoic and unhealthy, and that being SBNR and focusing on healthy spiritual integration and unity was vital to resist the societal addiction to the false self and to seek the true self:

> There is inconsistency in the world which says with one voice that you are not enough and then with the other love yourself to the extreme. There is a kind of self-love that is indulgent; it can be narcissistic. In such a situation you have to get over yourself. (Anton, Borough dialogue group, 25 July 2018)

17

Thinking about the false self and the true self, is there a link between this and society ... that society is constructed in a way that is not for me; that I need to make enough money, I need to try and get on top of life to be able to survive; so is the state of society the accumulative effect of all these false selves? (Anton, Borough dialogue group, 25 July 2018)

For Anton, spiritual practices were important because they were counter-cultural to forms of individual consumerism:

There is something about letting go of the need to keep consuming ... We can't just live in an experience-driven life because it is just about the next hit rather than authentic spirituality, which requires you to let go of endless consumption. This requires a paradigm shift, true spirituality to be transformative needs to be a paradigm shift. It becomes central to life. Once you have this type of transformative experience, nothing can take that centre ground quite like that experience, and it probably needs to happen more than once. (Anton, Borough dialogue group, 30 January 2019)

Calum was in his fifties and an unemployed sales manager on a low income who lived with his partner in north London and had previously completed graduate studies. His spiritual journey began through an emerging interest in spirituality following therapy after a period of painful depression caused by overworking. For Calum, there was a strong sense that there had to be more to life. He had grown up in a strictly atheistic family with a focus on scientific rationalism as the conveyor of truth. Spirituality was a totally new quest for him. For Calum, this experience catalysed his search to become an SBNR spiritual seeker away from the unhealthiness of post-secular society:

We live in a consumer society and ... the pressures around us, and the messages we all receive, are commercial messages, around how you can create yourself ... and issues around religion are avoided ... nobody has the tools that older generations might have been taught, to explore the spiritual self and religious existential questions ... consumerism ... takes over your life. (Calum, City dialogue group, 4 July 2018)

So I had to do some psychotherapy, for myself, I have not really thought about it as a spiritual experience, never crossed my mind, so that is a new thought, and I can see that the therapy was a spiritual quest now. (Calum, City dialogue group, 25 July 2018)

Trevor shared this same yearning for spiritual freedom and well-being, but for him it was driven by a desire to counter the consequences of a market society culture driven too much by materialism and money:

> Many people are completely defined by money. 'Am I successful or not?' for many is defined by money ... My sister and her boyfriend are organizing a wedding ... money is the first thing they think about ... all they can ask me about was money ... I have the money to live well, to live with sufficiency. It is almost like the wedding is only worth something if it is expensive. For me this is counter to spirituality. (Trevor, Battersea dialogue group, 8 January 2020)

Finally was Cathy. She worked in an NHS hospital on a low wage after completing vocational postgraduate studies; she was single and lived alone. Cathy's spiritual journey began with ill health. She started to explore spirituality, including attending a weekly Zen Buddhist class as well as a meditation group:

> Changing career was a big one for me. It was for well-being needs, my previous work was making me unhappy and stressed. So I wanted to get away from suffering. One of the reasons I started exploring spirituality was for the alleviation of suffering. Looking for well-being. (Cathy, Life History Interview)

For Cathy, engaging with spirituality was the means of healing and recovery from the context of a market society that makes many unwell.

In conclusion, living in a post-secular culture creates the underlying conditions to unsettle many, causing them to become SBNR and spiritual seekers. At the same time many of our churches are unable to respond to this need, because they are often caught in what has been called the 'immanent cultural frame'. Yet there is a need for a form of Christian mission to engage with spiritual seekers.

In the next chapter I will explore the characteristics of spiritual seekers, specifically those who define themselves as SBNR, and how they seek to resist post-secular materialism and consumeristic market gratification.

Notes

1 David Lyon, 'Being Post-Secular in the Social Sciences: Taylor's Social Imaginaries', *New Blackfriars* 91, no. 1036 (November 2010), p. 648.

2 Charles Taylor, *A Secular Age* (Cambridge, MA: Belknap Press of Harvard University Press, 2007).

3 Andrew Root, *Churches and the Crisis of Decline: A Hopeful, Practical Ecclesiology for a Secular Age* (Grand Rapids, MI: Baker Academic, 2022).

4 James K. A. Smith, *How (Not) To Be Secular: Reading Charles Taylor* (Grand Rapids, MI: Eerdmans, 2014).

5 Lieven Boeve, 'Religion after Detraditionalization: Christian Faith in a Post-Secular Europe', *Irish Theological Quarterly* 70, no. 2 (2005), p. 100. Also published in a slightly different version as Lieven Boeve, 'Religion after Detraditionalization: Christian Faith in a Postsecular Europe', in *The New Visibility of Religion*, ed. Michael Hoelzl and Graham Ward (London: Continuum, 2008), pp. 187–209.

6 Barry Taylor, *Entertainment Theology* (Grand Rapids, MI: Baker Academic, 2008), p. 170.

7 Taylor, *Entertainment Theology*, p. 201.

8 Abby Day, 'Non-Religious Christians', in *Post-secular Religious Practices*, ed. Tore Ahlbäck and Björn Dahla (Åbo/Turku, Finland: Donner Institute for Research in Religious and Cultural History, 2012), p. 44.

9 Ian Mobsby, *God Unknown: The Trinity in Contemporary Spirituality and Mission* (London: Canterbury Press, 2012), p. 5.

10 Bryan S. Turner, 'Post-Secular Society: Consumerism and the Democratization of Religion', in *The Post-Secular in Question: Religion in Contemporary Society*, ed. Philip Gorski, David Kyuman Kim, John Torpey and Jonathan VanAntwerpen (London: New York University Press, 2012), pp. 135–58.

11 Jürgen Habermas, 'Notes on Post-Secular Society', *New Perspectives Quarterly* 25, no. 4 (September 2008), p. 17.

12 Turner, 'Post-Secular Society'.

13 Habermas, 'Notes on Post-Secular Society', pp. 17–21.

14 Post-colonialism is the shift from a nation holding a cultural imperialistic attitude of a dominant culture over another to a post-empire situation, where this power dynamic needs to be redressed to find approaches to tolerant co-existence not based on power domination but on true cultural pluralism.

15 Boeve, 'Religion after Detraditionalization', p. 107.

16 Taylor, *Entertainment Theology*, pp. 12, 34, 79, 154.

17 Boeve, 'Religion after Detraditionalization', p. 104.

18 Colin Campbell, 'I Shop Therefore I Know That I Am: The Metaphysical Basis of Modern Consumerism', in *Elusive Consumption*, ed. Karim M. Ekstrom and Helene Brembeck (Oxford: Berg, 2004), pp. 27–44.

19 Boeve, 'Religion after Detraditionalization', p. 108.

20 Anne-Christine Hornborg, '"Are You Content with Being Just Ordinary? Or Do You Wish to Make Progress and Be Outstanding?" New Ritual Practices in Contemporary Sweden', in *Post-secular Religious Practices*, ed. Tore Ahlbäck and Björn Dahla (Åbo/Turku, Finland: Donner Institute for Research in Religious and Cultural History, 2012), p. 112.

21 Nicola David, 'Developing the Community Habit', *Church Times*, 22 March 2011, https://www.churchtimes.co.uk/articles/2011/25-march/features/developing-the-community-habit (accessed 07.08.2024); Boeve, 'Religion after Detraditionalization', p. 107.

22 David Lyon, 'Memory and the Millennium', in *Grace and Truth in the Secular Age*, ed. Timothy Bradshaw (Grand Rapids, MI: Eerdmans, 1998), p. 248.

23 Grace Davie, 'Believing without Belonging: Is This the Future of Religion in Britain?', *Social Compass* 37, no. 4 (1990), pp. 455–69.

24 Boeve, 'Religion after Detraditionalization', p. 107.

25 Tom Greggs, 'Religionless Christianity and the Political Implications of Theological Speech: What Bonhoeffer's Theology Yields to a World of Fundamentalisms', *International Journal of Systematic Theology* 11, no. 3 (July 2009), pp. 293–308.

26 Boeve, 'Religion after Detraditionalization', p. 103.

27 Jacintha Ashworth and Ian Farthing, 'Church Going in the UK: A Research Report from Tearfund on Church Attendance in the UK' (Tearfund, April 2007), pp. 5–26, http://news.bbc.co.uk/1/shared/bsp/hi/pdfs/03_04_07_tearfundchurch. pdf (accessed 07.08.2024).

28 Ashworth and Farthing, 'Church Going in the UK', p. 2.

29 Greggs, 'Religionless Christianity', pp. 296–303.

30 Boeve, 'Religion after Detraditionalization', p. 102.

31 Yves Lambert, 'A Turning Point in Religious Evolution in Europe', *Journal of Contemporary Religion* 19, no. 1 (June 2006), pp. 29–45.

32 Boeve, 'Religion after Detraditionalization', pp. 102–3.

33 Boeve, 'Religion after Detraditionalization', p. 105.

34 Thomas Hobbs, 'UK Ad Spend Hits Record £21.4bn as Digital Dominates Again', *Marketing Week*, 25 April 2017, https://www.marketingweek.com/2017/04/25/uk-ad-spend-digital/ (accessed 07.08.2024); Anon, 'UK: Advertising Industry – Statistics & Facts' (Statista), https://www.statista.com/topics/1747/advertising-in-the-united-kingdom/ (accessed 28.12.2017).

35 Sheree Johnson, 'New Research Sheds Light on Daily Ad Exposures' (S J Insights, 29 September 2014), https://sjinsights.net/2014/09/29/new-research-sheds-light-on-daily-ad-exposures/ (accessed 07.08.2024).

36 Zygmunt Bauman, *Consuming Life* (Cambridge: Polity Press, 2007), p. 46.

37 Bauman, *Consuming Life*, p. 47.

38 Bauman, *Consuming Life*, p. 47.

39 Bauman, *Consuming Life*, p. 57.

40 Bauman, *Consuming Life*, p. 100.

41 Bauman, *Consuming Life*, p. 114.

42 Oliver James, *Affluenza* (London: Vermilion, 2007), p. 65.

43 Christopher Lasch, *The Culture of Narcissism: American Life in an Age of Diminishing Expectations* (New York: W. W. Norton, Inc., 1991), p. 7.

44 Helga Dittmar, 'The Costs of Consumer Culture and the "Cage Within": The Impact of the Material "Good Life" and "Body Perfect" Ideals on Individuals' Identity and Well-Being', *Psychological Inquiry* 18, no. 1 (2007), pp. 23–31.

45 Gerda Reith, 'Consumption and its Discontents: Addiction, Identity and the Problems of Freedom', *The British Journal of Sociology* 44, no. 2 (2004), pp. 292–3.

46 Lasch, *The Culture of Narcissism*, p. 4.

47 Graham Cray, 'Doors to the Sacred through Fresh Expressions of Church', in *Doorways to the Sacred: Developing Sacramentality in Fresh Expressions of Church*, ed. Phil Potter and Ian Mobsby (London: Canterbury Press, 2017), p. 6.

48 Thomas Merton, *The Wisdom of the Desert: Sayings from the Desert Fathers of the Fourth Century* (New York: New Directions, 1970), pp. 3–24.

49 Lasch, *The Culture of Narcissism*, p. 4.

50 Bauman, *Consuming Life*, p. 124.

51 Bauman, *Consuming Life*, p. 126.

52 Bauman, *Consuming Life*, p. 80.

2

The Crisis of Personal Identity and the Rise of Spiritual Seeking and the 'Spiritual But Not Religious'

Graffiti Art, Leake Street Arches Waterloo, London 2021

In the last chapter, I identified why so many people today have turned to spirituality and spiritual seeking from experiences of being wounded by the dehumanizing effects of the global market and post-secular society. In this chapter, I explore who are the spiritual seekers, specifically the 'Spiritual But Not Religious' (SBNR). I do this in the belief that a more contemplative approach to mission will enable spiritual seekers to experience God as they approach God in pilgrimage. As part of this exploration, I will identify the conceptual understandings of the SBNR, drawing on the stories and perspectives of those who took part in the research study.

Who are the spiritual seekers and the Spiritual But Not Religious?

In the 1980s and 1990s, forms of non-religious spirituality appeared to emerge from within contemporary culture. David Tacey, an Australian interdisciplinary researcher writing on Christianity, culture and spirituality, said:

> I began to notice signs of spirituality in my students ... These were vague and indistinct at first and included hearing the word 'spirituality' used occasionally in tutorials and discussions ... most students using this language were not religious and had not been brought up by religious families.[1]

Tacey also attributes this rise in spirituality to a dissatisfaction within the secular culture of many post-industrial Western nations, an unease with much of the uncertainty of modern life.[2] Writing from a UK perspective, Steven Croft et al. identify the rise of secular spirituality as a reaction against Christians specifically: 'Research shows that many people don't trust us with their stories of spiritual search, the rituals and activities they've tried, because they believe Christians will laugh, humiliate them.'[3]

Paul Heelas, a British sociologist and anthropologist, and Linda Woodhead, a British sociologist of religion, attribute this rise of secular spirituality to the demise of Christianity and dissatisfaction with secular culture:[4]

> Such an 'inner' sacred offers people the freedom to find their own path rather than telling them the path which they ought to follow, and it enables them to test activities to find what works best for ... life ... The 'practice of experience' rather than the practice of belief systems.[5]

For Tacey, Croft et al. and Marie McCarthy, the label 'Spiritual But Not Religious' was quickly identified with this rise in post-secular spirituality. As Tacey said: 'A statement often heard these days, particularly by young people but by no means confined to them, is, "I am not a very religious person, but I am interested in spirituality". I have heard this said throughout Australia, Britain and Europe.'[6]

For Heelas and Woodhead, the language of the 'spiritual milieu' is used to describe what seems to have emerged through non-religious spirituality, as experienced by those who do not formally use the label 'SBNR'. They define this as a 'subjective-life' form of spirituality, as 'the holistic milieu activities that facilitate the convergence of the spiritual path and the personal path', suggesting that 'When the sacred flows from within subjective-life, it offers "inner solutions" which are uniquely appropriate to the challenge and opportunity of becoming fully alive in the here-and-now.'[7]

These ideas of the 'subjective-life' and the 'subjective turn' of non-religious spirituality are synonymous for Heelas and Woodhead: 'The subjective turn is thus a turn away from "life-as" (life lived as a dutiful wife, father, husband, strong leader, self-made man etc.) to "subjective-life" (life lived in deep connection with the unique experience of my self-in-relation).'[8]

Tacey recognizes this 'subjective turn' as an essential feature of how the SBNR spiritually seek: 'We have experienced a revolution of the spirit, in which spiritual authority has been placed in the hands of the individual person and his or her conscience.'[9]

As well as agreeing that this SBNR or spiritual milieu is a subjective response to a form of non-religious spirituality arising from the difficulties of modern life, the writers also agree that there is a connection between this desire for spirituality and issues of well-being and healing. As Tacey has said: 'It is our secular society realising ... we have outgrown the ideas and values of the early scientific era, which viewed the individual as a sort of efficient machine.'[10] Heelas and Woodhead see the focus on the spiritual milieu being connected with a desire for inner healing:

> the activities of the milieu provide the opportunity for participants to 'grow' ... So whether dis-ease has to do with the bad habits of the body (manifested as backaches, for example), emotional blockages or dysfunction (involving stress or anger, for example), or problems in relationships at home or at work (such as inability to assert one's needs or a sense of low self-esteem), the important thing is to move on or 'grow'.[11]

This connection to a desire for inner healing is also shared by Croft et al.: '"Spirituality" has become an "in" word ... the interrelatedness of all things, and holistic healing ... the notion of the spiritual affecting the physical has gained credibility even in mainstream healthcare.'[12]

From research results, Heelas and Woodhead (as demonstrated in Figure 2) argue that there is a clear connection between stress and unhappiness and a desire for healing and spirituality.[13] These results identify why people sought out spiritual activities within the spiritual milieu in Kendal, where the research took place. From my own experiences of dialogue with the SBNR, these factors ring true: many are seeking spiritual relief from inner pain, stress and difficulties.

Figure 2: The Holistic Milieu in Kendal

What are people spiritually seeking for?
In order of percentage

1. For health and fitness
2. Looking for spiritual growth
3. Stress relief
4. Relief of bodily pain or illness
5. Looking for personal growth
6. Pleasure, enjoyment or treat
7. Life crises
8. Time out of daily routines
9. To meet like-minded people
10. Emotional support or human contact
11. Dissatisfaction with mainstream medicine
12. To complement mainstream medical treatment

For Linda Mercadante, a theologian and ordained Presbyterian minister writing from in-depth American research, the SBNR as a movement was a protest against religion that was perceived to be too politically conservative and dogmatic and overly focused on 'organized hatred'.[14] At the same time, Mercadante identifies the SBNR as protesting against secularism and its overreliance on science to answer all problems while neglecting spirituality; instead, the movement promotes a focus on individual spiritual experience.[15] Further, Mercadante attributes some of the growth in the SBNR to a desire to innovate from personal experience.[16] Often the catalyst for becoming SBNR in a US context began in ill-health, addiction or bereavement.[17]

Mercadante's research echoes previous research into spiritual seekers which found that the negative stereotype concerning all religions was held across the whole SBNR constituency. This was a major challenge for mission: 'They all had certain ideas in common which prompted them to castigate, disdain, or simply ignore organised religion ... This happened in spite of differences in age ... spiritual journeys, and ... reasons for adopting the "spiritual not religious" label.'[18]

Again echoing earlier studies, it is clear that Mercadante's research epitomizes a myopic view of Christianity and religion reflecting more conservative 'fundamentalist' elements, to the absence of more progressive, contemplative and incarnational forms. In her conclusions, she suggests that if the church is going to be effective in mission it has to face truths understood by the SBNR, that religions, including Christianity, often promote:

- An exclusivism that rejects all religions but one's own;
- A wrathful and/or interventionist God;
- A static and permanent afterlife of glorious heaven and torturous hell;
- An oppressively authoritarian religious tradition;
- A non-experiential, repressive religious community; and
- A view of humans as 'born bad'.[19]

There are real issues for the Christian faith to face here if it is going to be involved in contextual mission with the SBNR. Further in her research, Mercadante identifies common features to the SBNR she encountered, which included:[20]

- Commencing being SBNR following some form of life crisis;[21]
- Seeking experimentation;
- Initial spiritual group or practices often do not last long;
- Spiritual beliefs have a part to play.

In Canada, researching into spiritual seeking with university students, Matthew Graham, Marvin McDonald and Derrick Klaassen[22] established similar themes to the work of Mercandante, which included:[23]

- Desire for profound spiritual connection;
- Transcendence in daily life;
- Questing as identity shaping;
- Growing beyond traditions.

Finally, and uniquely to her work, Mercadante identified five different types of the SBNR:

1. 'Dissenters' who had some previous form of a religion, largely Christianity, and felt angry about these experiences;
2. 'Casuals', interested in spirituality but it is not central to their life;
3. 'Explorers', seekers of consumerist spiritual experiences;
4. 'Seekers' who yearn for spirituality but never settle;
5. 'Immigrants' putting down roots and seeking to belong in a spiritual context and/or community.[24]

Reading through Mercadante's work, I can't help but think that her five designations of the SBNR relate more to different stages of spiritual development rather than being distinctly different types of the SBNR. Indeed, this is borne out by Mercadante herself in her assertion that not all those who start out as SBNR as dissenters make it through to being immigrants and putting down roots with a particular spiritual community.[25] These five areas, if instead understood as different spiritual stages of being the SBNR, would then make connections with the writings particularly of Tacey, McCarthy, Heelas and Woodhead.

However, this is where coherence and agreement break down between writers, reflecting the reality that they were writing from differing positions. For Steven Croft, an Anglican bishop and writer on Fresh Expressions and mission, and Heelas and Woodhead, there is a deep connection between the SBNR, 'spiritual milieu' and what has been called the 'New Age movement'. For Croft et al., this has been at the heart of the rise of non-religious spirituality: '"Spirituality" … is largely influenced by Eastern religions and the New Age movement, with the emphasis on attaining higher consciousness in the search for the divine, the interrelatedness of all things.'[26]

For Heelas and Woodhead, the New Age movement and the rise of non-religious spirituality are one and the same.[27] Further, for them, the plethora of differing forms of alternative spirituality fall under the New Age movement and include: 'the multifarious forms of sacred activity which are often grouped together under collective terms like "body, mind and spirit", "New Age", "alternative" or "holistic" spirituality, and which include (spiritual) yoga, reiki, meditation, tai chi, aromatherapy, much paganism, rebirthing, reflexology, much wicca and many more'.[28]

However, for Tacey, the New Age movement reflects a repressed impulse for spirituality and as such is inauthentic, having additionally become commodified and exploited by our consumeristic market society. For Mercadante, the SBNR she interviewed did not want to be associated with the New Age.[29] In Tacey's thinking, forms of spirituality become unhinged from religion (their usual containers) in times of major socio-cultural change, and the New Age has more to do with being a reaction against religion than anything authentic about spirituality.[30] He pulls no punches when he says:

The New Age interests are indeed a series of 'poor symbols', and bespeak a cultural impoverishment that education should correct. This realisation made me see the New Age in a different light and caused me to study it in-depth. It is a vulgar series of spiritual technologies that exist because there is nothing better on offer.[31]

Marie McCarthy, an American Catholic nun and pastoral theologian, agrees with this analysis in stating that she believes that the New Age is inherently dishonest and inauthentic:

> The designation 'New Age' itself is problematic. Many of the practices which are referred to as New Age are, in fact, centuries old ... much of New Age spirituality is marked by privatization and commercialization ... a product to be sold ... it is packaged and marketed to suit the taste of the consumer.[32]

For Tacey, Mercadante and McCarthy, there is a connection also between the desire of the SBNR for authentic expressions of non-religious spirituality and the influence of what they call post-modern culture (which for me is more to do with a post-secular culture) as the cultural world view and self-understanding of people. As Tacey has said: 'Although postmodernism became an elite enterprise that few citizens could understand, it did signify that the familiar world was over. From the spiritual point of view it loosened to the structures of rationality and provided openings for the return of mystery and spirit.'[33] For Tacey, post-modern spirituality (which I contend is post-secular spirituality) liberates the spirit with a 'new language and a new imagining to make it part of the postmodern intellectual landscape ... The key to this new development is conversation and listening.'[34]

In contrast, Heelas and Woodhead believed that post-modernism had made no impact at all on the context of Kendal, the site of their sociological research.[35]

The greatest differences between the writers is the relationship between the SBNR and spiritual milieu and religion. Heelas and Woodhead take quite a distinct approach, defining the difference between 'spiritual life spirituality' and 'spirituality as religion':

> One of the great virtues of the language of 'life-as' and 'subjective-life' is that it enables us to sharpen up the distinction between 'religion' and 'spirituality' by distinguishing between life-as religion and subjective-life spirituality. The former is bound up with the form of life-as – indeed it sacralizes life-as. By contrast, the latter is bound up with subjective-life – indeed it sacralizes subjective-life. Thus the former involves subordinating subjective-life to the 'higher' authority of transcendent meaning, goodness and truth, whilst the latter invokes the sacred in the cultivation of unique subjective-life.[36]

Tacey and Heelas and Woodhead argue in slightly different ways that religion (and they largely equate this with Christianity as the dominant religion) is about transcendence and spirituality 'out there' – as going to a church or temple to take part in a congregation of some description – whereas spirituality is about that which arises from within. They therefore make a distinction between spirituality as devotion and spirituality as experience regarding lived religion.[37] As Tacey has said:

> Devotion does not ask questions or raise doubts, but places the individual in a subordinate position to a mystery that the faith institutions seek to control. Spirituality might give new vitality and direction to the spirit, but if it comes at too high a price for the institution, spirituality is banned or even persecuted ... the creative spirit is a headache for religious authorities, since it is sometimes iconoclastic, original and radical.[38]

From my own reading, Tacey and Heelas and Woodhead are not consistent in their arguments. Their descriptions of religion as spirituality 'out there' is too simplistic and does not acknowledge the more mystical, contemplative or even charismatic traditions of the Christian faith that also emphasize spirituality as experiencing God 'from within'. Heelas and Woodhead acknowledge: 'This is not to deny that there may be forms of Christian spirituality that are essentially concerned with the cultivation of unique subject-life, particularly in the mystical tradition.'[39] Tacey goes even further regarding the relationship between religion and spirituality when he states:

> When the spirit is activated and recognised, the student tends to develop or rediscover (as the case may be) a natural interest in religion, because religion offers the spirit complex language, a sense of tradition and cultural memory ... The inward spiritual approach to religion is deeper, based on personal experience, tolerant towards difference, compassionate towards those who make different life-choices, and relatively free of ideological fanaticism.[40]

It seems to me that Tacey and Heelas and Woodhead all regard conservative and institutional Christianity as the prominent form, with an associated redemptive theology, and ignore expressions of the Christian faith and church that are more incarnational and contemplative in orientation. This reveals an approach that could be criticized as being too dualistic. Nancy Ammerman, an American sociologist of religion, questions this dualistic approach in the separation of religion and spirituality, drawing on recent and comprehensive research looking at 'lived religion' in Boston. From her research she noted:

> Our perception of declining 'religion' and growing 'spirituality' implies that as there is less of one, there will be more of the other ... Those who have tried to pay attention to both 'religion' and 'spirituality' have discovered that there is actually a good deal of overlap between the two domains, at least in the American population.[41]

Ammerman also questions whether the term SBNR is as counter to religion as currently understood. From her research she argues that those who say they are SBNR are often drawing on some form of religious resource:

> So what really fits the 'spiritual not religious' label? ... it is used to describe a hypothetical distinction between two categories, neither of which apply to the person making the distinction. When we look at practices instead of rhetoric, in the vast majority of our participants, religious participation and spiritual engagement occur alongside talk that intermingles the two.[42]

For Ammerman, this difference between what the SBNR said (that they were not religious) and the fact that they engaged in religious spiritual practices demonstrates that the SBNR were an inauthentic social grouping. For her, this inconsistency between practice and description meant that the SBNR were not a credible social grouping regarding lived religion or spirituality:

> Among our participants, being 'spiritual but not religious' is the way of describing the religious social world that fits prevailing secularization assumptions nicely, but reflects moral and political categories more than analytical ones.[43]

Although I understand and have sympathy with Ammerman's dualistic argument here, it has also concerned me that she has dismissed the SBNR as inauthentic a little hastily. In doing so, there is, as Meredith B. McGuire, an American sociologist and anthropologist, has stated, a danger that such sociology of religion research can 'simply fail to capture how multifaceted, diverse and malleable are the beliefs, values, and practices' of the SBNR.[44] Rightly, in my view, McGuire makes a distinction between 'logical coherence' and 'practical coherence'. She argues that lived religion (and by implication lived spirituality) is based more on spiritual or religious practices than on ideas or beliefs, which are not necessarily 'logically coherent'. This is clearly the case with the SBNR.[45] She suggests that a 'practical coherence' can exist that makes sense in the individual's everyday life, which needs to be effective or work for them, where this 'practical coherence' in terms of reasoning may seem irrational and inconsistent. By making a distinction between spirituality and religion the SBNR are seeking to 'delineate acceptable from unacceptable beliefs and practices, desirable from denigrated identities and statuses, and worthy from unworthy ideals and values'.[46] Drawing on McGuire's work I therefore disagree with Ammerman, because it seems to me there is a practical coherence to the SBNR, which means they are a credible social grouping even if they are logically inconsistent.

Regarding UK research, Ammerman directly criticizes the conclusions of Heelas and Woodhead in their study of the 'spiritual milieu' as making large claims with very little evidence and making unfair comparisons between religion and spirituality.[47] As an alternative, she offers interpretations drawing on a recent sociological exploration of 'lived religion' in Boston. From these findings she identified four different spiritual tribes, one of which was labelled the 'Extra-Theistic' (ETH). In her research she described this grouping:

> [The ETH] speak of a world of experiences that do not depend on the Christian (or any other) God but that nevertheless signaled transcendence, reaching beyond the ordinary. This genre of spiritual discourse encompasses attention to transcendent connections to others, the sense of awe engendered by the natural world and moments of beauty, life philosophies crafted by an individual seeking meaning, and the inner core of individual self-worth ... These ways of thinking about spirituality are often described ... as 'immanent', flowing from the person, the community, and the natural world needing no authority beyond the person's own experience.[48]

Ammerman goes further to identify the Extra-Theistic as seekers of spirituality. This description does appear to share some of the characteristics of what we have explored as SBNR. In summary she defines the ETH as:

- Seeking transcendence in nature and spirituality;
- Seeking integration, unity and connection;
- Seeking meaning to guide one's life;
- Seeking mystical truth that lies within.[49]

Although Ammerman makes a distinction between the ETH and other spiritual tribes in Boston, she does state that the ETH might stray into the terrain of what she labelled the 'Ethical or Moral' tribe; nevertheless, she makes a distinction between these two spiritual dispositions.[50] Ammerman defines the Ethical or Moral tribe as activists who live by an ethical understanding of the 'Golden rule' as 'acting in a way that you would like to be treated yourself'.[51]

While there is much to learn from Ammerman's research, it is not coming from a theistic frame of understanding, which might partly explain the lack of coherence between the different studies of spiritual seekers. So how do the SBNR and ETH relate? Clearly there is a connection between the SBNR, spiritual milieu (see page 23) and the Extra-Theistic as people who are seeking for forms of spirituality but do not explore this need in connection with religion. The fieldwork of my own PhD study unapologetically held a theistic world view when engaged in the ethnographic fieldwork. Drawing on this ethnographic data and the grounded theory of my research, I found that, in a London context, the SBNR, ETH and spiritual milieu did indeed reflect the same social grouping and thereby offered the same opportunity for missional engagement. To assist this beginning point for mission, I will first outline the key conceptual understandings of SBNR spiritual seekers.

What are some of the key conceptual understandings of spiritual seekers?

A number of concepts arose from participants' spiritual stories, identified in group dialogues and individual interviews, which were all transcribed in the fieldwork stage of the PhD research behind this book. The method focused on the terms that appeared repeatedly in the varying understandings of the participants in six SBNR dialogue groups held in central and south London. To ensure these spiritual concepts reflected the views of the SBNR, they were further raised in two focus groups formed from participants of the six dialogue groups, to check the accuracy of what was named and shared.

Spirituality as a path of evolving spiritual growth and well-being

Central to all the groups was the focus on spirituality as an individual and experiential journey of discovery and exploration: for some this was about attending specific events such as spirituality workshops, retreats and learning events while for others it was seeking to discern spiritual significance in the ordinariness of life or a regular spiritual practice; for many this journey was catalysed through either painful experience of life or the sense that there was something more beyond. For many, well-being was important because their spiritual seeking had begun when they were unhappy, stressed or unwell because of the consequences of living in a modern market society. As Sam states:

> Spirituality is an evolution, for me ... Your viewpoints change and get broader, the more in my world, the more you are evolved ... for well-being, it helps me deal with the everyday, it helps me to make sense of the everyday and the ups and the downs. (Sam, City dialogue group, 4 July 2018)

Such spiritual growth came from experiencing forms of awakening or enlightenment, of unexpected meaning or emotional connection: this often came as a deeper connection to themselves, or a sense of love and connection with others, or a sense of connection to the beauty of life and nature.

This concept is significant, because it begins to name the importance of spiritual journeying for SBNR spiritual seekers, and the fact that participants will continually grow and change in this process. This will become important later in the book when we explore a specifically contemplative model of mission.

Spirituality as trans-rational experiential knowing

A common understanding of SBNR participants was the perception that the world valued rational knowledge gained through forms of scientific rationalism but totally undervalued more spiritual knowing as forms of wisdom or insight, gained through spiritual practices or participation in forms of spiritual community. This form of knowing-as-wisdom tran-scended facts-based knowledge.

For some, raised in households where scientific rationalism was the only form of knowing, it required forms of therapy or attending 12-step fellowships or the like to learn to suspend this tendency to decide what was important by whether it was rationally true or not and to provide space for other forms of knowing. This required 'unlearning' an over-dependency on rationality almost like a form of addiction, and allowing space for learning to trust intuition concerning other modes of know-ing. There was a connection between forms of scientific rationalism and the desire to control, to tie everything down, make everything neat and tidy, which was unhealthy because life is inherently messy. In this way rational modes of knowing did not enable the ability to live with paradox or mystery, which are inherently part of the spiritual journey. Reference was made many times to the desire for scientific knowing as a form of seeking to control the world, and how dangerous this was concerning the human ego. For example, Mike made decisions in the light of experience as a form of trans-rational knowing and inspiration:

> I try to make meaning out of what I experience and get challenged by. It's just experiences leading to understanding. It is always something beyond me and I just go with it. This is why I am here, this is why I am curious. (Mike, Peckham dialogue group, 6 August 2018)

For Trevor, spirituality offered the opportunity not to live a life dictated by the human ego in the context of our materialist market culture:

> I do believe that spirituality can offer the separation from the dominance of your ego and the ability to prevent the ego overdominating your sense of self. (Trevor, Battersea dialogue group, 23 October 2019)

The importance of non-rationalistic modes of spiritual knowing is I believe vital for the valuing of spiritual experience in our post-Enlightenment, post-secular context and is critical if the spiritual path is going to enable the SBNR seeker to grow. Learning such an approach to transformation, through spiritual intuition, artistic experience or experience of nature, among other things, is indispensable if the spiritual path is to be truly transformative.

Human and divine consciousness, evolution of consciousness

The language of consciousness was key to those in the study who were SBNR and was akin to a growing awareness of spiritual significance. For some, this was a journey of developing and deepening a sense of the individual human self and participation in a greater sense of connectiveness to others and a collective consciousness; for others, it was a strong sense that there was no such thing as an individual self but only a collective consciousness. There were a number of disagreements between these two groups, the later arising from the 'non-duality' movement or from the teaching of some forms of Zen Buddhism.

It was true to say that a significant majority of participants were seeking to deepen and strengthen a sense of self by following the spiritual path. Those who held to non-duality were however involved in three of the six groups. Cathy in the City dialogue group with her experience of Zen Buddhism, and Bethan from the Battersea group and her experience of non-duality, were the most outspoken in their non-belief in the human self:

> We have this delusion of the self and it is kind of guided by not wanting to see things for what they are but driven by desires of what I want or what I do not like. (Cathy, City dialogue group, 4 July 2018)

> So, the 'me' is part of a collective consciousness ... there is no individual self, which is why our current cultural form is so damaging ... The market and competition and the whole 'I' focus is based on a lie and misconception ... What we see in the world doesn't make it real ... We can't really define reality through our own experience of the world, but we can know that we are part of something far bigger. (Bethan, Battersea dialogue group, 20 November 2019)

Further to this was the idea of an 'evolution of consciousness', which was raised in all the groups. Here the path of spiritual growth of the human self, gaining in trans-rational knowing through various experiences, was seen and named as an evolutionary process. For Elna, the path of an evolving sense of consciousness was critical for her own spiritual path and connection to the divine:

> It doesn't matter what path you follow as long as you are evolving ... 'spirit' ... feels to me like life and breath and it's the kind of vast stillness ... the thing that is always there, that is never moving, that is immovable. And it feels to me like – if that is God – then highly intelligent, very graceful, full of grace and we get to see that when we are very quiet ... and it feels like, if I am in touch with that, it feels like peace. It's utterly peaceful, and complete love. (Elna, Pilot dialogue group, 24 January 2018)

For some who did not feel comfortable using language for God talked about a strong sense of knowing that there was some form of intelligence that lay behind the whole of life, as a form of divine consciousness. In the responses in the groups this seemed to be an alternative to the use of language of God, where this divine consciousness could be experienced or encountered through being close to nature, through encountering the divine from within, from unexpected experiences in life or through the use of various spiritual practices. For Sophie, this divine consciousness is closely related to a God of love:

> God for me is divine love, source, great spirit, what the native Americans call it. It's just pure consciousness, a divine consciousness. God for me is pure: the highest highest point of pure consciousness and pure love that you can get. And I feel comfortable using the word God. (Sophie, Kingston dialogue group, 16 May 2018)

On occasion these encounters with a divine consciousness were talked about in the context of participation where the individual human consciousness participated in relationship with the divine consciousness. Anna, who had been atheist, following the deaths of some family members started a spiritual search after having what she interpreted as spiritual dreams. She spoke of a greater awareness of her sense of consciousness and of encountering a divine consciousness from within:

> I always felt that there is more to life: there is more. I felt so desperate to find some answers … so I felt like finally I had received some kind of insight into the fact that there is more than meets the eye, and spirituality to me means now, that I have a consciousness and that through this I am in connection to something infinite, I encounter something eternal and I am whole and I am in connection to the divine or a divine source that is in me. (Anna, Telegraph Hill dialogue group, 26 August 2019)

The importance of consciousness and an evolution of consciousness are critical concepts in the forming of a normative theology and missiology in Part Two: its basis in the forming of a contemplative model of mission will be explored in Chapter 5.

Universality and eco-disconnection

As stated earlier in the stories and understandings of participants, consciousness was often connected to the idea of a universality of connection, a universality of all things. On many occasions participants addressed the need to situate people and society in an ecological context in reaction to the modern period, which distanced people from an ecological interdependence with all other animals and plants. In these discussions post-secular culture was named as deeply unhealthy, not only in terms of the speed of life and dependence on technology, but because of the active dehumanization resultant from urbanization, increased social isolation and other consequences of market society. It was seen as an intentional withdrawal from an integration with nature, as a form of eco-disconnection that has done humanity great harm regarding human mental and physical health. A healthy form of reconnection was often named, along with a sense of a renewed responsibility to promote closer interdependence of all life on the planet in forms of ecological diversity.

This eco-reconnection was seen as a renewed, spiritual appreciation for a universality. Choosing to live focused on eco-reconnection was seen to be a life choice to live counter-culturally to the selfishness of extreme individualism. The market society and its focus on economics and money was seen as doing violence to all life, including humanity, because the sanctity of life is effectively enslaved to the advancement of the market and the commodification of all life, including every human being. This connected to the danger of the human ego, around power and control, so that a reappreciation for a renewed ecological universality and reconnection was seen as a vital focus on collaboration and the common good, rather than the barbarity of competition where all and the environment lose.

For Abigail, being close and integrating with nature through walking in beautiful places was a regular spiritual practice:

> I feel a deep connectedness to nature when I walk. That sense of feeling part of something that is much bigger than the individual person. That connectedness to all living things. (Abigail, Telegraph Hill dialogue group, 26 September 2019)

Isabel's spiritual journey was influenced by the experience of living in a SBNR eco-community, which changed her spirituality through eco-reconnection:

> I lived in a forest garden in the south of Spain, and just ate food that I foraged for ... no electricity or running water, but camping and living very close to the earth. I had an epiphany when I was there ... I had a literal bio-chemical transformation of my body ... and started to see things so much more clearly. ... I felt happy for the first time in my life on a deep level. I felt deeply connected to the place I was and a sense of union with living things, I felt like a child of the universe. Less of a feeling and more of an experience of one-ness. In that time I was much more tuned into things in a way much deeper than I had ever before through experience of the heart. It was quite profound really. It changed the direction of my life ... My deepest wish really is

to recreate something like that for other people to experience. (Isabel, Telegraph Hill dialogue group, 14 November 2019)

For participants of the PhD research study, spirituality was about a healthier appreciation of ecological interdependency, rather than plundering the planet for resources in an unsustainable way that creates ecocide and global warming. Eco-reconnection also emphasized a healthier appreciation of the importance of human community around mutual love and mutual benefit. Spiritual community was focused on a universal belonging. I will return to this concept in Chapter 4, when forming a responsive contemplative theology.

Participation and community

This understanding of interdependence had much to say about relationality and relational connection as something to be experienced. One of the reasons often given in the groups for the term SBNR was that religious practice was too rational and made faith and belief about forms of facts and thinking, whereas spirituality was about life and the desire for depth, the common good and mutual flourishing. This was often articulated as a radical return to relationality. Therefore, when thinking about the possibility of a God and connection between God and people, this was explored in a more relational way.

For the majority of participants, growing in spirituality was seen as a journey of the reintegration and participation of the human self, as many acknowledged the real issue of a fragmented sense of the human self. This journey of inner integration connected to the possibility of experiencing God from within, a more participative approach than just thinking about God and faith, instead focusing on mystery and connection. For those who believed in a human self (which was not everyone, as discussed earlier), participation was named as a key concept in understanding a healthy human self and the connection between the self, other people and the divine. This was true for Peter, who said:

You can learn that in an instant, by sitting in a beautiful mountainside, and have a transcendent experience, or it can take years to learn through trial and error but it means that your deepest contentment is found when you stop seeing the world as 'What can I get out of life?' and more about, 'How can I participate?' … And amazingly and paradoxically, by connecting outside of yourself, and other people, you find yourself – you find something unique and beautiful about yourself as well ... And that is something I think spirituality helps you to do. (Peter, Borough dialogue group, 25 July 2018)

This focus on spiritual participation is significant for the forming of an emerging contemplative theology in Chapter 4.

Human identity: the true and false self (ego fantasy self), the inner and outer selves

When it came to human identity, as I stated earlier, there was a division between those who affirmed the importance of the human self and those of the non-duality movement and Zen Buddhism who did not. However, in the dialogues and interviews both sides did agree that the egoic sense of self was deeply unhealthy, something that spiritual seekers sought to address. Here an egoic sense of self was that driven by power, success, money, materialism and the desire to define the self by these things, which was seen as deeply unhealthy and unsustainable. This egoic sense of self was seen as aligned to a fantasy or false self, since it was made up and not real. This false self was seen as central to our contemporary market society and the modern tendency to eco-disconnection and isolation resulting in ill health and forms of addiction. Participants generally agreed that the spiritual path addressed the need to let go of this false sense of self. For those coming from a non-duality and Zen Buddhist perspective, the focus was on letting go of a sense of self altogether. For the majority who did believe in the importance of the self, the spiritual path focused on the development of a healthier sense of identity, which may have involved counselling or therapy, beginning a spiritual journey, learning to know and encounter the true self and letting go of any attempt to define the self through the false self. Spiritual practices were named as a particular way to do this. For Teressa, there is a spiritual developmental journey on which the individual proceeds:

We humans are born, and we have to develop our egos, and then you do get to that place later in life ... when you integrate that, when you transcend the ego, where you need to let go of any false or fantasy sense of self and seek the true self and then you move on to the next stage of development with the trans-rational. It's almost like an amalgamation of the instinctual with the rational, and experiential. (Teressa, City dialogue group, 31 May 2018)

The spiritual journey was seen as having two parts, the inner self and the outer self. For Calum, this integrated approach to spiritual seeking was critical:

> I am interested in the dynamic of ... the inner and the outer life as they have to be interrelated ... if we like it or not, no matter how much we try to suppress the inner life into our unconscious, it will eventually invade the conscious and the outer life. So whether we like it or not they mirror each other ... hopefully you are ... committed to facing and exploring ... the ego, the false, the shadow, the things about yourself, as part of your spiritual journey of the inner spiritual life, that will then impact on the outer life as greater integration and peace and contentment. (Calum, City dialogue group, 25 August 2018)

For Barkley, this inner and outer self related to the idea that each human is a mix of 'spirit' and physicality or 'matter'. He talked of the importance of unity of the two, where any sense of a gap could cause harm. By implication, spirit relates to the inner self and matter and physicality to the outer self:

> Spirituality for me is knowing that I am a 'spirit' person first. Which is a mass of energy, consciousness and intelligence ... I think that our physicality and the spirit, the objective of having both is to have them to unite as one. Disunity is only going to cause pain. (Barkley, Kingston dialogue group, 6 June 2018)

As I will go on to explore, the connection between the true and false selves, and the self as both spirit and matter, will be critical to the forming of a normative contemplative theology in Chapter 4.

Multifaceted God

When I began the PhD fieldwork research, I assumed that most SBNR would not use language of God but would prefer to use looser language. I was therefore surprised by how many talked about God quite openly. The majority of references made in the dialogues and interviews talked of God in metaphorical terms – as source, creator, spirit, love and sustainer.

On several occasions God was named as a multifaceted God that could be experienced, and where that encounter might be in the form of participation in relational connection. However, language around God was not consistent between all participants. An appreciation for a multifaceted God does open up the possibility of a primitive form of Trinitarianism.

Unsurprisingly, traditional religious use of language for God did not occur, other than naming Jesus on a very few occasions as a human person and as an expression of divine spirit. However, at the same time, I was surprised how many drew on religious and Christian forms of contemplative practice to resource their spiritual seeking. Valeria, for example, expressed encounter of the complex God through a spiritual practice of writing:

I do believe in a form of God but also believe that I can see God in everything. I experience this God though in multiple ways, God for me is not simple, God for me is complex, there is a multiplicity or multi-facetedness in the nature of God. I want to see God in everything, and I write and I write poetry, and I write stories and I read a lot, and I like to think that I like to try and find something of beauty in everything whether it is spirituality or squalor. (Valeria, Telegraph Hill dialogue group, 26 September 2019)

The understanding of a multifaceted God has many resonances with a Trinitarian understanding of God in a basic form, which will be discussed in Chapter 4.

Individual and collective soul

I was surprised that there was general agreement about the term 'soul', articulated as a form of spirit, as something hidden that was intrinsically part of being human. I was surprised as it implied the concept of life after death and a hidden part of our humanity drawing on Judaeo-Christian understandings. However, there were differences stemming from this: where followers of non-duality and others believed in a collective soul, some believed we all had a little bit of the divine soul within us. Others believed that we each had an individual human soul, which when we died formed a shared sense of collective soul. Still others believed in an individual human soul that travelled beyond when the individual died. However, all agreed indirectly that every human being was made up of matter – our human flesh and embodiedness – and a form of soul as a form of spirit, whether collective or individual or a mixture of both. By implication each human being was then a mixture of matter and spirit/soul. For Rosaline, there was a link between consciousness and a collective soul:

I think they have access to their whole higher self. Which is a collective soul. (Rosaline, Telegraph Hill dialogue group, 14 November 2019)

For Isabel, not only were there an individual and collective soul, but also the dynamic of how this relates to the false and true self or consciousness:

I see that there is a collective soul, which could be called the collective unconscious, and I think at the centre of every human being, there is a connection to that collective soul. Although most of us most of the time don't feel it. As individual souls, we have separated ourselves from our sense of being one with the collective soul through the way that we are conditioned as we grow up and the development of our egos, the way that we are made to live in a false separate consciousness. Often the way people try to get over that is to transcend it. (Isabel, Telegraph Hill dialogue group, 26 September 2019)

Dialogue, prayer and meditation practices as the media for spirituality

Finally in this brief descriptive analysis, I was surprised at the agreement in all the groups concerning the importance of a rhythm of spiritual practices to assist development on the spiritual path of seeking. I was surprised because this focus on spiritual prayer and meditation practices did not figure so prominently in the research on spiritual seeking outlined in the last chapter; and, again, it draws on an almost religious level of commitment, quite counter-cultural to the consumerist spirituality of avoiding commitments. To the contrary, such practices were seen as an essential part of the experiential aspect of being SBNR, and it was these spiritual practices that enabled six key features of the ways the SBNR seek for spirituality, which we will return to in Chapter 3. These practices broke down into three different forms: first, dialogue seeking to hear and share wisdom and insights to resource the spiritual journey; second, forms of prayer that drew on religious prayer practices, including those of Christianity, and creative expressions of spiritual practice, for example, engaging with nature and labyrinths; third, forms of contemplation and meditation in silence for mystical encounter with the divine or God. Spiritual practices, therefore, were seen as central for spirituality. For Calum, being disciplined about meditation was critical for his focus in spiritual seeking:

Practice is incredibly important, particularly for meditation, because for me, that is the core of it, actually, it is the practice, it is experiential for my spiritual path. (Calum, City dialogue group, 4 July 2018)

In conclusion, I have argued that the SBNR are an authentic social grouping and therefore worthy of missional engagement. Drawing on PhD research, I have identified some of the key conceptual thinking of the SBNR who took part in six dialogue groups in London. With the insights of this chapter into post-secular spiritual seekers, and clarity concerning the conceptual understandings of those who self-identified as Spiritual But Not Religious, these perspectives will be useful when exploring a contemplative theological response in Chapter 4. In the next chapter, I again return to the PhD research, but this time to reflect on how the SBNR seek for spirituality in a London context.

Notes

1 David Tacey, *The Spirituality Revolution: The Emergence of Contemporary Spirituality* (London: Routledge, 2004), p. 49.
2 Tacey, *The Spirituality Revolution*, p. 2.
3 Steven Croft, Rob Frost, Mark Ireland, Anne Richards, Yvonne Richmond and Nick Spencer, *Evangelism in a Spiritual Age: Communicating Faith in a Changing Culture* (London: Church House Publishing, 2005), p. 64.
4 Paul Heelas and Linda Woodhead, *The Spiritual Revolution: Why Religion is Giving Way to Spirituality* (Oxford: Blackwell, 2005), p. 82.
5 Heelas and Woodhead, *The Spiritual Revolution*, p. 83.
6 Tacey, *The Spirituality Revolution*, p. 30.
7 Heelas and Woodhead, *The Spiritual Revolution*, pp. 27, 83.
8 Heelas and Woodhead, *The Spiritual Revolution*, p. 3.
9 Tacey, *The Spirituality Revolution*, p. 42.
10 Tacey, *The Spirituality Revolution*, p. 1.
11 Heelas and Woodhead, *The Spiritual Revolution*, p. 26.
12 Croft et al., *Evangelism in a Spiritual Age*, p. 8.
13 Heelas and Woodhead, *The Spiritual Revolution*, p. 91.
14 Linda A. Mercadante, *Belief without Borders: Inside the Minds of the Spiritual but not Religious* (Oxford: Oxford University Press, 2014), pp. 32–3.
15 Mercadante, *Belief without Borders*, pp. 34, 36.
16 Mercadante, *Belief without Borders*, p. 32.
17 Mercadante, *Belief without Borders*, pp. 46, 52, 173–4.
18 Mercadante, *Belief without Borders*, p. 69.
19 Mercadante, *Belief without Borders*, p. 230.
20 Mercadante, *Belief without Borders*, p. 52.
21 In her research she found that nearly a third of participants had some experience of a 12-step recovery group that started them on the path of being seekers of spirituality as SBNR.

22 All three are Canadian academic researchers of the psychology of religion including research into spiritual seeking.

23 Matthew D. Graham, Marvin J. McDonald and Derrick W. Klaassen, 'A Phenomenological Analysis of Spiritual Seeking: Listening to Quester Voices', *The International Journal for the Psychology of Religion* 18, no. 2 (2008), pp. 154–8.

24 Mercadante, *Belief without Borders*, pp. 56–64.

25 Mercadante, *Belief without Borders*, p. 64.

26 Croft et al., *Evangelism in a Spiritual Age*, p. 8.

27 Heelas and Woodhead, *The Spiritual Revolution*, p. x.

28 Heelas and Woodhead, *The Spiritual Revolution*, p. 7.

29 Mercadante, *Belief without Borders*, p. 70.

30 Tacey, *The Spirituality Revolution*, pp. 3, 63–4, 69.

31 Tacey, *The Spirituality Revolution*, p. 69.

32 Marie McCarthy, 'Spirituality in a Postmodern Era', in *The Blackwell Reader in Pastoral and Practical Theology*, ed. James Woodward and Stephen Pattison (Oxford: Blackwell, 2000), p. 198.

33 Tacey, *The Spirituality Revolution*, p. 16.

34 Tacey, *The Spirituality Revolution*, p. 60.

35 Heelas and Woodhead, *The Spiritual Revolution*, p. 32.

36 Heelas and Woodhead, *The Spiritual Revolution*, p. 5.

37 Heelas and Woodhead, *The Spiritual Revolution*, pp. 5–6.

38 Tacey, *The Spirituality Revolution*, p. 33.

39 Heelas and Woodhead, *The Spiritual Revolution*, pp. 5–6.

40 Tacey, *The Spirituality Revolution*, p. 77.

41 Nancy Tatom Ammerman, *Sacred Stories, Spiritual Tribes: Finding Religion in Everyday Life* (New York: Oxford University Press, 2014), p. 4.

42 Ammerman, *Sacred Stories*, p. 50.

43 Ammerman, *Sacred Stories*, p. 52.

44 Meredith B. McGuire, *Lived Religion: Faith and Practice in Everyday Life* (Oxford: Oxford University Press, 2008), p. 5.

45 McGuire, *Lived Religion*, p. 15.

46 McGuire, *Lived Religion*, p. 6.

47 Ammerman, *Sacred Stories*, pp. 33–4.

48 Ammerman, *Sacred Stories*, pp. 34–5.

49 Ammerman, *Sacred Stories*, pp. 40–1.

50 Ammerman, *Sacred Stories*, pp. 34–46.

51 Ammerman, *Sacred Stories*, pp. 44–47.

3

How the 'Spiritual But Not Religious' Seek for Spirituality

In this chapter, I continue to explore the stories and perspectives of the spiritual seekers who took part in the PhD research study but this time turning to the task of spiritual seeking itself. This includes a comparison between the findings of Nancy Ammerman's research concerning the Extra-Theistic (ETH) in Boston, and those of my research on the 'Spiritual But Not Religious' (SBNR) in London.

Analysis of both groups' dialogues and interviews identified six main modes that the SBNR use to spiritually seek. These modes appear to be driven by the spiritual searchers themselves and raise theological issues and concepts that will need theological and missiological analysis in the next chapter before exploring a contemplative model of mission.

Turning to comparisons between the work of Ammerman in Boston and the findings of the PhD research in London, I first want to address differences in the nature of these studies. Ammerman's study is focused on the sociology of religion, or 'lived religion', which is not necessarily theistic in its epistemology. The framework of the PhD research, as a basis of this book, was definitively theistic and specifically Christian, and therefore the emerging theory arising from it is focused on mission practice and has a different epistemological relative perspective. As such the PhD research study may be better able to inform mission practice. Yet at the same time Ammerman's insights and findings are important to reflect upon.

The emerging theory of the PhD research study of how the SBNR seek for spirituality affirmed Ammerman's findings of four features, numbered 1 to 4 in Figure 3 below, which were:

1. Seeking transcendence in nature and spirituality;
2. Seeking integration, unity and connection;
3. Seeking meaning to guide one's life;
4. Seeking mystical truth that lies within.

However, the grounded theory and coding that drew on the ethnographic empirical data of the PhD research established evidence for the expansion of feature number one to include forms of the arts, and the addition of two new modes or characteristics of spiritual seeking, which were:

5. Seeking mystical truth that lies outside of the self;
6. Seeking authenticity through responsibility.

Figure 3: How Do the SBNR Spiritually Seek?

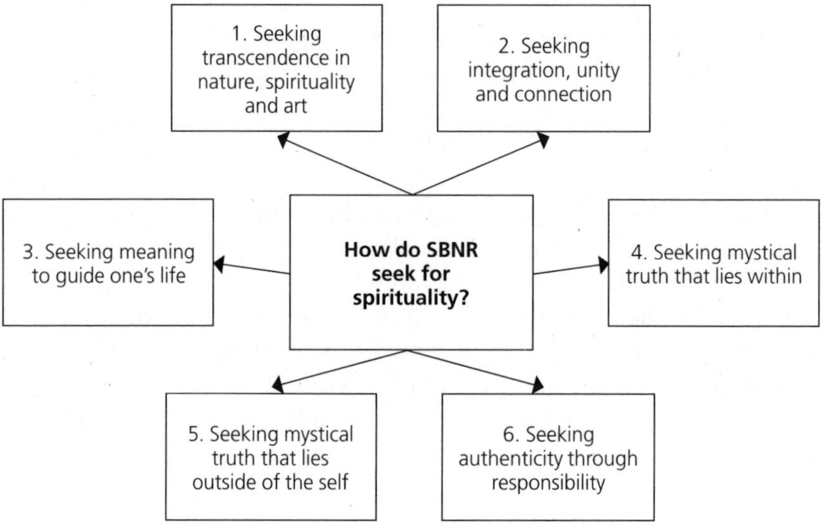

These six features therefore represent a strong typology and emerging theory for SBNR spiritual seeking.

Turning to Paul Heelas and Linda Woodhead and their work with the spiritual milieu, it is plain that the motivations and lived expression of the milieu in Kendal, explored in Chapter 2 and expressed in Figure 2, resonate strongly with the reasons why the SBNR became spiritual seekers in the PhD research study and these six characteristics or features of how the SBNR spiritually seek. This being so, this grounded theory drawn from the ethnographic empirical data of the PhD research study suggests that the spiritual milieu of Kendal and the SBNR of London in this study are the same social grouping.

1 Seeking transcendence in nature, spirituality and art: spiritually seeking mystical encounter

For Ammerman in her study of the ETH in Boston this first characteristic did not include the arts. In the PhD research study into the SBNR in London, this characteristic affirmed Ammerman's finding but went further to include the arts. Participants talked movingly of their sense of the experience of transcendence and spirituality when close to nature and when engaged in some form of artistic activity or experience.

For Peter, as for many, the palpable sense of awe as transcendent and mystical spiritual encounter when close to nature was profound and significant; he was clearly emotionally moved by the unexpected beauty and otherness of what he called 'spirit' when in a garden:

> Simply just by sitting in a garden and becoming aware of how bees are buzzing around flowers, and the birds are flying overhead, and the grass is growing, and just realizing that there is a whole universe that is already full of the most useful gifts that you can simply on a basic level just connect with. I belong in this universe, and I have to learn just to be. (Peter, Borough dialogue group, 25 July 2018)

Isabel indicated that she engaged in gardening specifically because it enabled the seeking of spirituality through proximity to nature and life, which brought a sense of well-being and connection:

> When you are in the garden, the garden is gardening you. It completely changed my relationship with being in the garden, I go out there every single day and just feel so connected. (Isabel, Telegraph Hill dialogue group, 26 September 2019)

An addition to that found by Ammerman's research team was the area of the arts and spirituality as transcendent moments of encounter through music, paintings, galleries and artistic performances. I was surprised how often the arts and experiences of transcendence were named in the groups. I was left asking the question: If this was so significant, why had this not been identified in the Ammerman research? Here Philippe describes the connection between the arts, consciousness and a form of transcendence that had moved him:

> It relates to consciousness ... in art you can see people and their eyes, you can see love and no conflict, passing on this experience from one generation to another ... so, spirituality then for me is about the

expression of love and therefore can be any expression or form of art – music, singing, painting, photography, movies. (Philippe, Borough dialogue group, 27 May 2018)

While Philippe hinted at this, Sam was pretty clear that not only does proximity to nature and engagement in artistic experience bring transcendence, but it further enables the SBNR seeker to experience breaking free from limitations as spiritual freedom:

Stepping out of your own little world into the world, experiencing the world in different ways, especially in nature, sunsets, the seascapes etc., just getting out there and experiencing the world again rejuvenates us, gives an appreciation of some kind of creation, creation force, what is behind all of this, and getting inspired by just simple things in life I guess, that are out there and exist in the world. (Sam, City dialogue group, 31 May 2018)

In addition to the sense of transcendence through nature and partaking in artistic activity to break free from limitations as spiritual freedom, for some like Sophie this progresses as a form of mystical encounter of the sacred and holy through being close to living things:

Sacredness for me is about finding the holy, holiness in something … You could do the gardening as if each flower and each plant are a very beautiful and incredible gift, and you could revere it with honour and respect, it's just about … acknowledging holiness and specialness in life I think. And seeing God in things. (Sophie, Kingston dialogue group, 6 June 2018)

2 Seeking integration, unity and connection: seeking spiritual fulfilment

This second feature of Ammerman's study of the ETH in Boston matches that of the SBNR in London. It was also clear that this feature was a key motivation and agency of the SBNR seekers in their stories of this study, as they sought to establish a healthy integration of self, particularly for those who became SBNR through a reactionary spiritual thirst driven by trauma, ill health and negative life experiences. This feature therefore shows the internal drive and the 'how' of their SBNR desire to find spiritual solutions and resources for a healthier sense of self. Further to this, I heard many times the commitment to seek to step away from the

more egoic forms of self-fulfilment through consumerism and materialism and instead a desire to face up to the delusions of the false self and
the spiritual task of focusing on being the true self.

Unsurprisingly, the largest area talked about in this study was the
seeking of spiritual fulfilment through an integrated approach to
'well-being, health integration and practices'. For many like Bethan,
seeking spiritual integration through spiritual practices that promoted
health and well-being were very important:

> I consider myself to be spiritual now ... for me, the well-being side
> is very important and crucial, my mental health is way stronger than
> it was five years ago. I have been able to deal with difficult family
> situations, work situations, manager situations, all kind of difficult
> situations including death and illness. All of that I have been able
> to handle drawing on non-duality as a spiritual principle. (Bethan,
> Battersea dialogue group, 20 November 2019)

In the stories of the SBNR of the PhD research study, it was clear that
many were taking a holistic approach to integration and connection,
particularly concerning emotions and dealing with fear and negativity,
as they sought for forms of spirituality as healing and restoration, often
through forms of self-help/spiritual mastery or self-improvement. For
Rosaline, this holistic approach of rebalancing the inner and outer life
was crucial for the alleviation of suffering from fear through feeling loved:

> My understanding of soul ... is that I am in contact with much more
> in my life, now that my inner life and my outer life are a much more
> aligned reality ... So for me spirituality has resolved a lot of the fears
> that I think I have because essentially at a deep level, I feel loved.
> (Rosaline, Telegraph Hill dialogue group, 16 January 2020)

For Jenny, engagement with spiritual forms of integration enabled her
to face and process negative experiences:

> These negative experiences help you to see and value the good things
> that you have in your life ... So I think facing spiritually, the shitty
> things that happen in life, is really important. Once you come out
> the other side, you can see them and the positive impact it can bring.
> (Jenny, Kingston dialogue group, 8 August 2018)

Engaging in spiritual practices that bring integration enabled SBNR participants such as Abigail to find peace with the self, with a focus on increased self-acceptance as a spiritual discipline:

> There is something about standing up to injustice and prejudice that is also very spiritual ... something about acceptance and self-acceptance are so important; that has been part of my journey of life as a person too. There is something about spirituality being about having peace with yourself. (Abigail, Telegraph Hill dialogue group, 3 April 2020)

The one area that I was surprised to hear named was the connection between seeking integration and unity and the ideas of the false self, true self and shadow self. Not only did this show the influence of therapy and reading of various self-help texts, it also connected to the more contemplative: the striving to dig deeper than the egoic self that has no depth, or those parts of us that are difficult to acknowledge like the shadow or false self.

For those who have faced illness and forms of trauma, it is not surprising that many are on a spiritual quest to engage with the true self. This also connects again with the perspective that there is much about a modern market society that colludes with the false, shadow and egoic self, hence the spiritual quest to dig deeper.

As explored earlier, for Anton, there was the awareness that our market society promoted the egoic and unhealthy, and that being SBNR and focusing on healthy spiritual integration and unity was vital to resist the societal addiction to the false self and to seek the true self:

> There is inconsistency in the world which says with one voice that you are not enough and then with the other love yourself to the extreme. There is a kind of self-love that is indulgent; it can be narcissistic. In such a situation you have to get over yourself.
>
> Thinking about the false self and the true self, is there a link between this and society ... that society is constructed in a way that is not for me; that I need to make enough money, I need to try and get on top of life to be able to survive; so is the state of society the accumulative effect of all these false selves? (Anton, Borough dialogue group, 25 July 2018)

Peter represents many of the SBNR in the PhD research study in demonstrating not only a depth of understanding of the false self, shadow self and true self, but also awareness of the consequences of these on the healthiness of the individual:

> The ego being this kind of fragile thing, that is us in our less mature state ... and in my false self, the one that is easily anxious, easily offended, thinks that I have got something to lose, thinks that another person's success means that I am less successful. Constantly making comparisons with others, that is the false self. The true self is that when you are living in a more sense of peace, you feel you have a place in the world, you feel that whatever happens you will be OK. (Peter, Borough dialogue group, 25 July 2018)

The importance of these insights cannot be overstated, and they will be explored in the context of contemplative theology and practice.

3 Seeking meaning to guide one's life: seeking experience leading to understanding

Again, this characteristic identified by Ammerman in her study of the ETH in Boston reflects the experience of the SBNR in London. Within the stories of those who took part in the PhD research study, the desire to seek varied spiritual experiences to open up understanding was seen as a key form of knowing that was distinctive for those who saw themselves as SBNR.

Seeking spirituality brought different forms of knowing to counter what was seen as an overfocus on rationalism and in particular scientific rationalism. Engaging with what I have labelled as trans-rationalism (although many SBNR in this study did not like this label) brought together the importance of the heart through instinctual, artistic, wisdom and other non-rational modes of knowing as the means for seeking meaning to guide one's life.

For Mike, spirituality was based on an approach of 'experience leading to understanding', needing to be based on non-judgementalism if it were to lead to real wisdom:

> For me, spirituality is a looser term ... it's something that's open to everybody. It's not something that judges harshly, not something that condemns, it's just something there the whole time without having to be anything in order to achieve it. (Mike, Pilot dialogue group, 24 January 2018)

While for Bethan, non-dualism was key to enable real learning that does not resist, avoid or overly simplify complex situations:

We seek to run away from pain, so there is always a seeking and always a resisting. When you are totally comfortable with conscious- ness, neither of those are present. So this means we have to stop run- ning away, and face non-duality as a basis of our existence. (Bethan, Battersea dialogue group, 20 November 2019)

On a different tack, but still relevant in their connection to knowing, were people's responses around existential questions of life and the need to face them as part of an explorative process of spiritually seeking as meaning-making. This was particularly so in the context of bereavement and loss, as experienced by John. Connected with this and prevalent with some, like Kitty, was a belief in reincarnation. For some, the seek- ing for meaning and guidance concerned the significance of this life, where people's spiritual search touched on the importance of whether there was life after death or not, and if there were, if this would relate to forms of reincarnation:

All this death has been very traumatic for my Mum and I. Spirituality has become more important to me on the loss of my father, brother and sister. I miss them a lot, and spirituality gives me comfort that I believe they live on in a different place. (John, Life History Interview)

I feel there must have been a bit of me that has been around before. This body, things that you have known intuitively, or you sense, or you go into places you recognize even though you have never been there before. Or meet other people and they feel familiar even though you have never met ... I do believe there is a connection between reincarnation and the soul. (Kitty, Telegraph Hill dialogue group, 25 September 2019)

Of interest to me as the researcher was the synthetic process by which many of the SBNR participants of this study made meaning. Often this was a fusion of internet blog posts, online materials, social media, You- Tube videos and the like that provided opportunity for people to engage with all sorts of information as part of a synthetic process, exploring influences to form experience leading to understanding. The responses of Caleb offer a good example of this form of synthetic process of knowing:

I am part of a number of Meetup Groups ... I do use the internet and email and social media for communication. I do visit spiritual sites not religious ones. (Caleb, Life History Interview)

Regarding this third feature, 'Seeking meaning to guide one's life', I turn to the articulated understandings of participants and the emerging theory around 'knowing'.

Given its complexity, I will seek to explore these codings in Figure 4, which relates to the largest group in this typology, those who made a distinction between rational and non-rational modes of knowing.

The rational was related to scientific truth and the need for order and the simplification of reality, whereas the trans-rational was seen as wild and unpredictable, or forms of wisdom and the following of the heart. Further, where the rational as scientific truth sets up a binary of being true or false, trans-rationalism affirmed the reality of something being grey and non-binary, where reality is far more uncertain.

Figure 4: Seeking Meaning to Guide One's Life

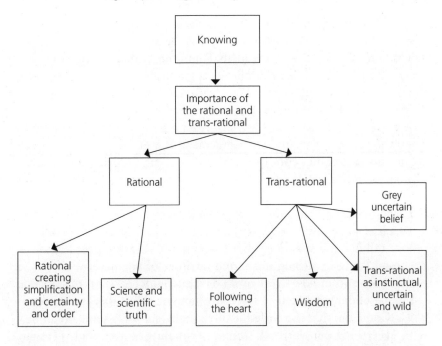

In the PhD research study group discussions, interviews and focus groups, it was clear that for many of the participants there was a connection between being a SBNR spiritual seeker and engaging deliberately in non-rational modes of knowing. While the importance of rationalism was acknowledged in our highly scientific culture, the importance of non-rational modes of knowing to inform the spiritual seeking for meaning to guide one's life was seen as central and essential for the SBNR. Indeed, non-rational knowing was seen as a necessary corrective to the overdependence on rational knowing which, many argued, was one of the reasons why the planet and human society was in a mess.

In both focus groups the terms 'rational' and 'trans-rational' were not liked. One participant offered 'head' and 'heart' as replacement labels but after reflection I decided against them because 'heart' was already a subordinate coding, and because the terms 'rational' and 'trans-rational' are already being used in a similar way by others in published works:[1]

> One of the surprises ... was this word 'trans-rational' and I have been trying to work out exactly what it meant ... I think it represents the heart, like the rational is the mind and the trans-rational is the heart. I feel concerned that the word 'trans-rational' for me is a way of bypassing ... the heart, is like a mental way of describing the heart without describing the heart. (Isabel, First Focus Group, 14 July 2020)

In the PhD study I kept the label 'trans-rational' because only one of the aspects of this experiential coding was the heart and the other terms – 'wisdom', the 'wild' and 'instinctual' and the 'reality of uncertainty' – were as important as 'heart' in the ethnographic coding of the empirical data. Likewise, I also kept the label 'rational' because many of the participants talked about rationalism rather than head knowledge.

For Trevor, the open-endedness of reaching beyond the rational into the trans-rational was an essential element of an experiential approach to spiritually seeking, core to the SBNR, seeking experience that leads to understanding:

> I love being on that journey of finding out more about spirituality, which is somehow free from the weight of science and rationality. I love talking and speaking about spirituality, hearing people's views ... and I love exploring uncharted territory of what spirituality is in other people's minds. Every time I have encountered or heard someone talking about spirituality I have not thought, 'Well that is not true is it', 'Come on, that is a little bit silly', there is always some credibility to everything people think about spirituality in my mind. (Trevor, Battersea dialogue group, 23 October 2019)

Teressa goes further to connect the spiritual journeying of the SBNR not only to reach beyond rationalism, but further to reach beyond the egoic into the instinctual, uncertain and wild:

> We humans are born, and we have to develop our egos, and then you do get to that place later in life ... when you transcend the ego, and

then you move on to the next stage of development with the trans-rational. It's almost like an amalgamation of the instinctual with the rational, or experiential. (Teressa, City dialogue group, 31 May 2018)

A few SBNR in the PhD study described times of feeling overwhelmed by the focus on trans-rational modes of experiential learning, because this non-rational mode of knowing and living was seen to be wild and unpredictable and therefore, at times, painful, exhausting and difficult.

For Mike, who worked in a health profession, the demands of the job meant that he could not function when he felt overwhelmed. In such situations, rational modes of knowing can provide comfort even if this is known to be oversimplified. When overwhelmed it can be easier to live with a strong sense of order than to live with everything being uncertain and grey, even if this makes things less interesting:

For me the head and rationalism are almost like a retreat when things are really hard, when at times the spiritual becomes confusing ... and the world and its pressures are unrelenting, the head takes over. It's a reflex, it's a coping strategy and I think many people do this. The inner life and engaging with it can be raw, yes at times exciting and rewarding, and sometimes ... uncertain, overwhelming and anxiety-making. This is the nature of the spiritual, it is raw and not easy. So in situations when I am not feeling great, I fall back into the head and rational to remain functional. (Mike, Peckham dialogue group, 7 November 2018)

However, Mike also acknowledged that non-rational modes of knowing were linked to the idea of a wisdom that goes much deeper than forms of rational knowing:

Lived experience, emotional experience, psychological experience, spiritual experience, all of this becomes the background of experience leading to understanding that informs my decision-making. Those things tend to go all together. This I think is called wisdom. There is a difference between logic and wisdom. So I base my decisions, I hope, on a growing wealth of wisdom. (Mike, Peckham dialogue group, 6 September 2018)

For the SBNR in the PhD research study, the focus on knowing through trans-rational experiential seeking was critical as a strategy for spiritual growth. This can be seen as a corrective to a culture that until recently has been driven by the overfocus on scientific rationalism as the only means of reliable knowing. The SBNR in the PhD research study are clearly reappropriating more trans-rational, experiential modes of seeking experience, leading to understanding and forming a spiritual wisdom out of these experiences. However, at the same time, participants did acknowledge the need for a both/and approach, the trans-rational and the rational. For Calum, this more non-dualistic approach was seen to be important:

> It seems to me that we need both, the rational and the trans-rational, the need for the tension or the assimilation of the two, because you cannot have one without the other. (Calum, City dialogue group, 31 May 2018)

This feature named by Ammerman of the ETH of Boston resonates with the SBNR of the PhD study in London, and therefore offers further evidence that the two terms are more connected than Ammerman stated.

4 Seeking mystical truth that lies within: spiritually seeking the divine and God from within

This feature arising from Ammerman's feature of the ETH is central to what makes the SBNR in this PhD research study spiritual seekers: the focus on using various forms of spiritual practice. In the coding of the ethnographic empirical data of the study, the SBNR spiritual seekers used various spiritual practices, motivated by the desire for a deeper and more comprehensive sense of encounter with the divine or spirit from within. Further, as expressed in the fifth feature later, for some, these spiritual practices enabled a deeper and more comprehensive encounter with God's presence.

For some, such as Anton, this internal spiritual search began by acknowledging the importance of each person having an individual soul. Any inner exploration then comes from the sense of a spiritual identity that touches deeply into the spirituality of that person, which is more than the body, mind and human emotions:

> We have a body, and a mind and emotions and beyond that we seem to have this thing called a soul, something that has hopes and dreams and that is crucial to spirituality. (Anton, Borough dialogue group, 25 July 2018)

This sense of a soul was also expressed as spirit. For Barkley, spirit was at the heart of a human being. As such the SBNR seek the life force, spirit or energy source that lies within:

> Spirituality for me is knowing that I am a 'spirit' person first. Which is a mass of energy, consciousness and intelligence, so beyond the physical self. (Barkley, Kingston dialogue group, 6 June 2018)

On listening to the stories of the SBNR in the PhD research study, spiritual practices were the essential means and activity by which participants actively sought spiritual experience by turning inwards, stating that such an approach often gave them life and a form of wisdom. Spiritual practices, then, enabled the formation of ancient wisdom, so often neglected by many in modern society with the overdependence on rational thinking rather than seeking spiritual experience of the transrational through participation in spiritual activities and practices.

Given the complexity of the theory concerning spiritual practices arising from this PhD research ethnographic study, I utilize the aid of a chart to map out the various elements of spiritual practices coming out of the stories of participants in this study, as listed in Figure 5.[2] This figure expresses the grounded theory concerning 'Seeking mystical truth that lies within', where forms of alternative spirituality and religious spiritual practices were utilized in this quest. Some participants used one or two different resources; the majority drew on many, while some drew on a mixture of all those listed in their own unique spiritual journey.

As shown in Figure 5, for Sam, engaging in forms of spiritual practices was essential to a life-giving spirituality:

> Spirituality ... it is definitely something that gives me life I guess, it enhances my idea of life. It helps me centre myself. I find that where I am now. (Sam, City dialogue group, 31 May 2018)

For Caleb, participating in spiritual practices shared within a community was important to his sense of growth and spiritual search from within:

> The spirituality that I follow ... it's ... about what I do with my life and how I progress, and how I grow in consciousness and the importance of an evolution of consciousness, and join in with a community that is also seeking to grow this way, into and guided by an ancient wisdom. (Caleb, Life History Interview)

Figure 5: Seeking Mystical Truth that Lies Within

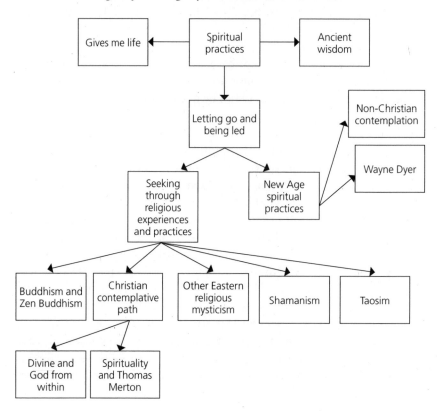

As I stated earlier in this book, I was surprised how important it was for those who were SBNR seekers in the PhD research study to be committed to forms of spiritual practice. Not only this, but a number were drawing on differing forms of contemplative prayer and meditation that focused on some form of 'letting go' or 'surrender' of the self or 'ego-self'.

For Anton, this focus on 'letting go' in spiritual practices was an important means of being counter-cultural to forms of individual consumerism, and then enabled a sense of deeper transformation:

There is something about letting go of the need to keep consuming … We can't just live in an experience-driven life because it is just about the next hit rather than authentic spirituality, which requires you to let go of endless consumption. This requires a paradigm shift, true spirituality to be transformative needs to be a paradigm shift. It becomes central to life. Once you have this type of transformative experience, nothing can take that centre ground quite like that experience, and it probably needs to happen more than once. (Anton, Borough dialogue group, 30 January 2019)

Before beginning the fieldwork for the PhD research study, I had assumed that most participants would be seeking approaches resonant with the New Age movement as exemplified by my experience of Mind, Body and Spirit festivals in a UK context, with their focus on energy and a whole host of more Eastern influences.[3] I had assumed that spiritually seeking SBNR participants would be highly suspicious or sceptical about engaging with spiritual practices associated with forms of religion, both Western and Eastern, but I was wrong. Some participants did name writers and New Age practitioners who had reinterpreted forms of religious practices, such as Wayne Dyer, who reframed forms of Taoism, but the vast majority drew on forms of religious spiritual practice.[4] Interestingly, many, like Cathy, were drawing on religious spiritual practices because they believed that such practices had credibility, having stood the test of time:

> I wouldn't say I was a Zen Buddhist, but I do follow their approach to meditation … I do not do anything that is not part of a traditional religion … I suppose I am very cautious. I want to know that something is tried and tested, and not dabble. (Cathy, Life History Interview)

I was less surprised that participants engaged with spiritual practices arising from Eastern mystical religions, including Zen Buddhism, Shamanism, Taoism and Indian Guru cult religions. I was not surprised, as this pick'n'mix approach drawing on Eastern mystical religions is core to the practice of adherents of New Age-focused Mind, Body and Spirit festivals in a UK context.

However, I was very surprised at how many used spiritual practices arising out of Christian contemplative traditions, with their focus on surrender and encountering the God from within. In one group the writings and practices of Thomas Merton were specifically talked about; a participant had walked into a bookshop randomly to explore the spirituality section and bought a book by Thomas Merton after being impressed by what he had experienced through YouTube clips and audios of Merton's work. Participants made a distinction between these spiritual practices and the religions they were associated with, so that the practices were seen as good and the religions as not relevant. There was a profound inconsistency here that reflects Ammerman's critical view of the SBNR, as she believed that partaking in religious spiritual practices makes you religious. Participants of the PhD research fieldwork disagreed with this understanding: it was possible to use a variety of differing spiritual practices associated with different religions and remain an authentic SBNR spiritual seeker.

For some of the participants, there was real surprise that there were contemplative traditions and practices associated with Christianity. Many had associated Christianity with fundamentalism, which was all about thinking and control, rather than forms of silence, meditation, surrender and giving away control. Connections here with the Christian contemplative traditions and theology will be discussed later in this book as critical to the formation of a normative theology.

5 Seeking mystical truth that lies outside of the self: spiritually seeking the divine and God from without

Beginning with the first of the two new features established in the PhD research study (in addition to Ammerman's features of the ETH), I explore the stories of SBNR spiritual seekers and how they intentionally use forms of spiritual practice largely drawn from trans-rational spiritual modes of encounter beyond the self. This feature of the seeking of the SBNR now begins in earnest to focus on an attempt to name various forms of encounter of spiritual significance beyond the self. This inevitably connects with the beginnings of an articulation of the divine and of God out of the differing experiences of the diverse SBNR participants of the PhD research study. Among differing understandings there are some resonances with a primitive Christian understanding of God. There are also a number of ideas and concepts that have theological implications, which will be discussed in later chapters.

Experience leading to understanding and transformative encounters with God and the divine

Transformative spiritual experiences enabled participants to make meaning out of largely trans-rational spiritual experiences of the 'other'. Given the complexity of this grounded theory evidenced by the empirical data, I have expressed the connections for this feature of the SBNR in Figure 6 below.

Within the stories of many participants of the PhD research study, there was an articulation of forms of transformative and mystical experience beyond the self, gained through engagement with some form of spiritual practice that gave rise to a trans-rational mode of experience

Figure 6: Seeking Mystical Truth that Lies Outside of the Self

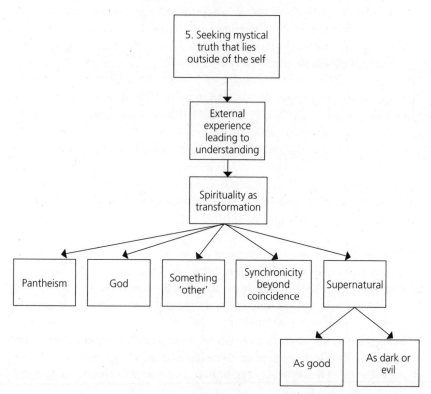

and encounter with something 'other', whether intentional, incidental or accidental. For many, this positive or negative experience led to some form of transformation as learning through experience. When seeking clarity about what other participants were seeking for as mystical truth, there was a variety of responses.

For some, like Elna, the articulation of an emerging understanding of this 'otherness' was difficult to name other than as a sense of encounter of something 'other' or a synchronicity beyond coincidence:

> When you look at coincidences in life, and synchronicity, and things that just seem beyond coincidence, like some sort of divine whatever the word is ... it feels to me sometimes like, things happen, almost as if there's something very intelligent, vastly intelligent life, holding everything or connecting everything. (Elna, Pilot dialogue group, 24 January 2018)

For others like Camila, the encounter with something 'other' is expressed specifically in the language of something supernatural, a sense of force either good or malevolent:

Negative forces are definitely present but also positive forces too. We as humans could not survive at all without these positive forces being present here on earth … there are supernatural forces in the world … Some are hostile forces that have unpleasant aspects as well. (Camila, Telegraph Hill dialogue, 1 May 2020)

A surprise to me personally was that many SBNR participants were happy to use the word 'God'. I thought this was something that many would not choose to do, preferring labels such as 'spirit', as reported by David Tacey, but in the PhD research study it seemed many were happy to use 'God'.[5]

Some, like Cathy, talked about seeking mystical truth that lies outside of the self through engagement with a pantheistic God who was present wherever there was life and in nature:

All things are connected. There was something very special about being on my way to work … and hearing this little bird sing its heart out. The bird didn't seem to know or care that the tree was set in the middle of a man-made, rather ugly concrete jungle. It seemed utterly content in the moment to do what is in its nature. It had no regrets about not being able to find a nicer tree in a nicer area and no worries about the past or future. It helped me to come back to the moment and to experience the joy of being present right here and now. (Cathy, Ethnographic Photo Interview)

Naming God out of spiritual experience

Within this fifth typology of seeking mystical truth that lies outside the self, as listed in Figure 7 below, the naming of God out of varied forms of spiritual trans-rational experience, from either being close to nature or engaging in the arts, brought forth a wealth of differing ideas associated with speaking about God. In this section, I explore the varied understandings drawn out of the stories of participants, some of which will require further theological and missiological reflection in later chapters in the naming of a normative theology, beginning with the central theory of the PhD research study, that the Trinitarian God will be unsettling for the SBNR who are spiritually seeking to encounter truths about God.

There were four elements of the typology of this subgrouping of the stories involving God:

- God as an unjust God;
- God as a less personal God;
- God as something other of great intelligence and divine consciousness;
- God as love and more personal and able to be encountered.

I commence this exploration with a paradox: some acknowledged their conviction that God existed, but that such a God was unjust given the state of the world. Mike was typical of this view:

> What is the nature of this God? ... the God who answers prayers, the God who intervenes, the God who rescues and the God who doesn't, the inconsistency of it. (Mike, Pilot dialogue group, 24 January 2018)

Reflecting forms of pantheism, some did not believe in a personal God or that there was only one way to God, considering this a mistake of religion. I was surprised in this research that there was little use of the language of 'many gods' as the focus when God was mentioned; the term 'God' was largely seen as unitive. For some, there was a sense that we and all life are part of God, so again touching on a more pantheistic idea of God:

> I struggle with the idea of God as a human person, God is not that for me, God is for me a force, a positive force, a creative force, which is impossible for us to understand. (Sam, Ethnographic Photo Interview)

For other SBNR seekers who used language naming God in their stories, there was an affirmation that God does exist as an entity beyond the self as a form of divine consciousness or great intelligence – as a form of mysterious 'other'. Caleb named this God of intelligence and consciousness, but such a God still feels impersonal:

> I have often felt a sense of synthesis or synchronization where things have come together at the same time – my consciousness, the consciousness of others and the divine consciousness: it is when it happens, a very deeply moving experience, where you seem to be able to see things more spiritually, when you seem to be able to experience the deep spirituality and love in people, you just can't miss it, almost like the divine consciousness. (Caleb, Life History Interview)

Of great significance was the theme of 'God is love'. Given this as potential evidence of a God revealing Godself in human experience, I have summarized all these codings for clarification in Figure 7 below. Of great surprise for me were the many who considered themselves SBNR who talked of a God and recognized that the source of love is God, as stated by Sophie:

> God is the highest form or expression of divine love ... I have encountered this love in personal experiences of Jesus through prayer, meditation and being close to nature ... which has been extremely restorative for me and affirming of me as a person ... such encounters of God go deep and get back to the real Jesus who inspires and brings love. (Sophie, Life History Interview)

Some, even though they were not Christian and considered themselves SBNR, used language that bordered on religious theological language, where God was simultaneously the 'ground of our being' and a unifying force:

> It's a God from within and a God from without ... where I experience God the strongest for me ... like this idea of the 'ground of being'. (Calum, City dialogue group, 31 May 2018)

> We grow in our connection with God as a unifying force. (Caleb, Borough dialogue group, 1 May 2019)

For some, the language of God was connected to a multifaceted entity that some named as 'God'. It seemed that respondents were grappling with the desire to seek spiritual mystical truth that lies outside of the self, and that they affirmed a multifaceted God as an expression of love. These views were not affirmed by all the SBNR of the PhD research study; nevertheless they were mentioned quite a few times, but in non-religious language and understanding, as expressed by Caleb and Anton:

> I do believe in a multifaceted divine consciousness, and if that is what you mean by 'God' then I am happy. (Caleb, Life History Interview)

> That was one of the first things that drew me to wanting to experience spirituality and God and to know about this Jesus that I had heard talked about, and hearing about God and the Trinity and the Holy Spirit, that could actually fill you. (Anton, Borough dialogue group, 1 May 2019)

Continuing with this theme, some of the SBNR seekers of the PhD research study used language that held a sense of paradox that God was 'source' and at the same time multifaceted, which again seemed to verge on the beginnings of a Christian understanding, as articulated by Isabel:

> God moves in mysterious ways. God can move through anything and anyone. So God is in connection with everything. Infinitely multifaceted. (Isabel, Life History Interview)

Further, some articulated an understanding of God as 'source' and God as 'creator', which again resonated with Christian theology of the first person of the Holy Trinity, as articulated by Barkley:

> Well, in the world, the first thing we have to understand, there is a creator, God is life. (Barkley, Kingston dialogue group, 6 June 2018)

A common theme was language of God as 'life force' and 'spirit'. This again resonates with Christian theology, as stated by Anton in his encounters with Christians:

> One of my first spiritual experiences was that I felt filled. Christians have said that was being filled by the Holy Spirit, and I definitely feel there was something about God in that moment. I felt this deep sense of reconnection from being isolated and alienated. I learnt to be happier with being with myself and feeling filled on the inside. (Anton, Borough dialogue group, 1 May 2019)

In summary, many SBNR of the PhD research study seemed to name a positive understanding of God, and a number articulated the idea of 'God is love'. Some talked of the idea of a multifaceted God, and of the idea of God as source, creator, spirit or life force. This could be the beginnings of an articulation of God as Trinity, but for the fact that language about Jesus was lacking.

A minority of participants used the language of Jesus the person, and others mentioned the idea of 'Christos' as the divinity of Christ, as stated by Rosaline:

> There is also the love aspect of God which we call the 'Christos'. Because if you have pure intelligence without love, then you come to this earth to experience and to understand and to know love. And then embodied in the man Jesus, Yeshua, his family name was Yeshua, so he then embodied it. (Rosaline, Life History Interview)

Clearly this has minimally drawn on some understanding of Christianity, but then taken it into the abstraction of a SBNR discourse that changes the meaning of these words. In the stories of SBNR participants of the PhD research study, language of God was strong on 'creator' and 'spirit' but there was little content about the significance of Jesus.

However, saying that, the language used for God was diverse. It is hard to escape the significance of the connection of some of the responses as resonating with the beginnings of a Christian understanding of God. I was anxious to ensure that my views and understandings were not being imposed on to the research, but when this point was raised in the two focus groups to check out reflexivity, there was no challenge to the diagrams laid out in Figure 7.

The use of language for God in the stories of the SBNR seems significant in that it affirmed a more open-ended understanding of God and an emerging panentheism. Yet at the same time, for some, there seemed to be the beginnings of an articulation of God resonating with Christianity (see Figure 7).

Figure 7: Naming God out of Spiritual Experience

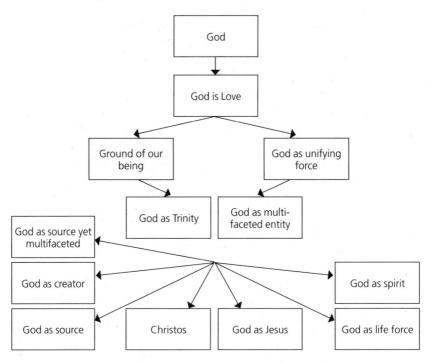

6 Seeking authenticity through responsibility: being counter-fundamentalist and counter-consumerist through spiritual activism

This is the second of the new features of 'How the SBNR seek for spirituality' identified in addition to those in Ammerman's work. As explored in Chapter 2, Ammerman names another of her spiritual tribes 'Ethical or Moral', defining them as activists who lived by an ethical understanding of the 'Golden rule' as 'acting in a way that you would like to be treated yourself'. In that study, Ammerman does say that some ETH might stray into the 'ethical' or 'moral', but nevertheless makes a distinction between these two spiritual dispositions.[6] However, in stories of the participants of this PhD research study, the SBNR not only stray into the moral or ethical, but express their spirituality deeply through seeking spiritual authenticity by choosing to live in a responsible way. This is a form of giving back to other people, all life and the planet – an expression of eco-reconnection, of spiritual love, of giving rather than taking. This depth of spiritual commitment can be seen as the consequence of all the previous features of the ETH and SBNR explored thus far.

Initially, participants of the PhD research study became SBNR spiritual seekers after experiencing a thirst for spirituality. This thirst often arose from an innate or reactive spiritual awakening, which led them to the path of SBNR spiritual seeking. Participants became open to the desire for trans-rational modes of experience leading to understanding as 'knowing', largely through forms of spiritual practice. These practices in turn opened up SBNR seekers to a transcendent encounter with God as the source of love, and a reality in and beyond the self that included the divine, or God, and all existence. Given that SBNR spiritual seekers have received this love, they therefore act to give back love, life and spirituality to God, the planet and others through spiritual activism.

For some, this spiritual activism was a direct response to the sense of an ecological dislocation or disconnection, and the loss of understanding of the place of each human being in a mixed ecology of life. In the research this was named as an 'eco-disconnection' caused by the increasing alienation between people and nature. In this context, spiritual activism was seen as critical for 'eco-reconnection'.

Many described this as a way of life, taking responsibility for your activities and the consequences of such actions on other people, animals and the planet. Such a way of living, a spirituality that sees the bigger picture and is therefore life-affirming, was seen as a corrective and as counter to the violence and lack of responsibility often shown by those who were religious fundamentalists or irresponsible consumers of a market society. Indeed, the focus on an activist spirituality being counter to religious fundamentalism as a way of life was a constant theme, not only in all the dialogue groups, but also in both focus groups, as expressed by Isabel and Caleb:

> One thing I had forgotten ... and it is a good thing, is about spirituality as being counter-fundamentalist, and yes that feels really right, promoting tolerance, diversity and inclusion, having space culturally for multiple ways of relating with spirit and ... including having a place where we can interact with people on the spiritual journey who are different from us. (Isabel, First Focus Group, 14 July 2020)

> I was hungry for change and for a deeper way of life, I was searching for something deeper than what is on offer in our secular culture. (Caleb, Life History Interview)

Qualities such as being open-minded and optimistic, facing the reality that life is short and we are impermanent, and having compassion and kindness for people, all life and the planet were seen as essential qualities of those who were SBNR. These values as a form of spiritual activism are expressed well by Jenny, Cathy and Imran:

> I think spirituality ... gives me a sense of stability and that I am valuing things in the everyday ... makes life meaningful ... to look for things that are good and to ... focus on those things rather than the bad things that happen. And to try and bring light to others who are having a bad time. Just deciding that you want to be a good person and pursue good things. (Jenny, Kingston dialogue group, 8 August 2018)

> ... the deeper problem of facing your own impermanence and fragility as the beginning of the spiritual journey, which begins with the need to deeply face yourself. (Cathy, Ethnographic Photo Interview)

> I don't think you can find real spirituality if it is all about you without responsibility of kindness, compassion and action with others. (Imran, Battersea dialogue group, 20 November 2019)

To live this way was seen as an important choice and as an expression of spirituality and love. This was learning to live in a way counter to the consumerism, materialism and greed of our market society by choosing to live more simply:

You are just not given the tools to answer questions about the spiritual in your life. And life has become so damned complex, that you have to put all your energies into just surviving and staying afloat. (Teressa, City dialogue group, 31 May 2018)

I try to give away a certain proportion ... I see the money as not mine and use it to help support people and charities in severe poverty and homelessness. It comes from the motivation about wanting to live a simple life. (Anton, Life History Interview)

Spirituality is all about the way of love at the end of the day. So spirituality then for me is about the expression of love. (Philippe, Borough dialogue group, 27 June 2018)

You can be right when having an argument or you can choose to be kind. You have a choice whether to be right or kind ... I use it as an opportunity to practise being more spiritual ... when you choose to practise compassion and kindness. (Ying, Kingston dialogue group, 10 October 2018)

Participants firmly believed that living this way not only brought freedom from the oppression of an overly materialistic, consumerist and addicted society, but also opened up the essential path of spirituality into a more fulfilled and deeper form of spiritual freedom:

Now there is so much more freedom and I am seeking the spiritual, the significantly spiritual which can be a whole new experience. (Neil, Borough dialogue group, 30 January 2019)

My greatest sadness as the researcher of this study was the general assumption of the majority of spiritual seekers and the SBNR that all religions are fundamentalist. However, the issue of the contemplative traditions and the SBNR arose many times. First, in the first locus of interpretation under 'innate spiritual thirst' concerning why participants became SBNR spiritual seekers, there was genuine surprise that there was a contemplative tradition to Christianity. Further, in the second locus of interpretation and in the fourth characteristic, 'seeking mystical truth that lies within', it was clear that many SBNR participants were drawing on Christian and other contemplative prayer practices for their own spirituality without participating in the tradition that formed the practice. The fact that the SBNR of the PhD research study used contemplative prayer practices and were interested in the writings of people like Thomas Merton shows that there were clearly resources within this tradition that need to be explored concerning a normative theology to engage with the views, perceptions and thinking of the SBNR.

Notes

1 See Chapter 2. See Richard Rohr's use of the term 'trans-rational' here: https://cac.org/orange-rational-organisation-2015-12-16/ (accessed 19.12.2020).

2 Wayne Dyer is a published spiritual self-help writer who is part of the New Age movement and draws on Taoism as a basis for his writing. See his official website here: https://www.drwaynedyer.com.

3 See https://www.mindbodyspirit.co.uk.

4 Wayne Dyer, *Change Your Thoughts, Change Your Life: Living the Wisdom of the Tao* (London: Hay House, 2007).

5 David Tacey, *The Spirituality Revolution: The Emergence of Contemporary Spirituality* (London: Routledge, 2004), pp. 2–5, 8.

6 Nancy Tatom Ammerman, *Sacred Stories, Spiritual Tribes: Finding Religion in Everyday Life* (New York: Oxford University Press, 2014), pp. 44–7.

PART TWO

A Contemplative Theology
and Model of Mission

Sculpture outside the Imperial War Museum, London.

4

Developing a Missional
Contemplative Theology

'Come and see' (John 1.39)

In this chapter, I explore Christian contemplative theology to engage with the concepts raised by spiritual seekers and the 'Spiritual But Not Religious' in the last two chapters. This is important to create a detailed theological framing to then explore a contemplative model of mission and the practical implications for this approach to mission practice.

Central to the stories of the SBNR in their spiritual journeying was the focus on human consciousness, and the process of changes in consciousness as they grew spiritually. Starting with consciousness, I draw on the writings of Elaine Heath, an American ordained academic theologian, and Sarah Coakley, a British ordained academic systematic theologian, regarding contemplative theology formed out of the experiences of prayer. I draw on the work of Thomas Merton, an American contemplative monk and theologian, Sarah Coakley and John Zizioulas, a Greek Orthodox bishop and theologian, to begin to explore a theological understanding of human consciousness. This leads to an exploration of the theory of an 'evolution of consciousness' for which I have followed the writings of Owen Barfield and Mark Vernon. Taking a theological understanding of an 'evolution of consciousness', I begin to explore the changing human consciousness as a form of spiritual path. I explore Barfield's three axial stages theory and how this relates to the biblical concepts of 'fall' and 'return', drawing on the ideas of the false self and true self, spiritual awakening and the significance of Jesus. Continuing with this exploration of human consciousness, I begin to address a theology of mystical participation with God. Beginning with the writing of Michael Gorman, I explore an understanding of 'participation in Christ' as a theology of theosis and *metanoia*. Within this, I identify a challenging dualism: of either holding a strong Christology and diminishing the spirituality of the SBNR, or attending to the spirituality of the SBNR and diminishing Christology. Drawing on the work of Kathryn Tanner concerning 'participation in Christ' as a theology of theosis, I address this dualism with a solution provided by her theological writing on a 'weak' and 'strong' participation. Finally, I explore the normative theology concerning other core concepts reflected in the stories of the SBNR named in the last two chapters. I then name some of the theological implications for mission practice that draw on contemplative theology explored in the stories of participants.

Spiritual seeking, human consciousness and contemplative theology

In the previous two chapters, I identified that many SBNR spiritual seekers search for meaning and significance largely on their own, in response to painful experiences or because they perceived that there was something more to life. In the preparation to write this chapter, I have wrestled with the paradox and tension between the narratives of participants as recognizing the individual freedom to engage in a conscious exploration through 'trans-rational' means, and the place of God in and above their seeking. I am reminded of the encounter between Jesus and Philip in the Gospel of John 1.43–51, where Jesus sought out Philip and said to him: 'Follow me' (verse 43). After his encounter with Jesus, Philip went to meet his friend Nathanael and said: 'We have found him whom Moses in the law and also the prophets wrote, Jesus son of Joseph from Nazareth' (verse 45). It is clear from this text that Philip perceived that he found Jesus, rather than Jesus 'calling him', and he then encouraged Nathanael to 'Come and see' (verse 46). This small but significant event in the Gospel throws up critical issues of autonomy, human consciousness, God's call and involvement and spiritual questing. I start this theological exploration by offering an understanding of what is meant by 'human consciousness'.

Defining human consciousness is not straightforward. In the narratives of SBNR participants of this study, connections were made between consciousness and forms of awareness, perception and knowing. The nature of human consciousness is therefore an epistemological question. The Lexico University of Oxford Dictionary defined consciousness as a: 'State of being aware of and responsive to one's surroundings, awareness or perception of something, awareness of the mind of itself and the world'.[1]

From a Western perspective, human consciousness is not a static concept, but something that evolves as understandings change. For Thomas Merton and others, there is a distinction between ancient forms of human consciousness, as expressed in the Old Testament, and more modern forms. For Merton, a contemporary understanding of consciousness begins with Descartes's *Cogito, ergo sum*, 'I think, therefore I am', where the individual 'self' has a self-awareness informed by thinking, observing, measuring and estimating as rational knowing.[2] This form of human consciousness makes the human subject distinctive by withdrawing from the world to be able to observe and learn from their interaction over and against objects that the individual learns to manipulate for their own benefit. However, as Merton emphasizes, such an approach to knowing comes at a cost:

> the more he tends to isolate himself in his own subjective prison, to become a detached observer cut off from everything else in a kind of impenetrable alienated and transparent bubble ... Modern consciousness then tends to create this isolated bubble of awareness: an ego self-imprisoned in its own consciousness, isolated and out of touch.[3]

For Merton, there is a more spiritual form of knowing: 'in self-giving, in love, in "letting-go", in ecstasy ... the self is not its own center and does not orbit around itself: it is centered on God, the one center of all, which is "everywhere and nowhere", in whom all are encountered, from whom all proceed.'[4]

From Merton's perspective, we counter the tension between the rationalist and egoic understandings of human consciousness with the more subtle trans-rationalist understanding where knowing is disposed to encountering 'the other' beyond the self. This form of ontological openness is attuned to the presence of God, indeed the sense that we and the whole of creation are in relation with this 'other' – a founding belief for those who are SBNR.

Owen Barfield and Mark Vernon address human consciousness from the perspective of Barfield's theory of the evolution of consciousness.[5] For Vernon and Barfield, this tension between the 'spiritual'/'immaterial' and 'material'/'matter' forms of knowing reflects the mystery of our human nature as being a mixture of both 'spirit' and 'matter'. The desire to seek consciousness through a more rationalist or materialist approach leads to Descartes's scientific understanding and takes the individual into their materialist nature. In contrast, the more open-ended desire for encounters beyond this takes the individual into their sense of 'spirit' and trans-rationalist identity and knowing.[6] For Barfield and Vernon, as we will explore later, imagination and the more mystical forms of prayer and meditation are important attributes of a more spiritual approach to human consciousness.[7]

The language of human consciousness resonates strongly with the writings of contemplative Christian theology and spirituality. We remember that the story of the Christian mystics and contemplatives, particularly in the Western church, has been a negative story of persecution and marginalization. The theologies of these traditions have not been taken seriously by many over the centuries. As Elaine Heath has said: 'Some Christians resist all talk of mysticism, as if mysticism and Christianity were mutually exclusive.'[8] Spirituality-informed theology is not some privatized numinous experience, but on the contrary, as Sarah Coakley states, brings deep reflection drawing on encounter with the living God.[9] Mystical theology resists the rigidity and certainty of an unquestioning form of faith that reduces Christianity to a set of principles, which then does not need any form of direct relationship with God where God in any sense leads. Instead, contemplative theologies, as Merton has articulated, understand that the Christian faith has to be lived in prayerful connection with God, and therefore goes through processes of refinement as people grow in their faith and understanding.[10]

Coakley reminds us that in the tradition of ascetical and contemplative theology there is a core commitment to the biblical language of 'heart' rather than 'head' as the organ for spiritual knowing.[11] She argues that this resonates deeply with our current post-modern/post-secular context of subjective experiential knowing as an 'urgent spiritual necessity sweated out of the exigencies of prayer', and therefore out of spiritual prayer and contemplation practices.[12]

This commitment to a theology arising from prayer has implications of joining in with creation and in the ministry of Jesus as the incarnation of God. Coakley comments on:

> the whole creation 'groaning' to its final Christological telos in God (Romans 8.18–21). What this underscores is the extraordinary ripple effect of prayer in the Spirit – its inexorably social and even cosmic significance as an act of cooperation with, and incorporation into, the still extending life of the incarnation.[13]

Merton also affirms that human spiritual consciousness of the heart rather than the head is key for authentic spirituality, but with a twist:

> To have a 'wise heart' ... is to live centered on this dynamism and this secret hope – this hoped-for secret. It is the key to our life, but as long as we are alive we must see that we do not have this key: it is not at our disposal.[14]

Merton reminds us that Christian theology affirms that we are not autonomous totally independent organisms on our own spiritual journey of
life, but that our spiritual questing also depends on God's allowing us to
experience mystical truths that can be concealed.

Yet at the same time, there is the mystery of Genesis 1.26: the balance
between dependence on God and human freedom. Each human being is
made in the mystery of the 'image of God', which affirms that our being
and therefore our consciousness are sustained by God. By implication
then, our chosen identity and self-consciousness are formed out of a
relationship with God. John Zizioulas, drawing on Eastern Orthodox
theology, reminds us that our journey of self-awareness must be influenced by God's direction in ways we may not be aware of:

> Man was created 'in the image and likeness of God' (Genesis 1.26)
> ... 'image' means that we may have our existence, not because we are
> obliged to by the way things are, but because we are able to receive it
> for ourselves willingly and freely.[15]

Returning to the encounter between Philip and Jesus, Philip responded
unaware of Jesus' call. By implication, we in our spiritual journey begin
with the gift of *imago Dei* that takes us on a journey of self-discovery
and self-awareness of (and by implication a denial or rejection of) our
true identity as God's image bearers.

Zizioulas questions the assumptions of Descartes by reminding us
that self-awareness and self-understanding come from our relationship
with others and God, which can never really be a truly self-objectifying
process: 'it is impossible to be conscious, to be a self, without a relationship. I am me because I am related to my brother, my nephew, my
neighbour, my employer or whoever ... You cannot say "me", in the
complete absence of any "you".'[16]

This relational perspective is a non-Western understanding of human
consciousness in contrast to the Cartesian world view, and is reflected,
for example, in the African concept of *Ubuntu*: '*Ubuntu* describes
humans as created by God. There is no independent existence without
the creative act of God.'[17]

This integrated way of understanding human self-consciousness is
not just limited to relationship with other people and God. Because
we are creatures living in a rich ecology of the living and inanimate,
our identity is formed by relationship with the whole of creation; our
human consciousness is 'constituted' by our connection to all things.[18]
This by implication has much to affirm of the SBNR focus on ecological
reconnection.

Our human consciousness, like our existence, is not a free choice, because we received it from God, and our continued being is in God.[19] This can be a very difficult truth to grasp or accept without the insights of contemplative practices or philosophical wisdom rather than the fruits of scientific explanation or analysis.[20] Zizioulas reminds us of a central truth of Christianity that most of the SBNR of this study would struggle to accept in our individualized culture: 'without God there is no creature called man ... The true definition of man is the creature who participates freely in the life of God – not a creature who lives from some resources of his own.'[21]

Yet there is a dynamic tension between our created dependence on God and our God-given freedom.[22] We are given the choice of self-determination, to be autonomous in deciding what we consider to be true or not, to self-determine our human self-consciousness.[23] This freedom can be exercised in two ways:

> It can be exercised negatively, when man decides to despise creation and disdain its Creator. Man can say that he does not acknowledge God as Creator, and that he does not consider this creation to be any concern of his. But equally there is the possibility that man will not reject creation.[24]

By implication we have a choice to operate more in our rejection of God: to live in our more material, rational, egoic self, drawing on a more scientific approach to knowing and consciousness, which as we will see has serious consequences. Alternatively we can choose to be in relationship, in 'union' with God through a more spirit trans-rational desire for a relational connection with God. Yet at the same time, as we saw in Jesus' encounter with Philip, who thought he found Jesus rather than Jesus calling him, and contrary to the norms of the immanent cultural frame of many churches and our liberal market society of self-determination, contemplative theology reminds us that it is God who continues to beckon and call us into relationship. We do not awaken ourselves, but it is God who chooses to awaken us, as Merton puts it so eloquently: 'a call from Him who has no voice, and yet who speaks in everything that is, and who, most of all, speaks in the depths of our own being'.[25]

Drawing on these theological reflections on human consciousness, I turn to the themes arising in the grounded analysis concerning an evolution of consciousness.

Evolution of consciousness and the people of God

In his writings, Barfield explores how the history and use of words change, and the way words reveal the human consciousness at that point in time.[26] For him, words are like 'human fossils' that reveal self-understandings, insights and perceptions in a snapshot of time.[27] Drawing on changes in how words are used in the Bible, Barfield argues that they indicate changes in consciousness: over time, human awareness evolved and consciousness shifted. He proposed a theory of three phases in this growth of human consciousness, which he named as 'original participation', 'withdrawal from participation' and 'final participation'.[28] Vernon, who has written on Barfield's ideas, preferred this third phase to be called 'reciprocal participation'.[29]

Barfield identified evidence in the biblical narrative of a form of ongoing process of spiritual 'participation', where there was a flow between the spiritual and material self and the human connection with God.[30] In time this flow of consciousness changes, leading to a period of withdrawal and focus on the material and 'isolated self'.[31] Then after a time the individual feels so isolated that they desire and seek reconnection with 'the other' beyond the self, which then leads to the seeking of a more reciprocal connection with others and the spirit.[32] For Barfield this process can take a very long time.[33] In this way individuals and human societies shift between the 'spiritual' and 'material' states of human nature almost like a continuum.[34] This process is reflected in Figure 8.

Figure 8: Barfield's Understanding of our Spirit/Matter and Union/Isolation

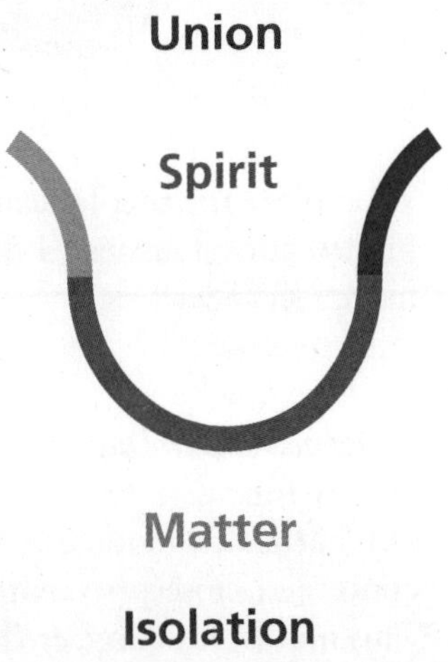

Union

Spirit

Matter

Isolation

In the shift from an 'original participation' through to 'withdrawal from participation' the individual and society shift away from the sense of 'spirituality' and 'spiritual truths' to a focus on objectivity, in what Vernon has called 'fall' and then later an eventual 'return'.[35] These ideas are full of latent theological meaning. The language of 'participation' is particularly important, and I reflect on it later in this chapter where I explore exactly what enables individuals and societies to shift from 'withdrawal' to 'final or reciprocal participation'. This is a key missiological issue.

I am also struck by how the language of 'fall' and 'return' resonated with the theological writings of Heath, Coakley and Merton, concerning the three stages of ascetical or contemplative prayer-led development, which may be viewed as 'purgation', 'illumination' and 'union'.[36] I will discuss these three stages particularly when I explore 'withdrawal from participation' and 'reciprocal or final participation'.

For Barfield, this evolution of consciousness was not a once-and-for-ever event, but rather an ongoing cyclical occurrence, where human consciousness never returns to exactly the previous 'original participation' state.[37] This process always leads to change as an evolution of human consciousness (see Figure 9 below).[38]

Figure 9: Barfield's Stages of the Evolution of Consciousness[39]

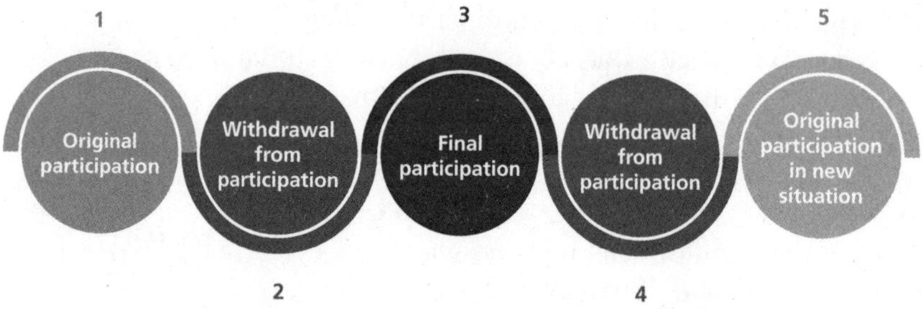

To explore the theological significance of these stages of an evolution in human consciousness, I draw on Barfield's original work and Vernon's more recent writing.

Original participation

For Barfield, the idea of 'original participation' (point '1' in Figure 9) concerned close proximity to the 'origin' or 'source' of participation.[40] This mindset is connected to a pre-modern epistemology, where human understanding and awareness are mythic.[41] Such cultures draw heavily on a nature-linked collective consciousness expressed in ritual participation of the tribe – you could only know something if you participated in it, sharing in its essence as a subjective experience in the present moment.[42] Knowledge and participation are intimately connected, and an individual could not be conscious of something if it was not shared with others.[43] With this understanding, consciousness becomes a flow from inner and outer processes, where there was no way of observing nature in a detached way, and a dependency on the collective, where the individual is shaped by the collective.[44] Human self-consciousness is severely limited, as the boundaries are not yet in place for this level of awareness.[45] Through studying the language in the Bible, Barfield identified that this form of human consciousness prevailed in Hebraic culture up to about 500 BC. Such cultures were not any less sophisticated than now but had a different way of knowing that was dependent on participation: for example, the expression of happiness, grief or penitence would be processed through the festivities of the year as collective mythmaking. For an Old Testament Israelite, a sense of justice meant cosmic balance, not personal rights.[46]

Withdrawal from participation

Through a transitionary, evolving process occupying significant time, an expansion of self-knowing occurred. Human consciousness shifted so that the individual became less shaped by the collective, and the collective instead began to be shaped by the individual (points 1 to 2 in Figure 9).[47] This shift from 'original participation' to 'withdrawal from participation', according to Barfield, occurred through an increased sense of self-consciousness (self-knowing) as distinct from the 'other'.[48] This retreat from 'spirit' and expansion into 'the material self' required an increased disconnection between human beings and nature and marked a distinction between 'inner' and 'outer' or the 'subjective' and the 'objective'. The individual became what Barfield calls an 'onlooker', and there began a journey into dualistic thinking:

> He has had to wrestle his subjectivity out of the world of his experience by polarizing that world gradually into a duality. This is the duality of objective–subjective, or outer, inner, which now seems so fundamental because we have inherited it along with language. He did not start as an onlooker.[49]

For Vernon, this shift in the evolution of consciousness of a growing sense of 'human-self' led the Jewish people to have a greater awareness of the 'God-self'. He argues that the ancient understanding of God as 'I AM WHO I AM', as revealed to Moses in Exodus 3.14, is reimagined with this new consciousness, as a God who has an identity, an internal life, a God who is knowable and distinct from nature and creation.[50] The self-conscious human is able to comprehend that they are also an 'I AM', able to have an understanding of a God who is 'I AM', as a new basis for human–divine connection.[51]

For Barfield and Vernon, this focus on dualistic thinking and the increasing focus on the objective over the subjective inevitably leads to the beginning of science.[52] They argue that the increased focus on religious reform of the faith of the Jewish people becomes an iconoclastic movement.[53] The Psalms in many places acknowledge the consciousness of God, and at the same time, God knowing the inner life of God's people, as in Psalm 139.1–2, 4: 'O LORD, you have searched me and known me. You know when I sit down and when I rise up; you discern my thoughts from far away ... Even before a word is on my tongue, O LORD, you know it completely.'[54]

For Barfield, this focus on the individual 'conscious self' will inevitably progress to isolation. Interestingly, he defines this as 'a kind of adolescence', by which I infer a kind of resistance or rebelliousness as a form of consciousness.[55] This inevitably connects to the central doctrine of original sin and the mystery of the 'fall': 'man decided to relate the world to himself instead of God ... It is an extraordinary mystery that by his possession of this God-given freedom, man was able to halt God's plan.'[56]

This sense of withdrawal from the 'spirit nature' of humanity, and increasing isolation from the source in original participation, inevitably leads to alienation, not only between the individual, the source and nature, but also alienation between people.[57] Pursuing the theory that alienation is the inevitable human consequence of the objective pursuit of science, Barfield writes of his interest in Theodore Roszak's work *Where the Wasteland Ends* (1972), and particularly the evolving consequences of this alienation.[58] He affirms Roszak's analysis that the focus on such scientific objectivity as a way of knowing is inevitably an act of alienation: it first results in alienation between the human self and nature, followed by a sense of alienation, first of the self from the body and finally of the self from the mind. This is deeply destructive and traumatizing to the human self. In such a stage, human beings believe that their inner life, their consciousness, is theirs alone and belongs to them in the separated and disconnected self.[59]

For Matthieu Ricard, Christophe André and Alexandre Jollien, writing about their shared conversations exploring spirituality from a religious, philosophical and health perspective, as a monk, philosopher and psychiatrist, this sense of destructive withdrawal and alienation is connected to the concept of the human ego and the false self. They state that, in the evolution of consciousness, the process whereby the individual develops a stronger sense of 'I' will also be accompanied by the dominance of the egoic self.[60] As the ego grows, the individual wants to satisfy and protect it: 'We manifest aversion toward anything that threatens it, and attraction for anything that pleases and comforts it. These two reactions give rise to a multitude of conflicting emotions –

anger, desire, envy, jealousy, and the like.'[61] It is no coincidence that there is a connection between the growth of the ego and the classic list of deadly sins.

Merton and Heath affirm that this destructive withdrawal and alienation is connected to the concept of the human ego and the false self. Heath reminds us that the growth in ego leads to the formation of the false self as a form of self-constructed consciousness.[62] This is a form of self that is crafted in the image of the individual and not in God or in participation.[63] This form of human consciousness then self-constructs a self-protective armour. The false self confuses identity with function, what we think with what we do. Life is haunted by fear, love becomes conditional and peace eludes the individual as they are driven by the false self to be continually vigilant against the failure of being found out, which in turn leads to fear and shame.[64] Merton makes the connection between the self that is overly defined by withdrawal to the material self, and the internal life of the pursuit of objective 'truth', which is more about the egoic need to be right:

> We are all convinced that we desire the truth ... But actually, what we desire is not 'the truth' so much as 'to be in the right' ... What we seek is not the pure truth, but the partial truth that justifies our prejudices, our limitations, our selfishness ... It is only an argument strong enough to prove us 'right'.[65]

The reality of the individual self-consciousness at this stage, then, is a strong sense of 'self' but with egoic self-construction that creates an 'ego self-imprisoned in its own consciousness, isolated and out of touch'.[66] This has profound implications for the mental health of such an individual and can lead to problems because of the psychological tensions of holding irreconcilable opposites in oneself so that personal unity becomes fractured.[67]

Such a false self is not in any way authentic to a sense of truth but is in fact, as Merton reminds us, a lie that has further negative effects:

> The lie brings violence and disorder into our nature itself. It divides us against ourselves, alienates us from ourselves, makes us enemies of ourselves, and of the truth that is in us. From this division hatred and violence arise. We hate others because we cannot stand the disorder, the intolerable division in ourselves ... This is not so far from the traditional doctrine of the Fathers of the church concerning original sin![68]

So the axial shift from original participation to a withdrawal from participation results in a stronger sense of 'self' but also the reality of alienation, egoic-false identity and, as a consequence, fear, shame, self-ishness and violence, so that everything humanity touches is tainted with these unintended consequences. Given this understanding there is, as I said earlier, a deep resonance between such a withdrawal of participation and chosen disassociation with God, and the theological understanding of 'original sin'. Ricard et al. connect these ideas of the consequences of the 'egoic' isolated self with the story of Adam and Eve in Genesis 3.7:

> The story of Genesis provides us with a luminous diagnosis. It says of Adam and Eve after they tasted the forbidden fruit: 'Then the eyes of both of them were opened, and they realized they were naked; so they sewed fig leaves together and made covering for themselves.' Shame, guilt, egocentrism – how can we avoid this infernal spiral? Losing one's innocence maybe means contemplating one's navel, beginning to cherish an image of oneself, a bunch of labels, a heap of illusions. This ... tendency toward narcissism is a source of a tremendous amount of pain and conflict. If I exile myself from the fundamental ground of my being, if I close myself off in my mental representations, if I continually play a role, how can I experience real joy?[69]

Traditional Christian theology interprets the story of Genesis with the motivation of rebellion, but from a more contemplative theological position the 'fall' is seen as the painful unintended consequence of the separation of the subjective and objective 'self'. This results in the alien-ation of our very selves and God, which then results in the idolatry of making our false self our God. As Merton says:

> The obstacle is in our 'self' ... the ... need to maintain our separate, ex-ternal, egotistic will ... when we refer all things to this ... false 'self' ... we alienate ourselves from reality and from God. It is then the false self that is our god, and we love everything for the sake of this self. We use all things ... for the worship of this idol which is our imaginary self.[70]

In this understanding, sin can be seen as the consequence of the person rejecting the true self and instead desiring the egoic false self, becoming blind to the consequences of this, as a process shifting from original participation to withdrawal of participation. Here the egoic desire of the false self leads to 'the desire ... for power, honor, knowledge and love, to clothe this false self and construct its nothingness into something objectively real'.[71]

The reality of this form of idolatry continues today in the context of our global market society, advanced through science and technology, but I will return to this later in the chapter.

There are important theological implications of the splitting off of the spirit and material self around the theme of wounding that need consideration from a contemplative theological position. Barfield talks of the consequences of such a gap between our 'spirit' and 'material identity'.[72] He offers a critical theological insight for the SBNR seekers concerning the theological idea of 'original wounding' as developed by Heath. This gap identified by Barfield matches Heath's original wounding in a new theological synthesis. As Barfield says:

> we live in that abrupt gap between matter and spirit; we exist by virtue of it as autonomous, self-conscious individual spirits, as free beings. Often ... it makes us feel lamentably isolated ... any way that involves disregarding the gap, or pretending it is not there, is a way we take at our peril ... so far from attempting to disregard the gap – or, if you prefer, the wound – between matter and spirit, to realize ... as human beings ... we can only live in it.[73]

For Heath, this focus on 'wounding' is critical to her reflections on the theme of original wounding as an understanding of mystical theology.[74] She draws on the wisdom theology of the medieval mystic Julian of Norwich, and her understanding of how the love of God meets humanity in loving healing rather than in judgement, and also the theological writing of Hans Urs Von Balthasar and his non-punitive doctrine of atonement. I shall outline both of these before returning to Heath's interpretation of the 'fall' in Genesis.

Drawing on the experiences of 16 visions, Julian of Norwich experienced and understood theologically that the Christian God was a God who did not seek vengeance but instead judgement without wrath, a God who sought to heal and restore the entire cosmos:[75]

> Julian's God loves with a power that is deeper than sin, that heals all wounds, and love that binds humanity to God forever ... God's overwhelming message to her is one of security for the saved ... Julian's stance becomes one of great hope for all people who are the wounded.[76]

According to Heath, Julian's theology of redemption is therefore therapeutic. She notes that Julian herself believed that it was easy for Christians to believe in God's power, but hard for them to believe in God's love, which results in a fixation with sin and judgement rather than the outworking of restorative love.[77] By implication, 'Wounds precede sin – original wounds – and for this reason ... God looks upon the human predicament with pity not blame.'[78] God then becomes a healing, strong mother, seeking to heal her children from brokenness and alienation.[79]

For Heath, Balthasar's theology is based on an eschatology of the love of God, where God's omnipotence and every aspect of God's character is love.[80] Accordingly, a doctrine of atonement for Balthasar is where God is in full solidarity with humanity and willingly suffers with people in our wounding, offering salvation to the whole world as restorative healing.[81] Balthasar therefore rejects all theories of substitutionary atonement that are punitive.

Drawing on this fusion of both Julian of Norwich's and Balthasar's writing, Heath proposes an alternative understanding of atonement in which 'God forgives our sin and heals the original wounds that lead to sin.'[82] This, then, for Heath, provides theological evidence to take a more archetypal reading of Genesis 1—3, where every human being is born blameless and vulnerable but is then caught in a web of wounds and sin from which we cannot abstract ourselves.[83] This is reflected in the story of Adam and Eve, who are born blameless and vulnerable and capable of being wounded. At the fall, the freedom, trust and relationship with God are broken, resulting first in alienation and then in violence: 'Future violence of every kind, future sin, begins with original wounds.'[84]

By implication, this withdrawal from participation, combined with the separation of the material and spirit nature of humanity, has led to a growing ego and false self, which in turn led to alienation, violence and isolation – the same background context to our problems now in the twenty-first century. In our context, the global market society that atomizes the individual, our addiction to consumerist gratification, the violence unleashed through technology and science, and forms of religious and political fundamentalism are all a result of this same consequence of 'withdrawal from participation'. This is why the majority of people who became SBNR spiritual seekers described painful experiences: addiction, violence, mental illness, stress and the struggle of life launched their search for spirituality. This also confirms why the language of human consciousness and an awareness of an evolution in consciousness were so strongly represented in the ethnographic empirical data and grounded theory of the PhD study. This is why I believe David Tacey is right when he makes the connection between alienation, violence and destruction:

Today, in the face of so much shocking alienation and destruction, our hunger for connectedness has broken through, and in this sense the hunger for spirituality ... is an involuntary and instinctive reaction against social conditions that are inimical to life and our planetary survival.[85]

Finally in her analysis, Heath makes a powerfully argued connection between forms of abuse and original wounding. I make this same connection between original wounding and the terrible cost of our global unrestrained market society, which clearly wounded the SBNR seekers of the PhD study. Many have been traumatized and damaged by the 'abuse' and the lie that the market society is about freedom, instead of the pain that has been created by the emptiness, addiction and dehumanization of lives enslaved by economics, commodification and addiction to consumerism:

The shattering of trust leads to deep wounds ... alienation, fear, and grief, the trauma leading to brokenness of body, mind, and spirit ... For some the patterns are around perfectionism in an attempt to overcome ... deep-seated shame. For some the wounds drive the attempt to control ... in order to feel safe. For others their wounds drive addictions ... and a multitude of other destructive behaviors ... because of the residual effects of the original wounds.[86]

By implication, contemporary society expresses itself as a culture of purgation: we cannot escape the wounds and conditions that lead to this form of sin, and so we participate in this cycle of hurt as the consequence of systemic sin as a form of wounding.

Final or reciprocal participation

However, as we reach the final stage of Barfield's theory of the evolution of consciousness, we turn from this sense of brokenness, loss and woundedness to a new axial shift, which he called 'final participation' but which Vernon calls 'reciprocal participation'.[87]

For Barfield, the coming of Jesus as Messiah, as the incarnation of God, at the time he did (around 4 BC) was critical.[88] Barfield argues that in the run-up to Jesus' birth the ancient divine name 'YHWH' or 'I AM WHO I AM', revealed in the Hebrew Scriptures, had ceased to be used or spoken in the temple or synagogue, and that God had become, through the Pharisees and Sadducees, 'essentially objective, remote, inaccessible, infinitely superior to, yet imagined as existentially parallel with man'.[89] Original participation was then so far away that either the situation would progress into ever more extreme forms of idolatry or it would require the intervention of God.[90]

In this withdrawal from participation, the knowledge of God had shifted to extreme objectification, or overly rational means, where God was literally boxed in with no room for mystical or contemplative encounter as a trans-rational means of knowing God on God's terms. Idolatry was expressed in the religion of the time in that they thought they fully knew God, which was in effect a form of idolatry by effectively trying to control God or at least control access to God. Therefore, Jesus' incarnation was a crucial happening to help humanity to shift from 'withdrawal from participation' to 'final or reciprocal participation', expressed as return to the source, a desire to freely connect with God, for union with God as they understood God, to be free from the pain and suffering of woundedness, alienation and disconnection. This then necessitates a shift from an overdominating material self to a balance of the individual consciousness of both spirit and the material. In other words, there is a shift here away from a sense of the false self to the desire for and pursuit of the true self, and reconnection to the source.[91]

According to Vernon, final participation as the connection with God as source is not in the same state of the 'no self' as original partici-pation. Instead there is a greater reciprocity of both the spirit–matter internal identity and a new form of I–God relationship.[92] For Vernon, Jesus comes when withdrawal from participation is in full flow: that it will take the intervention of God as incar-nation, life and resurrection to enable such a transition of return.[93] As Stephen Bevans and Roger Schroeder have said: 'In the full-ness of time (Galatians 4.4), the word of God became flesh … God's complete yet elusive presence, a human face. Jesus … now God is present in a visible, audible, and concrete way.'[94]

With this interpretation of Jesus coming as the Messiah, I modify Figure 8 to include Jesus' significance in this theory of the evo-lution of consciousness (see Figure 10). Jesus becomes the incarnation of God at a time of withdrawal from participation and, through the resurrection, points to a new final or reciprocal participation with God.

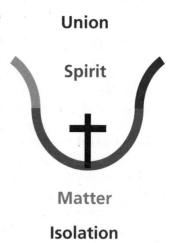

Figure 10: Jesus and the Theory of an Evolution of Consciousness

Union

Spirit

Matter

Isolation

For Zizioulas, the 'Logos' was required to become human so that all that had been created could be united with the uncreated, to bring salvation for all creation trapped in a cycle of life and death.[95] Such a mystical union is possible only through Jesus Christ, and from the very beginning of his ministry, as foretold by the Prophet Isaiah, Jesus did not delay. After reading the scroll he lived out the re-establishment, the reconnection of relationship between all that had become disconnected, all that had been wounded with and through the love of God:

> The Spirit of the Lord is upon me, because he has anointed me to bring good news to the poor ... to proclaim release to the captives and recovery of sight to the blind, to let the oppressed go free, to proclaim the year of the Lord's favour. (Luke 4.18–19)

Jesus bridges the infinite gap between God, humanity and creation by the supernatural mission of his life.[96] Jesus' ministry was therefore to reawaken humanity to the presence of God, and to do this through participation in the Holy Trinity, where the Son, the Redeemer, chose to enter the fallen world, through the Father, the Creator, who initiated the incarnation, through the power of the Holy Spirit supporting the Son.[97] Beginning with the disciples, he created a movement that sought to promote a new world view, to think differently about God and humanity, beginning with imagining a new form of Judaism.[98] Jesus spoke through parables and dialogue as forms of trans-rational experience, sought to inspire by engaging with the excluded, marginalized, ill and unclean, and spoke with passion about God and God's love for the world. At breathtaking speed, he said to many, like Philip, 'Come and follow me', and through teaching, healings, good works, parable telling, prayer and the miraculous, provoked humanity to move from withdrawal to re-engagement with God through wonder, awe, love and inspiration. He used parables and spiritual practices to actively encourage people to use their imagination as the means of re-encounter with God through him. As Vernon stated: 'Imagination is crucial because it can achieve a step out of individual isolation without losing the modern experience of personhood. It can become a reconciling agency, and answer to the yearning, without compromising the me that is me and you that is you.'[99]

Jesus also promoted prayer and mystical forms of direct encounter with God by seeking to engage with the God from within as much as the God who is transcendent:[100] 'whenever you pray, go into your room and shut the door and pray to your Father who is in secret' (Matthew 6.6); 'your Father who sees in secret will reward you' (Matthew 6.18); pray to God as your Abba, 'Father' (Matthew 6.9); 'the Kingdom of God is within you' (Luke 17.21, NRSV footnote).

For Vernon, the real revealing of Jesus' call to reciprocal participation is stated in the Gospel of John, where the relationship between Jesus, God the Father and the Holy Spirit is profound and interdependent and expresses the fullness of mutual participation: 'On that day you will know that I am in my Father, and you in me, and I in you' (John 14.20).[101]

Returning briefly to the ethnographic empirical data and grounded theory, the centrality of a Christology drawing on contemplative theologies is almost entirely missing in the narratives of the SBNR. For a few participants, the significance of Jesus as 'Christos' informed them of Jesus' key role in a form of reconnection or union with the divine, but they were a minority. For the majority, Jesus the Christ may be part of the story but rarely central. This may be because of the lack of spirituality in aspects of the contemporary Western church. As Vernon himself noted:

> He stood for something ... a thoroughgoing change in worldview and imagination ... when Christianity becomes a set of moral requirements, and the arrival of the Kingdom is deemed remote, the way it is offered drains of joy and power. The central promise of a discovered union with God ... gets lost ... this loss is central to the declining appeal of Christianity today.[102]

This is exactly why the SBNR consider Christianity as a religion in these terms, affected by a dominant rationalist form of knowing with little room for trans-rational spirituality.

Theosis and being 'in Christ'

One possible solution to this 'dumbing down' of the spiritual significance of Jesus by reopening it up to spiritual seekers could be to engage with Western mystical theology and practice and Eastern Christian understandings of 'participation', particularly the theology of 'theosis'. As Michael Gorman, an American New Testament scholar, states, this has never been widely understood in the West.[103] It draws on the theology behind Paul's letters and the Gospel of John, that Jesus became like us (human) so that we could become like him (God) – or, rather, that we can share in the divine life, which is not the same as becoming God. As Gorman says:

> The fundamental theological axiom of theosis is the formulation by Church Fathers … that God became what we are so that we might become what God is. The axiom is rooted in Pauline 'interchange' texts … As a spiritual theology, theosis is predicated as well on the Pauline and Johannine experience of Christ's indwelling.[104]

The use of 'theosis' as a biblical understanding of participation or union with God does not remove the need and purpose of salvation, but rather reveals the divine project as restoring all things back into right relationship with God (Colossians 1.19–20). For Paul, salvation becomes the act of God creating a new humanity made into the likeness of Christ (1 Corinthians 15.45–49). This vision is one of cosmic liberation (Romans 8.18–25), through the universal Lordship of Jesus (Philippians 2.9–11), as a process of theosis (Romans 8.29–30) and the mystery that then all will be one (1 Corinthians 15.28).[105] Such salvation, though offered universally to all humanity through grace and God's love poured out to humanity (kenosis), requires an active response from people to choose to follow the way of Christ, accepting Christ's Lordship of their lives.

Kathryn Tanner, an American Protestant systematic theologian, in her seminal work *Christ the Key* explores the theology of theosis as participation with God through being 'in Christ'.[106] For her, human beings are unique in creation through an attachment to the divine image of God. By implication, human consciousness and identity are 'remoulded, altered and transformed for the better out of this attachment'. Human beings do not simply reflect the image of God, they are changed through the process of theosis.[107] I will return to the work of Tanner further in this chapter and the next when I draw on her work to articulate a more contemplative model of mission as 'God's Kenosis, our Theosis'.

To explore the implications of this understanding concerning the SBNR responses in the grounded analysis of the previous chapter, I need to explore the theology of participation with the process of conversion and transformation. I will then continue the theme of theosis with a Pauline understanding of being 'in Christ' through Gorman's writing, before returning to the three stages of contemplative/ascetical theology and practice.

Metanoia and transformation as conversion through participation

Vernon reminds us that Jesus' life and message stood for something new in giving room for the Spirit to convert in this new situation of reciprocal participation in God: those who responded found the Spirit to be resident in them, working from the inside out:

> It was what the times required. When it works a *metanoia* takes place ... It is usually translated as 'repentance,' but its real meaning points to a revolution of awareness. *Meta* means 'beyond.' *Nous* means 'mind'. When Paul talked of being transformed by the renewal of your mind (Rom 12.2), he was offering a more accurate rendition ... The person is converted if they allow their mind to re-orientate ... If the Kingdom were within them, then it followed that the Spirit of God was within them too.[108]

With this interpretation the person, in response to encountering Jesus, has a choice to respond to the gift offered as a change of consciousness. This *metanoia*, through some form of encounter with Jesus, then becomes an invitation to full participation with God as Trinity, which results in a comprehensive transformation of 'conviction, character, and communal affiliation ... to be "in Christ"' (2 Corinthians 5.14–17).[109]

For Gorman, participation as theosis marks a progression from conversion in 'becoming like God by participating in the life of God'.[110] 'God was in Christ reconciling the world to himself, and to do so God in Christ became what we are so that in Christ we might become what God is, as Paul puts it in 2 Corinthians 5.14–21.'[111] Gorman identified seven places in the writing of St Paul that describe how this theosis as participation is to be fulfilled for the Christian: baptism, through dying, rising and being in Christ (Romans 6.3–8); joining in Christ through justification by faith (Galatians 2.16); the resurrected Christ being 'within' believers (Romans 8.1, 9–11); being clothed with Christ and participating in the divine nature (Romans 13.12–14); sharing in Christ through koinonia as communion (2 Corinthians 13.13); being transformed by relations to Christ into the same image (2 Corinthians 3.14–16); and being conformed to Christ through the Spirit (Romans 8).[112] Further, for Gorman, drawing on the Gospel of John, theosis connects participation in the life of God as being 'in Christ' with mission.[113]

It is at this point that we encounter a serious problem in Western Christianity. By pursuing a strong Christian Christology of being 'in Christ', I have effectively excluded the spiritual significance and experience of the SBNR of the PhD research study – because they have not explicitly named Jesus. However, if I had argued from a more liberal perspective and been inclusive of all spiritual experience, I would thereby diminish the need for any Christology and diminish the faith. I have ended up with a dualism that diminishes either Christ or the experience of the SBNR.[114] This is why mystical and Orthodox theologies are so important here (and the reason why mystics/contemplatives have been marginalized in the West), because they refuse to be dualistic. Both traditions argue that we need to take seriously the spiritual experience of the SBNR as potentially authentic participation in the divine nature through the Spirit, although they might not seek or know it, and even if they reject all talk of Jesus. At the same time, we must hold on to the need for a distinctive Christology. The SBNR, then, remind us of the importance of this non-dualistic stance, which resonates with mystical and contemplative theology. The writings of Tanner on participation in Christ as a theology of theosis offer a solution to this dualism.

'Weak' and 'strong' participation in Christ as a theology of theosis

Tanner, exploring participation and theosis in her book *Christ the Key*, offers a solution to the problem just identified with what she calls 'weak' and 'strong' participation.[115] By implication, weak participation affirms that every animal, including every human, is sustained through connection to God; whether they know it or not, they are a 'creature of God … a life derived of God'.[116] Here it is possible for participants of the PhD research study to seek as the SBNR and to have significant experiences of God without acknowledging or affirming understanding from a Christian perspective. At the same time, Tanner affirms that a strong participation also exists when people become followers of Jesus as a form of being 'in Christ'. Here Tanner's strong participation correlates with Gorman's understanding of St Paul's writings on being 'in Christ' as a form of participative theosis. Tanner's stress on the critical need of this strong participation as being 'in Christ' therefore affirms the importance of Christology, and so the importance of becoming and being Christian.[117]

Tanner therefore offers a theological solution to the problem I identified earlier, by naming two forms of participation in God: 'weak' and 'strong'. The former affirms the experiences of the SBNR spiritual seekers of the PhD research study, and the latter affirms the importance of becoming or being Christian and the importance of a Christology.

This both/and approach to participation in God, therefore, offers an understanding of theosis as a form of spiritual journey and mission, beckoned through the love of God. I will explore this in the next chapter.

Participation and the three stages of Christian contemplation

To begin to develop a contemplative model of mission that resonates with the path of SBNR spiritual seeking, I return to the premise that the three stages of purgation, illumination and union relate to the shift in the last two axial stages of Barfield's evolution of consciousness: purgation, as the experience of darkness, pain and angst, relates to the withdrawal from participation, while illumination and union relate to final or reciprocal participation, and any reference to original participation is in fact a devolutionary moment. Starting with the latter, there were a number of responses drawing on non-duality and Zen Buddhist ideas to conclude that there was no such thing as the human individual self.[118] As confirmed by Vernon, I consider this a retreat from withdrawal of participation in an attempt to go back to original participation rather than going forward to reciprocal participation of the self with God as the source.[119] Further, I agree with Barfield, when considering the Jungian concept of a collective consciousness, that this too is a form of regression to original participation and therefore also inauthentic.[120]

The emerging normative theology in the stories of participants and its missional implications

At this point I return to the stories of the SBNR to underline how the contemplative theologies explored thus far create a theological framework that engages with the emerging theory of this and the previous chapter, and thereby begins to be missiologically useful.

I return to the theological understanding of human consciousness as a central concept repeatedly used by the SBNR in their stories of spiritual journeying. The language of consciousness was expressed by the SBNR who spiritually sought a change in consciousness as forms of spiritual growth in the six characteristics defined in Chapter 3. Such changes in consciousness were expressed through experiences of transcendence, unitive integration, guidance and meaning, mystical truth from within and without, and authenticity through spiritually responsible behaviour. A good example of this in the SBNR stories is expressed by Isabel. Here Isabel is choosing to seek spiritually, although, given my theological argument so far, there is a tension here between her choice and awareness of the spiritual path. Her brothers are not aware of this path, where her search touches on seeking spiritual experience to explore truths and to undergo a change in consciousness through living authentically and spiritually responsibly:

> I have two brothers who had similar experiences to me growing up who have no interest in spirituality at all. If I mention consciousness to them I will have lost them already ... Experiential learning has always been essential to me. Self-consciously I know I need to experience something to work out if I think it is important, or to understand something ... a lot of people aspire to be of service to the community ... without necessarily thinking of themselves as being spiritual or making that association. Many are completely unaware of this level of consciousness. Even with Extinction Rebellion you can say there is a spiritual thread in it wanting to wake people up, and reveal the truth, but many I would presume do not think of themselves as being spiritual. (Isabel, Telegraph Hill dialogue group, 14 November 2019)

Isabel is consciously choosing to be open to the path of spiritual experience. Theologically, I have argued that this is not just an autonomous spiritual choice, but one where God is seeking to awaken the seeker through a deep connection with God even if they are unaware of this.

Yet for some there was an acknowledgement that this desire for change in spiritual consciousness was not just about individual freedom, but depended on other factors in connection to something spiritually other or divine, or on factors outside the control of the seeker. On one occasion, Caleb expressed through the language of predestination a growing awareness, through experiences of transcendence, of a dependence on a spiritual other, although for him, this awareness is not yet an acknowledgement of God as source:

> We obviously have a choice, or we all would be unevolved, but our freedom is limited, because there is an evolutionary context of development that we exist in, so it is not a complete freedom of choice, as there is a sense of predestination in this process. I do believe that we are on a path that was predestined for us, and that we are all following in these separate unique paths. (Caleb, Peckham dialogue group, 7 November 2018)

So missiologically, mission strategies that engage with people's active individual experiences and meaning-making are critical for this form of mission practice. Each SBNR seeker is on their own unique spiritual path, which opens up the role of the missioner to be a guide or a sharer of wisdom, always willing to encourage the seeker to engage with the source of their spiritual experiences, where such seeking is part of the freedom to spiritually explore, and of an evolving awareness of their relationship to God as source.

In the context of the dialogue groups, there is an important focus on active listening for the missioner or pioneer, who should expect people to have all sorts of spiritual experiences as God seeks to awaken people to the reality of God – which is God's mission not ours – or, as Tanner suggests, as God remoulds or transforms people through the Spirit.

Many participants of the PhD research study named an evolution of consciousness which, by applying the work of Barfield, I understand through processes of original participation, withdrawal from participation, and reciprocal participation, where this participation relates to God, whether the individual acknowledges it or not. Caleb described in an interview a sense of participation with a multifaceted God:

> I think we are all connected to the divine, and those focused on spirituality and gaining in wisdom are growing through a process of developing evolutionary consciousness to reach a higher level of consciousness and awareness. I do believe there is a divine consciousness, there is a source, a single entity, but it is complex, a multifaceted entity … A creative or creator divine consciousness. So I do believe in a multifaceted divine consciousness. (Caleb, Life History Interview)

In the first stage of Barfield's theory of the evolution of consciousness, original participation, I made connections between this stage and those who did not believe in an individual self, who were largely coming from understandings of the non-duality movement or Zen Buddhism, as by implication these approaches believe in a collective identity as a collective consciousness. A good example is Bethan, who actively uses this approach of denying her human self-identity to manage painful life events and reject those experiences that catalysed her spiritual journey as 'baggage':

> What I called baggage later on didn't look like baggage originally, it looked like it was true. And when I had understood more, I became aware that it was baggage, and definitely not true … understanding non-duality has helped me cope with loss … Once you realize that who we are never is born and never dies, it reframes everything. (Bethan, Battersea dialogue group, 20 November 2019)

Missiologically, this understanding rejects not only the central Christian human identity as 'made in the image of God', but also the divine 'I–Thou' connection between the individual and God as Creator, Redeemer and Sustainer, forming instead an alternative divinity made up out of the connections of individuals. This understanding is clearly contrary to Christian theology and, if followed, could actively take people away from God. By implication, those who follow this particular path are effectively rejecting the promptings of the Spirit to an awakening to a deeper sense of participation in God. This disables the individual seeker from engaging in at least two of the six ways of spiritual seeking identified in Chapter 3, because there is an active denial or rejection of seeking integration, unity and connection, and seeking mystical truth that lies within.

Regarding the second stage of the theory of an evolution of consciousness, withdrawal from participation, I believe the pain, alienation, disconnection, sense of marginalization and wounding named by most of the SBNR participants were forms of purgation caused by the cultural context of systemic sinfulness of the world's global market system, forms of purist scientific-rationalist thinking and egoic consciousness. It was this that catalysed the move to their becoming SBNR spiritual seekers, responding to the beckoning of the Spirit to seek to return to God. Language about a multifaceted God, as spirit, creator and source, resonates with an encounter with a Trinitarian God, while, for a few, the language and desire for the presence of Christ was there in the dialogues although not central, as for example in the experiences of Isabel and Rosaline:

> In my own experience of growing up, I had quite a traumatic childhood … Facing stuff in my family required me to break out of the box that I was given. Something in me opened and became receptive to a life that reflected me. (Isabel, Telegraph Hill dialogue group, 14 November 2019)

> Jesus or Yeshua was born in order to bring the Christos love energy to the earth. Through his teachings and his being, not particularly as they were then written down later and put in the Bible, unfortunately … to start spreading the energy, the Christos through humanity … So he was here to bring love to the earth, to leave an example of what it is to be human … and that is why it was important he came as man. (Rosaline, Life History Interview)

The place of pain or difficulty in life in these examples, or an increasing awareness that there was more to life, has missiological implications. In some expressions of Christianity, pain or difficulty is seen as an aberration to Christianity, particularly in forms of theology influenced by the prosperity gospel. In contemplative theologies, the spiritual path sometimes begins with a spiritual awakening followed by a 'dark night of the soul' as an experience of pain and suffering, often in connection with unhealthy attachments and addictions.

The reality of painful experiences galvanizing spiritual seeking was evident in the PhD research study and has been outlined in the previous two chapters. Therefore, regarding missiology and mission practice, the missioner needs to reassure the SBNR spiritual seeker that, for many, the spiritual journey begins with pain and suffering.

Considering the third stage of the evolution of consciousness, reciprocal or final participation: this resonates with the contemplative spiritual movement from illumination, and the return or desire for union was evidenced in most of the transcripts of the research study.

I contend that some of the language around a unitive consciousness and soul, 'all are one', an emerging panentheism, 'ground of our being' and seeking God from 'within and without', are evidence of the desire for mystical union with moments of illumination. Engagement with spiritual practices and ethical living revealed the desire to get beyond an egoic consciousness and to seek the true self.

Some of these experiences clearly were authentic mystical experiences. For example, Elna's mystical encounter of the divine when visiting a garden was so palpably moving that it reminded me of the famous mystical experience of Thomas Merton on a street corner in Louisville, Kentucky, and even had elements of the transfiguration of Jesus:

> I sat in a garden last October ... I walked up with my daughter, and we kinda went [gasp in awe]. It was this garden where light shone out of the ... light. Like it was illuminated space. It was beautiful, and as we walked in there, the feeling was of complete and utter peace and love. And we sat down there, and it was honestly you know ... words, the trouble is words don't describe any of this ... because they fail. You can't come, you can't experience, I don't think, spirit directly. Which is why it doesn't work for cynics. You can't experience spirit through language and the mind. It's transcending beyond that. The feeling for me was of, I could just sit there. Nothing needed to be done. I didn't have to be anywhere, do anything, achieve anything, nothing, I didn't have to speak. I could have pitched a tent there and lived on the grass for the rest of my life, and it ... was perfection and

completion and there was nothing lacking. And I thought, if I could go through life connected to that feeling, wow. (Elna, Pilot dialogue group, 24 January 2018)

As we have already stated, few named the significance of Jesus in their spiritual experiences, except for Rosaline, who articulated an understanding of the 'Christos' and mystical encounters of Jesus:

I feel loved by the Christos. So that is not a romantic love or a love in this world, it is a love that says ... you face the problems of life, and the Christos will give you the resources to deal with that. (Rosaline, Telegraph Hill dialogue group, 16 January 2020)

However, there was little talk resonant with an emerging Christology even though there were the beginnings of an articulation of the Trinity: this again demonstrates the missional challenge that we will explore in the next chapter.

Missiologically, clearly these spiritual examples are beginning to acknowledge a source of this form of love as illuminated in human experience. The challenge for the missioner is to help attribute these experiences to God as the source of such love.

Finally, I turn to the theology of participation with God as theosis. Missiologically, theosis has emerged as a critical theological frame for the engagement of mission with the SBNR, which I have begun to articulate in this chapter and will develop further in the next.

It is the process of transformation or remoulding that takes place behind the entire spiritual journey, beginning with a spiritual awakening and the process of spiritual pilgrimage towards God through purgation, illumination and union. This theological understanding lies behind all six characteristics of spiritual seeking.

In the stories of the SBNR of the PhD research study, Peter's contribution to a group dialogue stood out as deeply resonant with theosis in that it incorporates contemplative spiritual practice, seeking for the true self, and letting go of the egoic and false self, driven by the deep connection and beckoning of a deeper relationship with God:

Spirituality ... you could define it as ... connecting to something greater than yourself and the search for meaning beyond the daily grind, and ... about well-being as an issue in our society ... if we were to talk about spiritual well-being ... are you generally feeling like you have a place in the world in that you are living in the flow of a life that is worth living? And I think we are in a sort of crisis in the Western world, of a lot of people experiencing life as being fractured, and not whole, and not quite sure who they are, or what the point of life is ... each of us has a self and the effects of the ego. The ego being this kind of fragile thing, that is us ... It is what we see in terms of everything we have to lose. And my false self, the one that is easily anxious, easily offended ... thinks that another person's success means that I am less successful. Constantly making comparisons with others ... The true self is that when you are living in a more sense of peace, you feel you have a place in the world, you feel that whatever happens you will be OK. You feel generous, and what is really fascinating is how as an individual any one of us can flip between the false self and the true self, several times each day ... So the question for me then is what can you do to centre yourself, to find balance in yourself and find wholeness? And that is the task I think for spirituality ... I personally believe in a spirituality in the fullest sense, with a connection with the supernatural, something divine, someone greater than ourselves, some sense of creator ... spirituality is something where there is a practice where you seek to go deeper into who you are ... You can either learn that in an instant, by sitting in a beautiful mountainside, and have a transcendent experience, or it can take years to learn through trial and error, but it means that your deepest contentment is found when you stop seeing the world as 'What can I get out of life?' and more about 'How can I participate in what is already happening in the world?' ... there is true healing to be found. (Peter, Borough dialogue group, 25 July 2018)

Peter's understanding here names a pathway or process of purgation, illumination and union in relationship to God and the call to be the true self, rather than the egoic and false self that has much to do with the unhealthy consequence of living. Missionally, then, theosis suggests that as people progress out of purgation they may grow in confidence to face existential and religious questions of life. This requires the missioner to be enrolled as a mystic or contemplative, seeking to share wisdom and offer spiritual prayer practices that could potentially assist the individual at their stage of spirituality.

Such wisdom should not shut down questioning, as has been experienced by some SBNR in their dialogue with Christians. For Trevor, this was a particular issue:

When I am in the SBNR discussion group, these are significant for me in the practice of coming and participating to the process of questing spiritually ... In the past I have been to lots of Christian things ... but no real room to question, doubt or explore ... I think that curiosity and openness in these conversations I have found to be spiritually enlightening. (Trevor, one-to-one interview, 16 December 2019)

Given Trevor's responses, a theosis-informed approach to mission, where such mission is God's not ours, requires a non-directive approach, where the missioner offers wisdom.

In conclusion, there were many connections between the emerging theory and an emerging contemplative normative theology. I began this chapter using contemplative theologies to explore human consciousness and its relationship to God. I have explored the three-stage pattern of contemplative prayer and a theory of the evolution of consciousness as a progression of three axial shifts and how these relate to the biblical narrative of original sin and the fall. I have again drawn on the insights from mystical theology to explore theological themes of original wounding and the relationship between egoic consciousness and the turn to violence, alienation and dislocation. I explored the significance of Jesus whose life, death and resurrection have given humanity the choice to respond to the final axial shift of an evolution of consciousness through being 'in Christ' as an act of participation, and theosis as the path to union with God as an expression of seeking for the true self and non-egoic consciousness. Reflections on the responses of the SBNR grounded analysis showed that the minority followers of non-duality desired the retreat to a devolution of a collective consciousness as an original state of participation. However, the majority who believed in an individual self recognized the need for an evolution of consciousness to progress to a form of reciprocal union with God. Yet saying all of this, responses did not name the significance of Jesus or the necessity of being 'in Christ' as a form of mystical experience. I surmised that this may be because of the forms of Christianity that participants may have experienced, which were not spiritual but reduced the faith to forms of moral certitude. I then returned to the example of Philip, as recorded in John 1.43–51, who had a direct experience of Christ, and I posed a number of questions. How do we respond to the missional imperative of enabling SBNR spiritual seekers to encounter Christ in their questing, and how does the church respond to this missional need and also allow itself to be transformed to engage far more deeply in Christian contemplative practice? Drawing on the stories of SBNR seekers and with reflections on the emerging normative theology, I explored how these key theological frames provided useful missiology and mission practice. Turning to the work of Tanner, I was able to find an approach to the use of theosis that honoured the spiritual insights of the SBNR and the importance of a strong Christology. Tanner's work emphasized a 'weak' and 'strong' form of theosis, which also provided the frame of understanding the missional journey through multiple epiphany moments towards God. I ended the chapter by offering evidence of the normative theology that we have been exploring in the stories of participants of this study. These SBNR narratives provide evidence of an awareness of the love of God or the divine that draws them on a continuing spiritual journey. In this way, these SBNR stories and this chapter's emerging normative contemplative theology join in with the words of Philip, who beckoned his friend Nathanael to 'Come and see.'

In the next chapter, I build on the theology of this chapter by turning to revised practice and the missiological frame. I develop a new approach to a contemplative model of mission as central to this revised praxis. This will continue to explore the theology of theosis and participation 'in Christ', and the significance of mystical and contemplative theological resources for the practice of mission.

Notes

1 Anon, 'Consciousness', in *Lexico.Com*, https://www.lexico.com/definition/consciousness (accessed 3.12.2020).

2 Thomas Merton, 'A New Christian Consciousness?' (Essay for Monastic Novices, February 1967), https://conversi.org/wp-content/uploads/2018/03/A-New-Christian-Consciousness-TMerton.pdf, p. 6 (accessed 3.12.2020).

3 Merton, 'A New Christian Consciousness?', p. 6.

4 Merton, 'A New Christian Consciousness?', p. 8.

5 Mark Vernon, 'Barfield and the Evolution of Consciousness', transcription following Zoom interview, 18 December 2020, p. 8; Owen Barfield, *The Rediscovery of Meaning and Other Essays*, 2nd edn (Oxford: Barfield Press, 2013), p. 212.

6 Barfield, *The Rediscovery of Meaning*, p. 212.

7 Barfield, *The Rediscovery of Meaning*, pp. 213, 219.

8 Elaine A. Heath, *The Mystic Way of Evangelism: A Contemplative Vision for Christian Outreach* (Grand Rapids, MI: Baker Academic, 2008), p. 4.

9 Heath, *The Mystic Way of Evangelism*, p. 5; Sarah Coakley, *God, Sexuality, and the Self: An Essay 'On the Trinity'* (Cambridge: Cambridge University Press, 2019), pp. 11–12.

10 Thomas Merton, *Conjectures of a Guilty Bystander* (New York: Doubleday, 1966), p. 70.

11 Coakley, *God, Sexuality, and the Self*, p. 15.

12 Coakley, *God, Sexuality, and the Self*, p. 12.

13 Coakley, *God, Sexuality, and the Self*, p. 114.

14 Merton, *Conjectures of a Guilty Bystander*, p. 212.

15 John D. Zizioulas, *Lectures in Christian Dogmatics*, ed. Douglas H. Knight (London: T&T Clark, 2008), p. 95.

16 Zizioulas, *Lectures in Christian Dogmatics*, p. 113.

17 Joe Kapolyo, 'The Conversion of Ubuntu – an African Vision of Human Nature' (Henry Martyn Seminar, Cambridge Centre for Christianity Worldwide: www.cccw.cam.ac.uk, 2010), p. 1.

18 Zizioulas, *Lectures in Christian Dogmatics*, p. 115.

19 Zizioulas, *Lectures in Christian Dogmatics*, p. 92.

20 Merton, *Conjectures of a Guilty Bystander*, pp. 220–1.

21 Zizioulas, *Lectures in Christian Dogmatics*, p. 115.

22 Zizioulas, *Lectures in Christian Dogmatics*, pp. 96–7.

23 Thomas Merton, *New Seeds of Contemplation* (New York: New Directions Books, 1972), p. 31.

24 Zizioulas, *Lectures in Christian Dogmatics*, p. 95.

25 Merton, *New Seeds of Contemplation*, pp. 3, 10.

26 Barfield, *The Rediscovery of Meaning*, pp. 249–50.

27 Owen Barfield, *Saving the Appearances: A Study in Idolatry* (Oxford: Barfield Press, 2011), p. 65.

28 Barfield, *Saving the Appearances*, pp. 318–20.

29 Mark Vernon, *A Secret History of Christianity: Jesus, the Last Inkling, and the Evolution of Consciousness* (Winchester: Christian Alternative, 2018), pp. 2–4.

30 Barfield, *The Rediscovery of Meaning*, p. 219.

31 Barfield, *The Rediscovery of Meaning*, pp. 311–12.

32 Barfield, *The Rediscovery of Meaning*, pp. 212–13, 311–12.

33 Barfield, *Saving the Appearances*, pp. 249–50, 265; Vernon, *A Secret History of Christianity*, p. 3.

34 Barfield, *The Rediscovery of Meaning*, p. 220.

35 Vernon, 'Barfield and the Evolution of Consciousness', p. 7.

36 Heath, *The Mystic Way of Evangelism*, p. 10; Coakley, *God, Sexuality, and the Self*, p. 87; Merton, *Conjectures of a Guilty Bystander*, p. 70.

37 Vernon, *A Secret History of Christianity*, pp. 4–5; Barfield, *The Rediscovery of Meaning*, pp. 249–50.

38 I interviewed Mark Vernon about Barfield's thinking given his own published work, and used the transcription as evidence as recorded 18.12.2020, 9.30–10.45 a.m., see https://docs.google.com/document/d/10GVFCxYXj_MGzf3X3uMMuUqBWOToX7l3/.

39 Vernon, 'Barfield and the Evolution of Consciousness', p. 7.

40 Vernon, 'Barfield and the Evolution of Consciousness', p. 8.

41 Barfield, *Saving the Appearances*, p. 41.

42 Barfield, *Saving the Appearances*, pp. 38–9.

43 Vernon, 'Barfield and the Evolution of Consciousness', p. 8.

44 Barfield, *Saving the Appearances*, pp. 41, 318–20.

45 Vernon, *A Secret History of Christianity*, p. 3.

46 Vernon, 'Barfield and the Evolution of Consciousness', p. 1; Vernon, *A Secret History of Christianity*, p. 11.

47 Barfield, *The Rediscovery of Meaning*, pp. 319–20.

48 Barfield, *The Rediscovery of Meaning*, pp. 203–4.

49 Barfield, *The Rediscovery of Meaning*, pp. 21–2.

50 Vernon, *A Secret History of Christianity*, p. 40.

51 Vernon, *A Secret History of Christianity*, p. 40.

52 Barfield, *The Rediscovery of Meaning*, p. 265.

53 Vernon, *A Secret History of Christianity*, p. 164.

54 Vernon, *A Secret History of Christianity*, p. 41.

55 Barfield, *The Rediscovery of Meaning*, pp. 318–19.

56 Zizioulas, *Lectures in Christian Dogmatics*, p. 105.

57 Barfield, *The Rediscovery of Meaning*, pp. 311–12.

58 Barfield, *The Rediscovery of Meaning*, pp. 276–7.

59 Vernon, *A Secret History of Christianity*, p. 4.

60 Matthieu Ricard, Christophe André and Alexandre Jollien, *In Search of Wisdom: A Monk, a Philosopher, and a Psychiatrist on What Matters Most*, 1st Eng. edn (Boulder, CO: Sounds True, 2018), p. 45.

61 Ricard, André and Jollien, *In Search of Wisdom*, p. 45.

62 Heath's writing here resonates with the understandings of the groups about the false and fantasy self; see the ethnographic descriptive analysis in Chapter 2, section 'Human identity', and the grounded theory analysis in Chapter 3, section 'Seeking integration, unity and connection'.

63 Heath, *The Mystic Way of Evangelism*, p. 72.

64 Heath, *The Mystic Way of Evangelism*, p. 72.

65 Merton, *Conjectures of a Guilty Bystander*, p. 78.

66 Vernon, *A Secret History of Christianity*, p. 3; Merton, 'A New Christian Consciousness?', p. 6.

67 Merton, *Conjectures of a Guilty Bystander*, p. 208.

68 Merton, *Conjectures of a Guilty Bystander*, p. 85.

69 Ricard, André and Jollien, *In Search of Wisdom*, p. 39.

70 Merton, *New Seeds of Contemplation*, p. 21.

71 Merton, *New Seeds of Contemplation*, pp. 34–5.

72 This theme of the gap between spirit and physicality in the human person and the need for a healthy unity of the two was talked about in the groups; see Chapter 2, section 'Human identity'.

73 Barfield, *The Rediscovery of Meaning*, pp. 219–20.

74 Heath, *The Mystic Way of Evangelism*, p. 29.

75 Heath, *The Mystic Way of Evangelism*, p. 31.

76 Heath, *The Mystic Way of Evangelism*, p. 34.

77 Heath, *The Mystic Way of Evangelism*, pp. 36–7.

78 Heath, *The Mystic Way of Evangelism*, p. 37.

79 Heath, *The Mystic Way of Evangelism*, p. 37.

80 Heath, *The Mystic Way of Evangelism*, pp. 38–9.

81 Heath, *The Mystic Way of Evangelism*, p. 39.

82 Heath, *The Mystic Way of Evangelism*, p. 42.

83 Heath, *The Mystic Way of Evangelism*, p. 42.

84 Heath, *The Mystic Way of Evangelism*, pp. 41, 46.

85 David Tacey, *The Spirituality Revolution: The Emergence of Contemporary Spirituality* (London: Routledge, 2004), p. 222.

86 Heath, *The Mystic Way of Evangelism*, pp. 46–7.

87 Barfield, *Saving the Appearances*, p. 158; Vernon, *A Secret History of Christianity*, p. 165.

88 Barfield, *The Rediscovery of Meaning*, pp. 349–50.

89 Barfield, *Saving the Appearance*, pp. 184–5.

90 Barfield, *Saving the Appearances*, pp. 184–5.

91 Merton, *New Seeds of Contemplation*, pp. 40–1.

92 Vernon, 'Barfield and the Evolution of Consciousness', p. 8.

93 Barfield, *The Rediscovery of Meaning*, p. 349; Vernon, 'Barfield and the Evolution of Consciousness', p. 2.

94 Stephen B. Bevans and Roger P. Schroeder, *Prophetic Dialogue: Reflections on Christian Mission Today* (Maryknoll, NY: Orbis Books, 2011), p. 11.

95 Zizioulas, *Lectures in Christian Dogmatics*, pp. 102–3.

96 Merton, *New Seeds of Contemplation*, pp. 40–1.

97 Zizioulas, *Lectures in Christian Dogmatics*, p. 106.

98 Bevans and Schroeder, *Prophetic Dialogue*, p. 116.

99 Vernon, *A Secret History of Christianity*, p. 165.

100 Vernon, *A Secret History of Christianity*, pp. 113–14.

101 Vernon, *A Secret History of Christianity*, pp. 103–4.

102 Vernon, *A Secret History of Christianity*, p. 103.

103 Michael J. Gorman, *Becoming the Gospel: Paul, Participation, and Mission* (Grand Rapids, MI: Eerdmans Publishing Co., 2015), p. 3.

104 Gorman, *Becoming the Gospel*, p. 4.

105 Gorman, *Becoming the Gospel*, p. 5.

106 Kathryn Tanner, *Christ the Key* (Cambridge: Cambridge University Press, 2009), p. 13.

107 Tanner, *Christ the Key*, p. 16.

108 Vernon, *A Secret History of Christianity*, pp. 117–18.

109 Gorman, *Becoming the Gospel*, pp. 23–4.

110 Gorman, *Becoming the Gospel*, p. 268.

111 Gorman, *Becoming the Gospel*, p. 6.

112 Gorman, *Becoming the Gospel*, pp. 26, 28–30, 32, 33–4.

113 Michael J. Gorman, *Abide and Go: Missional Theosis in the Gospel of John*, Didsbury Lectures Series (Eugene, OR: Cascade Books, 2018), p. xvii.

114 I surmise this is why so many Western spiritual seekers call themselves 'SBNR'.

115 Tanner, *Christ the Key*, pp. 8–12.

116 Tanner, *Christ the Key*, p. 8.

117 Tanner, *Christ the Key*, p. 13.

118 As distinct from non-dualism, which is about getting beyond either/or to a state of both/and.

119 Vernon, 'Barfield and the Evolution of Consciousness', p. 5.

120 Barfield, *Saving the Appearances*, pp. 154–5.

5

Developing a Contemplative Model of Mission: 'God's Kenosis, Our Theosis'

Now there was an Ethiopian eunuch ... He had come to Jerusalem to worship and was returning home ... he was reading the prophet Isaiah ... the Spirit said to Philip, 'Go over to this chariot and join it.' So Philip ran up to it and heard him reading the prophet Isaiah. He asked, 'Do you understand what you are reading?' He replied, 'How can I, unless someone guides me?' And he invited Philip to get in and sit beside him ... The eunuch asked Philip, 'About whom, may I ask you, does the prophet say this, about himself or about someone else?' Then Philip began to speak ... about Jesus. As they were going along the road, they came to some water; and the eunuch said, 'Look, here is water! What is to prevent me from being baptized?' ... Philip and the eunuch went down into the water, and Philip baptized him. (Acts 8.27–38)

In this chapter, I begin to specifically develop a contemplative model of mission, continuing with a contemplative understanding of God's mission (*missio Dei*) through the work of Sarah Coakley, Thomas Merton, Ion Bria, Paul Fiddes, Joshva Raja, Stephen Bevans and Roger Schroeder. Drawing on the work of Paul Hiebert, I explore how 'set theory' relates to mission with SBNR spiritual seekers, and in particular a form of mission that draws on the theology of theosis and set theory. Returning to the work of Kathryn Tanner, I continue to explore this missional theosis as 'participation in Christ'. I address some of the criticisms of Tanner's work articulated by Simeon Zahl, particularly concerning the real spiritual experience of conversion as the action of the Holy Spirit; I then draw on the work of Hiebert and set theory to challenge some of Zahl's criticisms, as well as briefly exploring how different church traditions assert different expectations of conversion to being 'in Christ'.

Drawing on the theology of the last chapter and the revised mission practice discussed in this chapter, I propose a new approach to a contemplative model of mission with SBNR spiritual seekers, which I have called 'God's Kenosis, our Theosis', as a particular articulation of the PhD research study and this book. This model will draw on a synthesis of the 'three positions' of Charles Taylor's work, and how these relate both to traditional understanding of the Christian contemplative spiritual path, as reaffirmed by Elaine Heath and Sarah Coakley, and to Owen Barfield's stages of his theory of the evolution of consciousness. The coming together of these different perspectives will be explored in the context of a 'centred-set' understanding of the mission of God through a focus on the conversion and spiritual growth of the inner self through transformation and awakening. This will draw on the writings of Michael Gama, Michael L. Yoder et al., Christopher Lasch and John Schumaker. I then turn to the work of Walter Brueggemann to consider the conversion process of the outer self through the reality of a constant movement of orientation, disorientation and reorientation. I then briefly return to differing understandings and approaches to spiritual conversion and draw on the work of Rupen Das and Catholicos Aram. Finally, I return to the issue of Christology, drawing on the writings of Hyun Kyung and Sister Anne Nasimiyu-Wasike to find a contextually appropriate and authentic expression for an understanding of the significance of Jesus that relates to the world view of SBNR spiritual seekers.

Mission as participation in God

I begin this missiological chapter with the encounter and dialogue between Philip the Evangelist and the Ethiopian eunuch as recorded in the Acts of the Apostles. We are told the eunuch had been on some form of pilgrimage to Jerusalem – which might have had something to do with his work – and that he was clearly a spiritual seeker. Philip, open to the Holy Spirit, is invited (both by God and the eunuch) to dialogue with the eunuch, enabling him to explore the meaning of a mystical scriptural text. As a result the eunuch has some form of spiritual experience through which he gains insight regarding the significance of Jesus as God. He then desires to be 'in Christ' and asks to be baptized in the moment, a request Philip dutifully fulfils. This all happens in the spontaneity of the moment as both Philip and the eunuch are open to God, on a road from Jerusalem to Gaza through the desert.

This scriptural encounter is rich with missiological themes that frame several key questions explored in this chapter. The eunuch, much like the SBNR spiritual seekers who participated in the PhD research study, viewed his spiritual life as a deeply personal journey of meaning-making and exploration. His spiritual thirst was part of a unique pilgrimage, reflecting the broader experiences of many SBNR individuals identified in earlier chapters. These spiritual seekers often express a profound yearning for spiritual encounter, striving to articulate their desire for a deeper union with the source of all life and being. Most of the SBNR seekers were on their own unique journeys as roads through the desert and tough places. The biblical text reveals the role of the Holy Spirit as a central presence or centrifugal force that reveals (in this case through Philip) the reality of God, and particularly Jesus as the Christ, and the place of baptism as a response to a transformative experience of God. Further, I was struck by the role of Philip: his availability as a form of spiritual discipline to God and the roles he plays here – part dialogue partner, part missioner, part prophet.

Participation in the *missio Dei, missio in Trinitate*

Continuing our exploration of a contemplative approach to Christian mission, we begin by acknowledging the centrifugal presence of God through the Holy Spirit. This *missio Dei*, the mission of God, as I affirmed earlier through the work of Coakley and Heath, is a mission of restoration, of healing from a sense of 'original wounding'. Here God seeks restored relationship through kenosis, the pouring out of love from God to the world and to all that exists. For Merton, this more contemplative Christian approach to mission assumes a focus on the inner and outer human 'selves'. Any journey of restoration into relationship with God requires a journey of the whole person, both inner and outer, where conversion can be understood as the act of inner awakening and outer saving.[1] In other words, we are acknowledging the essential mystery of the human self – both spirit and matter: conversion is understood as an inner converting, awakening to the fullness of life, and an outer saving from the brutalities of our material contexts of survival and existence.[2]

This 'inner' and 'outer' journey of conversion, then, explains the interest in and use of Christian prayer and meditation practices by SBNR spiritual seekers, as I noted earlier in this book. The first four characteristics relate to the inner quest of awakening through prayer and meditation: 'seeking transcendence in nature, spirituality and art'; 'seeking integration, unity and connection'; 'seeking meaning to guide one's life' and 'seeking mystical truth that lies within'. The last two characteristics relate to the outer journey as 'saving' through encounter of God in the world, through 'seeking mystical truth that lies outside of the self' and 'seeking authenticity through responsibility'. This outer quest as 'responsibility' encounters God through living with greater respect for all life, as a form of ecological reconnection in a time of global warming and growing ecocide.

Regarding the inner 'awakening', Coakley in her recent writing on the Holy Trinity takes this deeper by suggesting that an understanding of the Triune God is only conceivable when developed out of the experience of prayer, particularly contemplative or ascetical prayer. She argues that the Trinity emerged in the first three centuries of the Christian era through a 'crucial prayer-based logic'.[3] Prayer as experience then becomes critical to forms of encounter with the Trinitarian God that deepen an inner sense of awakening:

> Prayer (and especially prayer of a non-discursive sort, whether contemplative or charismatic) is the chief context in which the irreducible threeness of God becomes humanly apparent ... as one ceases to set the agenda and allows room for God to be God ... It is not I who autonomously prays, but God (the Holy Spirit) who prays in me, and so answers the eternal call of the 'Father'. Drawing me by various painful degrees into the newly expanded life of 'Sonship'.[4]

For Coakley, God 'the Father' becomes the 'source' and ultimate object of human desire, to be experienced through the Holy Spirit, the 'enabler and incorporator', through being 'in Christ'.[5]

This has significance for mission, in that the Holy Trinity becomes a loving attractional force, seeking to draw human beings into relationship with God through the medium of contemplative prayer: 'we ... need to speak of the Father's own reception ... as 'source' ... via the Spirit's reflexive propulsion and the Son's creative effluence. Here ... then, is a 'source' of love unlike any other.'[6]

This understanding of God as centrifugal source has implications when looking at set theory and mission, to which I will return shortly.

This contemplative form of the mission of God is ultimately focused on human flourishing and transformation, personal experience and encounter with the divine. It is a more trans-rational understanding, in contrast to modern, Enlightenment 'facts-based' approaches based on rational understanding. As Bria, a Romanian Orthodox priest and theologian, has said:

> Trinitarian theology points to the fact that God is in God's own self a life of communion and that God's involvement in history aims at drawing humanity and creation in general into this communion with God's very life. The implications of this assertion for understanding mission are very important: mission does not aim primarily at the

propagation or transmission of intellectual convictions, doctrines, moral commands, etc., but at the transmission of the life of communion, that exists in God.[7]

Mission, then, is about the reality of a context where God is inviting everything through kenotic love to participate in communion with God's very being. For Bevans and Schroeder, God's character is love but it is also mission: God seeks to draw people into 'God's very life ... of radical communion, spilling forth in the world, drawing humanity and even creation itself into that communion ... "in Christ God was reconciling the world to Godself ... and entrusting the message of reconciliation to us" ... (see 2 Corinthians 5.19–20)'.[8] In the context of SBNR seekers on a spiritual journey of encounter with God, both their inner-self explorations of awakening and their outer-self desire for salvation become opportunities for encounter with the missional God. Holding the tension between our 'material' and 'spiritual' selves regarding mission is important in order to avoid some of the mistakes of mission movements of the past; as Bevans and Schroeder remind us: 'There cannot be a material gospel and a spiritual gospel; these have to be one, as was true of the ministry of Jesus. There is no evangelism without solidarity; there is no Christian solidarity that does not involve sharing the message of God's coming reign.'[9]

For Fiddes, a British Baptist systematic theologian, any engagement with a Trinitarian God must be connected to the making of freedom and liberation from all forms of human oppression.[10] This also has implications for understanding mission, as being not just about 'conversion' but, more deeply, the 'outer' seeking of liberation from situations of wounding, including economic injustice and the unhealthiness of our market society, to which I will return later.

Fiddes also affirms the same position as that outlined by Coakley: that God's love going out into the world is the story and medium of salvation, the sharing of divine being in a communion of love. The God of salvation lives eternally in relationship.[11] For Fiddes, this understanding of God is critical, where God on the one hand is relationship and on the other an event. For him, the Triune God is essential for a Christian-informed approach to understanding the nature of being (ontology), a way of knowing (epistemology) that gets beyond the weaknesses we identified in the last chapter as a consequence of the Enlightenment. As Fiddes states: 'Only by bringing together being as relation and knowing as participation, will we begin to overcome the view of the human subject stemming from the Enlightenment in which observation is the basic paradigm of knowing.'[12]

By implication, therefore, this connection between God's mission and deep relationship, communion and participation with God (theosis) takes us from an understanding of the *missio Dei* (mission of God) to the idea of *missio in Deo* (missional theosis as participation in God) and therefore to *missio in Trinitate* (missional theosis as participation in the Trinity); however, as Raja, an Indian practical theologian and missiologist, has written, these ideas still need further development in theology and missiology, which I hope to expand here.[13] I turn now to set theory and its missional implications.

Set theory and mission practices

The focus of the mission of God and the individual missional journey from shopper to participant resonates with the writing of Hiebert, an American missiological anthropologist, and what he calls 'set theory'. Hiebert's writings on set theory have highly influenced contemporary mission practice in the UK context, including Fresh Expressions of Church.

Hiebert identified different approaches to mission activity and becoming Christian, which were driven not only by different missiologies but also by his set theory.[14] At the heart of his thinking were three different forms of 'set' which differed in their understanding of conversion, salvation, considerations for baptism, factors regarding the Holy Spirit and understanding around losing faith.[15] These differing sets he named 'fuzzy sets', 'bounded sets' and 'centred sets'.

For Hiebert, in fuzzy sets there are no distinctions, no membership or ownership of anything; they combine all sorts of things from differing spiritualties: 'They might participate in both Hindu and Christian services, or combine Buddhism and Confucianism in responding to the needs of life.'[16] This fusion of different influences becomes a 'mash-up' of different spiritualities and religions. The danger of such an approach to mission is that it promotes a pick'n'mix approach that loses the distinctiveness of Christianity, and therefore would not really promote an effective path to form a Christian faith.

A centred-set missional approach has a defined centre and everything in this set relates to the centre.[17] Further, there are boundaries that individuals freely cross into or out of in connection with the centre, where crossing into such boundaries creates a sense of belonging in these boundary areas.[18] Such an approach to mission does allow for the sense of progress where God is at the centre of the set. This would correlate strongly with the understanding above about mission being led by the

Holy Spirit, enabling people to journey towards God through multiple experiences of God through the Spirit. However, this missional understanding also recognizes that people can become Christian and later reject that identity to become post-Christian, dechurched or unchurched. This is a theological issue for those coming from a more conservative theological position concerning conversion and baptism.

Finally, there is the bounded set. According to Hiebert, when somebody crosses the threshold into a bounded set, then that person has arrived, and there can be no further change.[19] A bounded set is effectively uniform and static with a complete change of the former state of the individual.[20] There is therefore a major distinction between being 'not Christian' and outside the category, and being inside and 'Christian'. Conversion, then, when understood as entering into a bounded set, requires immediate and dramatic change, for the person to meet all expected beliefs and practices with a total disassociation from their identity before conversion, requiring immediate ontological change.[21] Salvation is then demonstrated by consistency in maintaining expected beliefs and behaviours. For such a dramatic change, traditions that hold this expectation require a decisive experiential event of transformation led by the Holy Spirit. The bounded set can correspond to the journey from shopper to participant, but this cannot be a slow process of change – it has to be something far more dramatic. This approach relates to more conservative or traditional understandings of evangelism and conversion.

As explored earlier, each of these sets has different understandings of conversion, salvation, expectations for baptism, factors regarding the Holy Spirit and understandings around losing faith.[22]

Drawing on set theory, we can begin to identify how a contemplative form of mission theology and practice can take shape. The descriptive analysis of previous chapters revealed differences in understanding what was going on between those who believed in the individual self and those who did not.

For those who did not believe in a personal self, spirituality was focused on forms of meditation and deconstructive thinking drawing on Zen Buddhism or 'non-duality' practices. There was no perceivable path to follow and certainly no centrifugal pull of any benevolent spiritual force behind the universe. For example, Bethan, a follower of the non-duality movement, articulated consistently her disbelief in a human self:

> I certainly used to want to have a firm set of beliefs, but that had to change as I have gone deeper in my explorations of non-duality ...

There is no I before the eyes, that is pretty mind-blowing. So many of the things I used to believe, I am now letting go of, letting go of a belief is a process ... And beliefs often pop up, and so I name them and let them go. (Bethan, Life History Interview)

Bethan's perspective reflected the view of a small subgroup of participants whose spirituality was an erratic process with no real spiritual path or journey other than deconstruction. Such an approach to spirituality correlates to Hiebert's fuzzy set theory.

Figure 11: Hiebert's Fuzzy Set

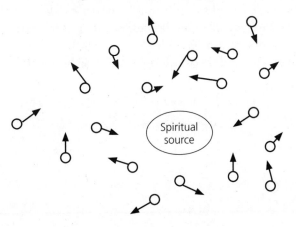

In fuzzy sets there were no distinctions, no shared direction and no connection to a form of spiritual source, as shown in Figure 11.[23] For my PhD study and this book, the small grouping of those who did not believe in the individual self are a form of fuzzy set and therefore have the same issues identified by Hiebert: there is no clarity, no uniqueness of any of the spiritualities; everything becomes a fusion where there is no ownership of anything in particular other than deconstruction and denial of the self.[24] By implication there is no path and no spiritual source, just a never-ending search for spiritual experience to deconstruct. God, if ever perceived, becomes just another experiential option or something to deconstruct. Using Barfield's understandings outlined in the last chapter, there is no evolution of consciousness, only a perpetual 'original participation' that leads nowhere. This, however, applied only to a small number of the participants in the PhD research study.

The vast majority did believe in a human self and the language of consciousness. As I have identified in previous chapters, for many there was evidence of a sense of a divine source and force, with language around unitive consciousness or union with the divine, or the beginnings of a language of God. With this grouping, drawing on the theological analysis of the previous chapter, I want to argue there is evidence of a centrifugal force of love seeking relationship, fullness and restoration. I therefore consider there to be a deep connection between the majority of SBNR spiritual seekers in the PhD research study – those who have a sense of self and are on their own individual spiritual life journeys, wanting a deeper, more fulfilling spiritual life – and what Hiebert has named as mission through a centred-set understanding, as expressed in Figure 12.

This has a defined centre and everything relates to the centre of the set.[25] Further, as I explore in Tanner's understanding of theosis and participation in God, there are boundaries that individuals freely cross into or out of in connection with the centre, where crossing into such boundaries creates a sense of belonging in these boundary areas.[26]

Figure 12: Mission Based on Hiebert's Centred Set

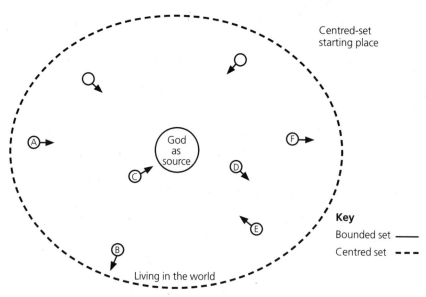

In Figure 12, I outline a missional centred-set understanding that I pro-pose to develop. God, the Holy Trinity, is the source at the centre of the centred set, where individuals A to F are on their own individual journeys living in the world, where you can journey to God but also away from God. This sustains both the centrality of God but also indi-vidual freedom. Further, there is, I believe, a connection between this centred-set approach to mission and the theology of participation of theosis. As Fiddes states:

> Participation in the triune God provides an all-embracing dimension ... a movement of relations which is as wide as the universe, as God, in an act of self-limitation, opens the divine communication of life to enable all created beings to dwell within it ... The Spirit is constantly ... giving our relations a place in the movement of God's purposeful journey towards new creation.[27]

Mission, then, begins as God's intention to restore all things into right relationship through the centrifugal force of the Holy Trinity, through the power of the Holy Spirit beaconing the SBNR spiritual seeker into relationship with God.

This centred-set approach to mission as theosis is reflected in the stories of spiritual journeying of the SBNR of the PhD research study. Caleb is an example of this, although he did not believe in a formalized sense of God but instead spoke of journeying to and with a loving source:

> In my experience ... I became aware of the things that were not good ... focusing on consciousness I was challenged to face forms of addiction through my spiritual connection to the loving source ... It is important to spiritually journey through little steps, lots of little moments of spiritual change and growth ... to help us be free for consciousness development. Freeing up our dreams and getting beyond the negative effects of lack of well-being and looking after ourselves. This work is never finished ... as we continue on our spiritual journeying. (Caleb, Peckham dialogue group, 15 August 2018)

This centred-set understanding of a spiritual journey towards God as source was reflected in the story of Sam:

> I have sensed the force of something hidden that was full of love behind all that brings life and goodness. I have felt at times guided by this, and as I said earlier I have little conversations in my head which I do believe are to and with God. I have felt a deep guidance at times, particularly when things are hard. (Sam, Life History Interview, 26 October 2018)

So there is evidence for this centred-set understanding resonating with the stories of spiritual journeying of the SBNR of the PhD research study.

Tanner, Christian becoming and 'participation in Christ'

I now return to the work of Tanner and her writing on theosis as 'participation in Christ', and the concepts of 'weak' and 'strong' participation that I explored in the last chapter. In that analysis I established that weak participation affirms that every living animal and human being is sustained in life through connection to God; whether they know it or not, they are a 'creature of God … a life derived of God'.[28] It was therefore possible for the SBNR in the PhD research study to seek spirituality and have significant experiences of God without yet acknowledging or affirming understandings from a Christian perspective.

Tanner's writing also affirmed a strong participation that exists when people become followers of Jesus Christ and are thus 'in Christ'. Here Tanner's strong participation correlates with Gorman's understanding of St Paul's writings on being 'in Christ' as a participative theosis. There are, therefore, important missiological implications for this understanding of theosis.

This both/and approach to participation in God opens up theosis as a form of spiritual journey and mission, beckoned through the love of God. Returning to the centred-set evolving understanding of mission through a missional theosis as participation, this new detail of weak and strong participation can be added to this growing mission framing, as expressed in Figure 13.

Figure 13: Centred-Set Model of a Missional Theosis through Participation

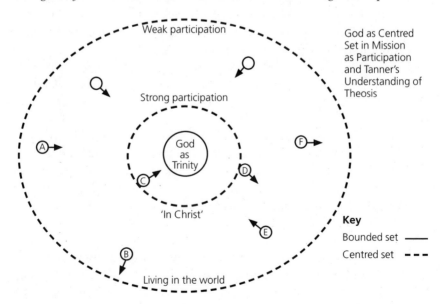

For Tanner, strong participation in being 'in Christ' is about attachment, where our salvation and being is sustained through participation: 'This turning of one's whole attention to Christ in faith constitutes a form of attachment to him ... By way of faith in him, Christ is in and with us and thereby we are justified.'[29]

Such participation is not just passively received; it is a process where God seeks to draw us from weak to strong participation through transformation in which our consciousness and awareness are changed through encounter with the God with whom we become deeply in relationship. As Tanner says: 'Humans do not simply reflect the image of God ... Humanity takes on, in short, its own perfect shape by being reworked through attachment to the divine image.'[30]

Drawing on Tanner's writing, we now have space between weak and strong participation where those who are SBNR can spiritually seek either towards God the Trinity as source and central to the set, or away from God. This space between weak and strong participation then becomes the space for mission and evangelism. Further, choosing to cross into strong participation, becoming 'in Christ', crosses a boundary, which reflects the process of becoming Christian through being 'in Christ' as a new allegiance, but also a process of going much deeper into a relational theosis, of participation 'in Christ'. Person 'C' in Figure 13 has crossed such a boundary and become Christian, and continues on this missional theosis journey of discipleship deeper into participation in God as Trinity through Christ in the power of the Holy Spirit. However, individuals are totally at liberty not to be in strong participation with God, as expressed in the diagram at person 'D'. This would correlate with those who had previously been Christian but have become post-Christian or dechurched.

In the course of the PhD study only one participant was known to have made the spiritual journey from unchurched SBNR spiritual seeker to being 'in Christ', thereby experiencing the shift from weak to strong participation. In the first City dialogue group, Calum began as someone who was changing from being a radical atheist to a SBNR spiritual seeker aware that there was a loving spiritual source to his spiritual seeking that was drawing him into relationship:

It seems to me that there is something going on about the life force, that kind of ... that realization or perception that there is something called life which exists in different levels ... these different shades of consciousness or life force ... I think as humans, inherently, we realized the sacredness of that life force, so we are really drawn back to it. And we really get a sense of when it is missing, and when we move away from it, and our society does have a tendency ... can easily move away from that life force, and we do start to suffer when we feel disconnected from that life force, so they can only go so far away from it. (Calum, City dialogue group, 31 May 2018)

After Calum had decided to be baptized and become a Christian, it was clear that this decision was not only based on a personal choice, but that he had had significant experiences of transformation. He had been transformed through his spiritual journey, marked by changes in consciousness that led him to publicly acknowledge this transformation through baptism with the Moot Community.[31] In so doing he was entering into a strong participation of being 'in Christ':

I think I found over time that I could identify with the spiritual message of Jesus and it was an exploration I wanted to continue with others, specifically Moot ... I have become comfortable with the mystery of faith and I no longer feel the need to apply rationalist thought to the teachings of the Bible. I think I used to view much of the Bible and Christianity as simply culturally accepted superstition. I now believe the Bible speaks to deeper truths about the needs of humanity, our relationship with others and with the universe, the heavens and God ... I feel Christianity is something I carry in my heart ... I'm feeling my own way in the company of others. (Calum, 'Additional Interview', 2 July 2019)

By implication, regarding an emerging missiological frame and mission practice, and in the context of Calum's spiritual journey, we are naming God the Holy Trinity as the source who pours out God's love to the world (and universe) as kenosis, and seeks to evoke a fervent human response, beckoning the human person into deep relationship with God and ultimately into participation in God as theosis.[32]

This coming together of God's love being poured out as God's kenosis and, in response, God's desire to draw us into greater relationship, begins to affirm the theological basis of a more contemplative model of mission, which I am naming 'God's Kenosis, our Theosis'. This further adaptation is expressed in Figure 14 below as a way of understanding salvation as a form of 'exchange formula' initiated by God's love mission to the cosmos as kenosis, giving human beings the opportunity to choose to respond to such love through a spiritual journey towards becoming 'in Christ' as theosis.

Figure 14: Contemplative Model of Mission –
'God's Kenosis, our Theosis' Centred Set

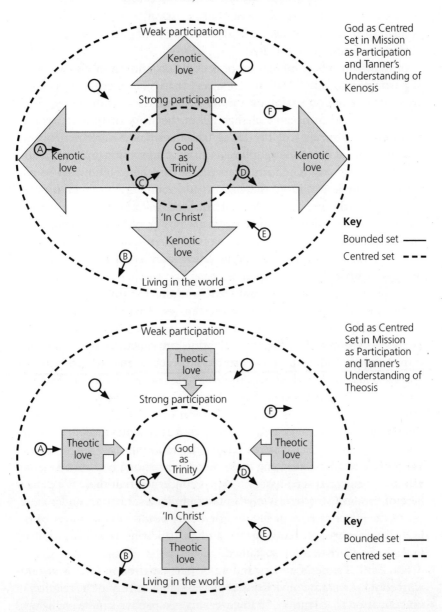

I now explore the implications of this missiological frame and model drawn from the stories of the SBNR of this study and their spiritual journeying, which I will illustrate later in the chapter.

Using this approach based on the writings of Tanner on participation and its inclusion of weak and strong theosis, a mission model takes shape based on a missional theology that understands mission as a form of *missio in Deo*, where restorative love is at the heart of this theosis-inspired understanding of God's mission, and importantly here, as mission to the inner self as God seeks to restore all things back into right relationship with the divine.

Drawing on this combination of centred set and Tanner's two levels of participation, the SBNR spiritual seeker can be interpreted as being on a journey of conversion as a move towards God at the centre. This can be in the form of slow change (as in the story of Calum), as part of an ongoing process of becoming Christian based on experience of, and, in time, the choice to follow, Christ. Conversion in this process is linked to *metanoia* as turning to Christ through relationship to and with God. By implication, this process of becoming Christian does not require a decisive experience of the Holy Spirit in one significant spiritual moment. Rather, through the centrifugal power of God, the individual grows and heals while journeying from original wounding into deeper relationship with God to the point where they cross the boundary of being 'in Christ'.[33]

Tanner's work is not beyond criticism, and for this we turn to the writings of Zahl, an American Protestant systematic theologian, who offers a comprehensive critique of Tanner's work. Zahl's writing focuses on the work of the Holy Spirit in salvation and sanctification and is concerned that it should be recognizable in practice and accord with the Spirit's work as described in Scripture.[34] He is concerned that Tanner's model of participation in God is somewhat 'anti-experiential' regarding significant change and is driven by a form of moral agency or modern Enlightenment improvement, rather than a real moment of transformation to becoming a Christian led by the Holy Spirit.[35] As he says: 'I am convinced that something more directly emotionally compelling and affectively engaged is necessary.'[36] He is concerned that there is a danger here of modernist progress myth undermining a Christian understanding of the effect of human sin, and that only in the salvific power of the Holy Spirit, through God's grace and the doctrine of justification by faith, is the Christian life sustained.[37]

For Zahl, Tanner's understanding of participation in God is at odds with core Protestant convictions about human nature and the relation of sanctification to salvation.[38] However, his perspective can be challenged by drawing on Hiebert's set theory, particularly the difference between centred set and bounded set and differing expectations of conversion depending on differing Christian traditions.

According to Hiebert, when somebody crosses the threshold into a bounded set, then that person has arrived, and there can be no further change.[39] The bounded set is effectively uniform and static with a complete change in the former state of the individual.[40] There is therefore a major distinction between being 'not Christian' and outside the set, and being inside and 'Christian'. Conversion when entering a bounded set requires immediate and substantial change for the person to meet all expected beliefs and practices, and a total disassociation from who they were before conversion – immediate ontological change.[41]

Salvation, then, is demonstrated by consistency in maintaining expected beliefs and behaviours. For such a dramatic change, traditions that hold this expectation require a decisive experiential transformation led by the Holy Spirit. This expectation of a bounded-set understanding of salvation and conversion is expressed in Figure 15 with person 'C'.

Figure 15: Hiebert's Bounded-Set Expectations

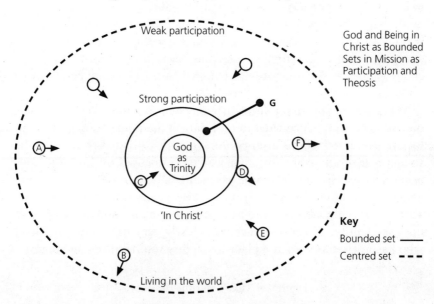

Given Zahl's writing, for person 'C' to cross into becoming a Christian, they must have a dramatic experience of the Holy Spirit to enable lasting change where conversion is a decisive moment.

Transformation

Zahl's views of conversion and soteriology in this situation match Hiebert's analysis of bounded-set expectations, whereas Tanner's writing on participatory soteriology and conversion is based on Hiebert's centred-set expectations, and therefore each reflects different yet authentic understandings of both soteriology and conversion within differing church traditions. However, saying that, I do want to critique the consequences of Zahl's writing and the weakness of bounded-set practice and theology in a missional context.

I turn to the spiritual journey of Mike to highlight the problem with Zahl's argument. Mike was an Irish qualified nurse in his thirties who had completed graduate training and moved to London for work and a relationship. He now lived in a house-share and was on a low wage. He had previous experience of a conservative church as a child and young adult, which he had later rejected over issues of human sexuality. Mike was dechurched and became interested in exploring the more existential and philosophical questions of life, and began a new spiritual journey catalysed by personal emotional pain arising from his experiences of family and church.

Mike, whose spiritual journey is expressed in Figure 16 below, was one of those who was invited to take part in the pilot group as he lived locally. He described his disappointment with Christianity and how he sought a form of spirituality that was more focused on love and connection with all life. His explorations as an SBNR spiritual seeker became a focus as an adult, catalysed by life experience in his teenage and young adult years when he knew the pain of rejection and non-acceptance of his gay identity. This experience was clearly very traumatic for Mike, who has not yet arrived at a place to explore returning to Christianity.

Figure 16: Mike's Spiritual Journey

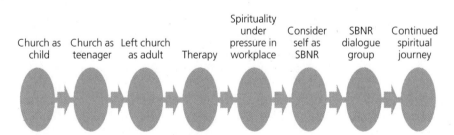

| Church as child | Church as teenager | Left church as adult | Therapy | Spirituality under pressure in workplace | Consider self as SBNR | SBNR dialogue group | Continued spiritual journey |

In Mike's story (which was shown in the line from point 'G' in Figure 15 above), only the first two stages in his spiritual journey can be expressed in a bounded-set approach to mission, those where Mike became a Christian and participated fully in a Pentecostal expression of church. However, there is no way of expressing Mike's decision to stop practising being a Christian when the church was unable to accept his coming out as gay, and his becoming dechurched and moving from strong participation to weak participation, using Tanner's understanding of theosis, which took a conservative view that this was incompatible with being Christian.

The presuppositions of a bounded set are that, once a Christian, it is a case of being Christian or being 'damned', with no room for the other six stages of Mike's spiritual journey. By implication, then, in a bounded-set understanding, once someone becomes Christian there is no place to become post-Christian and no space for 'doubt', in order to maintain orthodox uniformity of understanding and behaviour and to prevent 'backsliding'. As evidenced in the story of Mike, there were a number of the SBNR who were post-Christian, and who had negative experiences of Christians not tolerating or understanding this process. In Figure 15 above, this position can be expressed by person 'D', who by implications of Zahl's analysis must leave and is effectively damned or outside of God's love.

It is interesting that writers such as Tanner and Gama, an American theologian, writing as Protestant and Evangelical Christians, would disagree with the implications of Zahl here. For both, theosis and a missional theology of human becoming and participation in God in response to God's kenotic love provide an authentic way forward. As Gama has written:

> I am suggesting that the road forward for evangelicalism lies in a radical re-examination of the fundamentals of our faith – one certainly embracing mystery, wonder, and an openness to the ancient Christian understanding of salvation itself. I proposed ... that the ancient ... Christian doctrine of salvation – theosis, or union with God ... can provide a road map for an evangelicalism caught between two ages.[42]

In contrast to the limitations I perceive in Zahl's bounded-set understandings, Tanner's writing similarly resonates with centred-set expectations, leaving plenty of space for the individual in their own unique spiritual journey to oscillate between forms of faith and doubt as part of an ongoing process of God's grace expressed as kenotic love that is both reconciling and healing, and recognizing that the process of such a healing of the distortions of Heath's 'original woundedness' is never going to be a form of linear progress no matter how dramatic the conversion experience. Again, this more contemplative approach to mission is focused on an inner awakening corresponding to the inner self that leads to conversion and salvation through participation of being 'in Christ' through the centrifugal draw of a kenotic, wild and loving force expressed through the Holy Spirit beckoning people into deep relation to God as source.

Building a new approach to a contemplative model of mission: 'God's Kenosis, our Theosis'

At this point I want to draw together a synthesis of Tanner's two stages of participation and Hiebert's centred-set theory, along with the insights of Barfield, Coakley and Heath as explored in the previous chapter, but with new insights gained from the work of Charles Taylor, a Canadian philosopher and sociologist of religion.

I consider this critical to an expanded understanding of the context of *missio in Deo* in the model of mission I am proposing of 'God's Kenosis, our Theosis', and this emerging missiology frame building on the contemplative theology of the previous chapter.

In this new model, lying between Tanner's two levels of weak and strong participation, the gap between a human consciousness of existence and becoming Christian, are a number of other thresholds akin to the stages of the contemplative path as purgation, illumination and union.

In Chapter 3, I affirmed that in Barfield's and Vernon's writing on the evolution of consciousness, 'withdrawal from participation' related to the stage of purgation while mystical union related to the stage of 'reciprocal or final participation'. Further to this, I draw on Taylor's three conditions of 'alienated below condition', 'stabilized middle condition' and 'fullness condition' and argue that these relate to the stages of purgation, illumination and union.[43] In exploring these resonances, I also draw on the writing of Merton to explore this idea fully to build a particular approach to mission as God's Kenosis, our Theosis in practice and theology. This synthesis is expressed in Figure 17 below.

I return now to the work of Taylor. His writings are a curious reflective mix of his discipline as a sociologist along with his faith as a Roman Catholic Christian. He briefly touches on three conditions that have implications for a contemplative approach to mission.

Figure 17: Mission Model 'God's Kenosis, our Theosis': Inner Journey

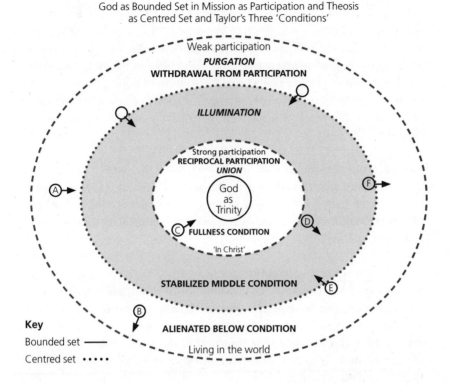

God as Bounded Set in Mission as Participation and Theosis as Centred Set and Taylor's Three 'Conditions'

Alienated below condition

For Taylor, this first of the three conditions is a negative space marked by 'a distance, an absence, an exile … an absence of power; a confusion, or worse, the condition often described as melancholy … the misery of absence or loss'.[44] This correlates to Barfield's understanding of the effects of alienation. It is a deeply unhealthy condition. For Lasch, an American historian and social critic, this also relates to the consequences of a culture of narcissism driven by a sense of hopelessness: 'Impending disaster has become an everyday concern … having no hope of improving their lives in any of the ways that matter, people have convinced themselves that what matters is psychic self-improvement.'[45]

This first of Taylor's conditions also relates to the writing of Schumaker, a retired psychologist now living in Canada, and his academic psychological critique of the consequences of living in a consumerist market society resulting in forms of mental illness and addiction:

Western consumer culture is creating a psycho-spiritual crisis that leaves us disoriented and bereft of purpose ... Rather than a depressive disorder, demoralization is a type of existential disorder associated with the breakdown of a person's 'cognitive map' ... As it is absorbed, consumer culture imposes numerous influences that weaken personality structures, undermine coping and lay the groundwork for eventual demoralization. Its driving features – individualism, materialism, hyper-competition, greed, over-complication, overwork, hurriedness and debt – all correlate negatively with psychological health and/or social wellbeing.[46]

By implication this space is a hostile environment, where the market society becomes a context of oppression and sin. Here it is God's kenotic desire to free people from such oppression, which we have brought upon ourselves. As Catholicos Aram, an Armenian Oriental Orthodox theologian, has stated:

The present global economic system is an idolatry ... It is creating ecological destruction, social injustice and high-level consumerism, alienating people from each other and from creation. The present economy must be restructured in order to ensure participation and justice ... Any economic structure that is not participatory produces economic and ecological injustice, and thus is sinful in both a theological and an ethical sense.[47]

This is a situation that Merton also deplores:

Selling my soul for the sake of money, and what money can buy ... Today, as a matter of fact, there is very little freedom anywhere because everyone is willing to sacrifice spiritual liberty for some lower kind. He will compromise his personal integrity (spiritual liberty) for the sake of security, or ambition, or pleasure.[48]

From the stories of the SBNR in the grounded theory analysis of the PhD research study, it is clear that participants experienced momentary encounters with God's kenotic and missional love. This enabled them to seek forms of spiritual liberation from this condition, to reach beyond and liberate themselves from this level of bondage through the healing of therapy, 12-step support groups, and spiritual exploration and practices. It also inspired the desire to seek authenticity through responsibility: being counter-consumerist through spiritual activism. The detachment from unhealthy consumeristic thinking and egoic life-practices is essential for the receptivity of the love of God towards relationship and the missional pathway to participation in God through being 'in Christ'. As Heath affirms: 'Until we actively resist the evil of unrestrained consumerism we participate in sin.'[49] Drawing on the centred-set focus, God's centrifugal love mission seeks to help people shift from this deeply traumatizing position to the next of Taylor's conditions through inner 'awakening', as expressed in person 'E' in Figure 17 above. Here mission is directly related to the alleviation of suffering, the promotion of well-being and the liberation of oppression both social and economic.

Stabilized middle condition

For Taylor, the spiritual seeker will have 'found a way to escape the forms of negation, exile, emptiness, without having reached fullness'.[50] In this middle condition there is an openness to the fullness condition, and also 'slow movement towards it over years'.[51] However, at the same time there is a sense that the person is 'treading water' in a form of routine, 'getting by', that keeps at bay the trauma of the alienated below condition. Thus, for many, fulfilment might be projected into work, vocation or love of family with a focus on finding an ordinary happiness. This condition approximates to the 'illumination' stage of the contemplative path, emerging from the state of purgation, aware of the need of change and the spiritual path, and the possibility of fullness or union with the divine. Taylor states: 'this sense of fullness is something we just catch glimpses of from afar off; we have the powerful intuition of what fullness would be, were we to be in that condition, e.g., of peace or wholeness ... fullness, of joy and fulfillment.'[52]

Taylor makes a statement that I believe to be true for many in contemporary society who are not religious or SBNR: 'there are surely many unbelievers for whom this life in what I've described as the "middle condition" is all there is. This is the goal. Living well and fully is what human life is about.'[53]

However, I am certain that this is not true for the majority of the SBNR of the PhD research study, who are clearly seeking beyond just making peace with the alleviation of suffering. They are seeking something more deeply, which I also believe to be the missional centrifugal force of the Spirit, beckoning people on to a fuller level of a missional theosis as participation with God. This leads to the final condition.

Fullness condition

This last of the three conditions brings a 'fuller, richer, deeper and more worthwhile position' that Taylor himself identifies as 'coming from a power which is beyond me'.[54] Critically for Taylor, this fullness condition is possible 'in prayer, in moments of fullness, in experiences of exile overcome, in what I seem to observe around me in other people's lives – lives of exceptional spiritual fullness'.[55] This resonates with Heath's writing on the contemplative path of union where: 'We believe in and experience love as God's meaning, love becomes our meaning, for we become like the God we worship.'[56] As Vernon states:

> To move to the next stage of self-awareness ... embraces once more a rich engagement with life and a renewed rootedness in reciprocity. The way forward, I believe, is to return to the centrality of religious experience, the intuition that there's more, and the realization that Christianity ... can make surprising sense.[57]

Taylor's fullness condition resonates with the crossing over into union with God, where the individual passes through the boundary and enters into Tanner's strong participation and Barfield's and Vernon's 'final or reciprocal participation' by choosing to be in a deep relationship of theosis with God – which Gorman describes as becoming 'in Christ'. In so doing the individual is profoundly caught up in the *missio in Deo* bringing deep human flourishing and fulfilment. It is at this point that the individual SBNR seeker has progressed through various stages of transformation and moments of conversion, now fully realized as the person self-identifies as a follower of the way of Jesus and in deep relationship with the Trinitarian God. In Figure 17 above this entry into strong participation and Taylor's fullness condition can be expressed as person 'C', whose spiritual journey has taken them into a full expression of theosis 'in Christ'. This final stage of mission, from a centred-set perspective, represents a key moment of the fulfilment of conversion. As I stated earlier, there are different understandings of conversion, and to explore conversion missiologically I turn to the writings of Rupen Das, a Canadian mission-focused theologian and writer.

Conversion and participation in God (theosis)

For Das, Christian denominations have differing understandings of conversion, which involve three elements – personal decision, socialization and liturgical acts.[58] Das argues that the evangelical/Protestant expectation of a dramatic conversion event is comparatively recent, being traced back to the missions of Jonathan Edwards in the early 1700s.[59] From a historical perspective, conversion was seen in a more centred-set spiritual path, as Das states: 'For the early church, conversion was not primarily a moment or event, but a journey, an extended period of intentional formation. It started with informal contact with the potential believer, and it moved ... to the second stage, that of catechumen.'[60] For Das, drawing on a historical context, conversion tended to be a protracted process 'usually containing various stages or elements'.[61]

Returning to the scriptural text of Philip the Evangelist and the Ethiopian eunuch, this Gospel story demonstrates a centred-set understanding of mission. Clearly the eunuch was on his own unique spiritual journey, which I am surmising as being a protracted process containing different experiences, including moments of mystical fulfilment and transformation. His encounter with Philip, led by the Spirit, seemed to represent a significant moment that assisted the eunuch to move from a state of illumination and the Taylor middle condition to union and the fullness condition. In so doing, he entered into strong participation with the Trinitarian God by deciding to be 'in Christ' as a consciously meditated decision to follow Jesus and taking the initiative as an outward sign of this conversion by asking Philip to baptize him.

From analysis of historical texts of conversion to Christianity from other faiths, Das identifies that such conversions were directly related to experiences of prayer, healing and mystical encounter with God. This again was a form of conversion as 'a process punctuated with spiritual encounters and a series of decisions, rather than a single crisis event'.[62]

Das's writing, coupled with Taylor's insights about the fullness condition, reiterates the importance of prayer and mystical encounter as being a critical medium for mission rather than the preserve of those who are already Christian. Even today it seems that prayer and meditation are largely overlooked and underappreciated resources for mission and softer forms of evangelism.

At this point, I want to acknowledge that my more contemplative argument and understanding of salvation and conversion has so far focused on the awakening of the inner self and somewhat neglected the need for mission and conversion of the outer self through modes of being 'saved' in the reality of the lived environment. I now explore this before returning to the stories of participants to consider the God's Kenosis, our Theosis model of mission, and then turning to reflect on the place of dialogue and prayer as critical media for mission. I then explore the role of those seeking to facilitate or lead events and gatherings focused on the proposed contemplative model. But first I will draw on the writings of Walter Brueggemann to explore the conversion of the outer self.

Conversion and the outer self

As I stated earlier, conversion by the awakening of the inner self is only part of mission, where the 'saving' of the outer sense of self is still important. As I reflect on the argument and the diagrams so far, I have become concerned that there is a danger of the import of 'modern progress myth' where individuals go in straight lines either to or away from God in response to God's kenotic love. There is, however, another force or dynamic that comes with just seeking to live and survive in the world, and for this I turn to the work of Brueggemann, an American Old Testament theologian, and his analysis of the people of Israel and the Psalms.

In his analysis of the Psalms, Brueggemann explores how the people of Israel seemed to go through a continuing cycle of 'orientation, disorientation and reorientation' as they sought to make sense of what was happening in their lives when there was drought and starvation, invasion by other armies and people groups, and times of death and great difficulty.[63] The process of survival was seen as being dependent on the good will and right standing of the people with God.

Here 'orientation' was seen by Brueggemann as a life characterized by the 'absence of tension and the holding of peace'.[64] Moments of death and threat to survival then became disorientating experiences for the people struggling to make sense of what was going on, times of 'dislocation, disorientation and lament',[65] whereas the movement to reorientation was characterized by 'the accent being on the new' and the letting go of 'dislocation and disorientation'.[66] These insights deeply reflect the human condition relevant for today, as Brueggemann says: 'The movement of our life, if we are attentive, is the movement of orientation, disorientation, and reorientation. And in our daily pilgrimage, we use much of our energy for this work.'[67]

By implication each human spiritual seeker does not exist in a vacuum, but rather in the reality of the experiences of living on this planet. This means that the outer self has to weather the storms of orientation and disorientation through to reorientation as consequences of life. Here I want to make an important connection with Barfield's writing in the previous chapter, about the mystery of each human 'becoming' as a mixture of both spirit and matter.

The inner journey of awakening pertains, I believe, to the spirit part of us whereas the 'matter us' relates to our embodiment and enfleshedness, and is therefore connected to our outer selves seeking survival and salvation. Turning back to the centred-set understanding of a missional theosis as participation in our model of God's Kenosis, our Theosis, I develop the model diagram further by expressing the centrifugal kenotic love of God in the context of an inner journey of awakening, but also in the complex situation of the outer self weathering the storms of life. This final development is expressed in the figure below.

Figure 18 is a further advancement of the developing model of God's Kenosis, our Theosis as a particular contemplative approach to mission, based on a centred-set model of mission where God as the Holy Trinity is central.

Figure 18: Mission Model 'God's Kenosis, our Theosis': Inner and Outer Journey

God as Bounded Set in Mission as Participation and Theosis as Centred Set and Taylor's Three 'Conditions' and Heath's and Coakley's Three Stages of Ascesis or Contemplation

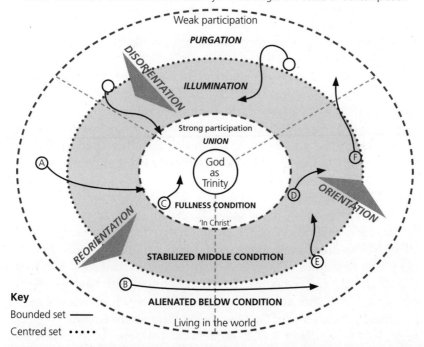

The figure maps out the stages of awakening needed for the individual's inner self to go on a gradual non-linear path from the outer space of purgation through illumination into union with God. This will largely be a protracted spiritual journey with steps forward and backwards as part of this path from weak participation into strong participation in response to God's kenotic love. At the same time, the model allows the individual person freedom to respond to the kenotic love of God or to repeatedly reject it and continue in a path away from God if so desired. Figure 18 demonstrates the two elements of the self – the inner and outer selves. As I have explored previously, the inner self is subject to the beckoning of the Holy Spirit to awaken to the reality of God. The outer self is subjected to the impacts of living on this planet in human societies that are external to the self and therefore outside the individual's control. These external experiences that affect the outer self impact the person as an ongoing flow of orientation, disorientation and reorientation.

It is therefore quite possible for the inner self to be in a place of purgation and trauma but for the outer sense of self to feel orientated. Again, the individual could be in the space of union with God, but at that point of time might – through illness or the death of a relative, for example – be experiencing disorientation. This understanding of the spiritual journey of the self as an integration of the inner and outer selves seems to me to relate to the full reality of human experience as well as the realities of a God who seeks human restoration. Figure 18 offers a credible framework to understand a missional theosis as a basis of the proposed missional model for engagement with the SBNR as God's Kenosis, our Theosis or *missio in Deo*, and a way to approach practical missional engagement. This new approach to a contemplative model of mission is founded on the grounded theory of Chapter 3, the theological reflection of the previous chapter, and the missiological frame and mission practice of this chapter.

Drawing on the now full God's Kenosis, our Theosis contemplative model, I return to the story of Mike I outlined earlier, and turn to Figure 19, which expresses his spiritual journey.

For Mike, who was brought up in a strongly conservative church in Ireland, starting out at point 'A' in Figure 19, with an unstable family life, early experiences of Christianity were deeply formative. Mike talked of a spiritual awakening experience as a child. This led at an early age to the formation of faith and deep spirituality that took him from a space of pain and purgation to a form of union with God. However, coming to terms with his sexuality against the conservative teachings of the church, and a sense of God 'not being there for him in times of great need', led him to doubt his Christian faith. This sense of disconnection from conservative Christianity led in turn not only to a loss of faith, but also to deep pain and anguish and a concern not to be too open to any form of spirituality, as it could bring further wounding.

However, Mike acknowledged a sense of paradox, believing in the existence of something more spiritual but not religious, but also fearing it in equal measure. However, positive experience of some less conservative Christians, developing interests in spirituality and spiritual practices,

Figure 19: 'God's Kenosis, our Theosis': The Spiritual Journey of Mike

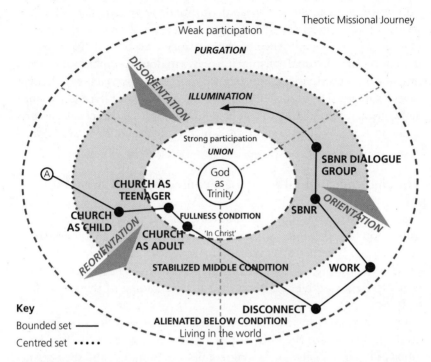

and participation in the dialogue group led to a shift away from purgation into a space of illumination. His work in the NHS in London was
a mixed blessing, it being a tough and costly vocation which meant that
he had to manage his exposure to spirituality. However, the combination of life, spiritual practices, dialogue and relationships with some
Christians had resulted in an openness to more contemplative forms of
Christian spirituality. Mike remains on a spiritual quest, continuing in
the space of illumination.

The missional praxis significance of this new model of contemplative mission as God's Kenosis, our Theosis

The first thing that needs to be said about mission practice, based on
this study, is the focus on heart rather than head. Any attempt to construct some form of missional non-experiential, 'fact-based' course is
going to be ineffective. This model, however, does suggest the need to
provide different forms of missional support for SBNR spiritual seekers,
reflecting the different needs of the stages of awakening, purgation, illumination and union.

What is clear is the critical need for the missioner to be also a practitioner of contemplative Christian spirituality, so that the sharing of wisdom and support for SBNR spiritual seekers draws on the authenticity of the lived experience of the missioner. Second, if the missional focus is on an individual spiritual journey with lots of epiphany moments, this not only takes a long time, but requires an approach that is open to spontaneity. The model emphasizes the centrality of lived experience, and consideration of how to resource SBNR spiritual seekers at the three different stages requires reflection, which I explore in the next chapter.

The challenge and difficulty of a contemporary Christology

I have argued thus far that becoming 'in Christ' is critical to this approach to mission as a missional spiritual journey of theosis as God's Kenosis, our Theosis. Whether this takes a long time with many twists and turns or happens through a number of intense conversion experiences, there needs to be a credible and accessible understanding of the significance of Jesus.

I was, however, struck that there were only 96 mentions of 'Jesus' in all the transcripts of the PhD research study. In a world of reduced religious affiliation, dislike of fundamentalist Christianity, and the injustice of male patriarchy, Jesus can be seen in strongly negative terms. Opening up a Christology that has relevance and resonance with the SBNR remains a significant challenge. What approaches can enable the SBNR to encounter Christ in their experience of God?

As Tanner reminds us, strong participation – being 'in Christ' – is critical for the 'gaining of the power of the Holy Spirit to renovate our lives' and for this more missional theosis and contemplative approach to mission.[68] At the same time, conveying a contextually accessible yet authentic understanding of Jesus is not easy – a Jewish man living in Palestine 2,000 years ago standing for a faith and church that are seen by many today in negative terms. As Merton affirms: 'Christ has indeed conquered the world and it does indeed belong to Him alone. This cannot help but be rejected in a world where all men ignore Him and misunderstand His Kingship.'[69]

One approach to an authentic and resonant Christology is to creatively engage with this idea of 'Lordship'. Das reminds us that the early church presented Jesus as *Kyrios* or Lord because it resonated with the Greek-speaking pagan context and the title used for cultic deities.[70] Viewed from an Asian woman's perspective in the writings of Chung Hyun Kyung, a Korean feminist theologian, the concept of 'Lordship' can be viewed as counter to Western colonialism and patriarchy; instead, Jesus the Christ and Lord of justice seeks to support the rights and privileges of the poor and oppressed.[71] This resonates with a few of the responses in this study, such as that of Isabel:

> When I say Jesus, I think I mean the Christ actually, which feels like a light that shines through the heart. (Isabel, Life History Interview)

However, as Das reminds us, when viewed from an experience-based understanding of Jesus from those who have converted from other faiths, it was the stories of the life and teachings of Jesus and the mystical experience of Jesus being the Christ in prayer, healings, visions, dreams and answered prayer that opened people to the reality of Jesus being divine.[72] Ultimately the path of inner awakening corresponds to the central claim of this thesis, that Jesus has to be experienced as the Christ from within, through an inner journey and revelation. Such a Christology becomes understandable from the revelation of God in human experience – where the Kingdom of God is within.[73] Such experience then speaks of the resurrected Jesus who lives in us as we experience resurrection in our own lives by choosing to follow this Jesus and thereby find spiritual liberation and freedom.[74] Akin to this are ideas that did resonate with a few participants of this study, of Jesus as 'cosmological restorer'. Anne Nasimiyu-Wasike, a Ugandan nun, theologian and missiologist, writing from an African woman's experience, affirmed the place of Christ as 'cosmological liberator' or 'spiritual liberator' who reconciles all things with God.[75] As Anton of this study expressed it:

> There is significance in Jesus who is unspectacular on the outside, but on the inside is totally transformative, full and weighty … I felt something deep about being more generous as Jesus was generous with those who have nothing … focusing on a calling of service to the poor. (Anton, Borough dialogue group, 30 January 2019)

Returning to the concept of Lordship, Hyun Kyung helpfully makes the distinction between a Christology that is 'top down' and one that is 'bottom up', saying that the former is difficult for ordinary people to accept and understand:[76]

> Christology from above (God becomes human) is difficult to understand for the ordinary masses of people … However 'a man becomes a God' is easy for them to understand. Jesus Christ as Messiah can be better understood in the image of historical Jesus who has loved his

neighbours more than himself and for this great love he went through surmounting suffering and sacrifice to become the Messiah, the Savior of humankind. Whereas the theory which says that because Jesus was God he was Messiah does not appeal too much.[77]

In an Asian woman's perspective this bottom-up approach to Christology helped Korean women to understand the significance of Jesus drawing on gospel values of the Kingdom, where the Emmanuel was less 'God with us' and more 'God among us', a God who lovingly understood the need for liberation.[78] This idea of bottom-up Lordship as 'cosmological liberator' would probably resonate with many of the SBNR spiritual seekers of this study, because it reflects a centred-set understanding of the significance of Jesus as human and God.

Further to this metaphor was the idea of Jesus as shaman that arises from Asian and South American understandings. Hyun Kyung explains that shamans are usually women who help other women to experience spiritual liberation from resentment, indignation, a sense of defeat and sickness, all largely a result of the patriarchal model of Korean society.[79]

It is interesting how this description resonates with the spiritual path from wounding to healing and from purgation to union with God as part of the God's Kenosis, our Theosis model I have outlined previously. The Christological significance of Jesus as shaman would resonate with a few in the study, like Sophie, who were exploring spirituality from a shamanistic perspective:

In the shamanic tradition they bang a lot of drums ... because the banging ... corresponds to the heartbeat and it takes you into a different state of consciousness ... I have met Jesus a few times in the upper world ... It is an ancient tradition ... it's called journeying in the shamanic tradition ... So in this practice I sometimes get answers to questions I am living with and seeking direction ... So I find this form of spiritual practice, the practice of shamanic journeying makes you feel better. (Sophie, Life History Interview)

For some, such as Rosaline, this idea of a spiritual guide with supernatural power was extended to the idea of Jesus as 'mystic teacher':

Jesus was born in order to bring the Christos love energy to the earth ... Jesus came at that point ... He was God in man. Through Jesus it became possible for God to be in every man. There was, at the time, a high level of spiritual intelligence and consciousness ... The news of this spiritual truth then spread widely through social contact and by word of mouth. (Rosaline, Life History Interview)

Drawing on this exploration of Christology and the content of the grounded theory, I suggest that the use of various metaphors for Jesus as the second person of the Trinity might resonate well with the SBNR spiritual seekers of this study. Such a bottom-up narrative might be effective: of Jesus as cosmological liberator, whose Lordship is about promoting and enabling spiritual freedom through kenotic love that can be experienced through forms of dialogue, prayer, meditation and contemplation. I will explore the missiological significance of this in the remaining chapters.

Conclusions

To conclude, in this chapter addressing revised praxis and missional framing I began by exploring a more contemplative understanding of God's mission as *missio in Deo*, seeing it as a form of spiritual journey into participation with God. I then named this the 'God's Kenosis, our Theosis' contemplative model of mission. I explored the importance of a 'centred-set' approach to understanding how it may work in practice. I explored the writing of Tanner in particular to help define a basis of the model in missional theosis, so that mission and evangelism became the focus of the spiritual path between a 'weak' and 'strong' theosis as two states of participation in God. Further, I explored criticism of Tanner's approach by Zahl and drew on centred-set theories and other writings to suggest that these criticisms were based on differences in church traditions. Drawing on a number of writers, I explored a more contemplative understanding of an approach to mission for the awakening of the inner self, and for the saving of the outer self – where both were important for a whole-person approach to mission. I then reflected on how the developed model of God's Kenosis, our Theosis resonated with the stories of participants.

From this I explored the need for an authentic and resonant approach to Christology accessible to the SBNR, offering a more bottom-up, 'Christ among us' approach rather than a traditional top-down understanding. I suggested that the ideas of Jesus as cosmic liberator, mystic teacher and shaman might resonate with some. The challenge remained how to open up these metaphorical understandings of Christology in a spiritually experiential way.

In the next chapter, I continue to explore a new approach to a contemplative model of mission as God's Kenosis, our Theosis in the context of the first stage of the model and the importance of dialogue, contemplative prayer and meditation as significant media to encounter God.

Notes

1 Thomas Merton, *New Seeds of Contemplation* (New York: New Directions Books, 1972), pp. 10, 37; Thomas Merton, *The Inner Experience: Notes on Contemplation*, ed. William H. Shannon (London: SPCK, 2003), pp. 3–5, 24–5, 28, 93.

2 As we explored in the last chapter with the writings of Owen Barfield and Mark Vernon.

3 Sarah Coakley, *God, Sexuality, and the Self: An Essay 'On the Trinity'* (Cambridge: Cambridge University Press, 2019), p. 4.

4 Coakley, *God, Sexuality, and the Self*, pp. 55–6.

5 Coakley, *God, Sexuality, and the Self*, p. 114.

6 Coakley, *God, Sexuality, and the Self*, pp. 332–4.

7 Ion Bria, ed., *Go Forth in Peace: Orthodox Perspectives on Mission* (Geneva: WCC Mission Series, 1986), p. 3.

8 Stephen B. Bevans and Roger P. Schroeder, *Prophetic Dialogue: Reflections on Christian Mission Today* (Maryknoll, NY: Orbis Books, 2011), p. 57.

9 Stephen B. Bevans and Roger P. Schroeder, *Constants in Context: A Theology of Mission for Today* (Maryknoll, NY: Orbis Books, 2004), p. 309.

10 Paul Fiddes, *Participation in God: A Pastoral Doctrine of the Trinity* (Louisville, KY: Westminster John Knox Press, 2000), p. 98.

11 Fiddes, *Participation in God*, p. 7.

12 Fiddes, *Participation in God*, p. 39.

13 Joshva Raja, 'Mission in Theological Education: Review and Prospects' (London: USPG), p. 4, https://d3hgrlq6yacptf.cloudfront.net/uspg/content/pages/documents/1596795184.pdf (accessed 04.01.2021).

14 Paul G. Hiebert, 'Conversion, Culture, and Cognitive Categories', *Gospel in Context* 1, no. 4 (1978), pp. 24–9; Michael L. Yoder, Michael H. Lee, Jonathan Ro and Robert J. Priest, 'Understanding Christian Identity in Terms of Bounded and Centered Set Theory in the Writings of Paul G. Hiebert', *Trinity Journal* 30, no. 2, 2009, http://hiebertglobalcenter.org/wp-content/uploads/2014/04/199_Chang_Critical-Contextualisation.pdf, pp. 177–88.

15 Paul G. Hiebert, 'Sets and Structures: A Study of Church Patterns', in *New Horizons in World Mission: Evangelicals and the Christian Mission in the 1980s*, ed. David J. Hesselgrave (Grand Rapids, MI: Baker Book House, 1979), pp. 217–27.

16 Paul G. Hiebert, 'The Category "Christian" in the Mission Task', *International Review of Mission* 72, no. 287 (1983), p. 427.

17 Hiebert, 'The Category "Christian"', pp. 223–4.

18 Hiebert, 'The Category "Christian"', pp. 223–4.

19 Hiebert, 'The Category "Christian"', p. 422.

20 Hiebert, 'Sets and Structures', pp. 220–1.

21 Yoder et al., 'Understanding Christian Identity', pp. 180–1.

22 Hiebert, 'Sets and Structures'.

23 Hiebert, 'The Category "Christian"', p. 427.

24 Hiebert, 'The Category "Christian"', p. 427.

25 Hiebert, 'The Category "Christian"', pp. 223–4.

26 Hiebert, 'The Category "Christian"', pp. 223–4.

27 Fiddes, *Participation in God*, p. 54.

28 Kathryn Tanner, *Christ the Key* (Cambridge: Cambridge University Press, 2009), p. 8.

29 Tanner, *Christ the Key*, p. 92.

30 Tanner, *Christ the Key*, p. 16.

31 The Moot Community was one of the sites of the PhD research. It held a 'Spiritual But Not Religious' dialogue group and meditation group, which became the spiritual home of Calum.

32 Michael P. Gama, *Theosis: Patristic Remedy for Evangelical Yearning at the Close of the Modern Age* (Eugene, OR: Wipf & Stock, 2017), pp. 103–4.

33 Hiebert, 'Sets and Structures', pp. 224–5.; Hiebert, 'Conversion, Culture, and Cognitive Categories'.

34 Simeon Zahl, *The Holy Spirit and Christian Experience* (Oxford: Oxford University Press, 2020), p. 80.

35 Zahl, *The Holy Spirit*, pp. 105–7, 117–18.

36 Zahl, *The Holy Spirit*, pp. 117–18.

37 Zahl, *The Holy Spirit*, pp. 105–18.

38 Zahl, *The Holy Spirit*, pp. 117–18.

39 Hiebert, 'The Category "Christian"', p. 422.

40 Hiebert, 'Sets and Structures', pp. 220–1.

41 Yoder et al., 'Understanding Christian Identity', pp. 180–1.

42 Gama, *Theosis*, p. xviii.

43 Charles Taylor, *A Secular Age* (Cambridge, MA: Belknap Press of Harvard University Press, 2007), pp. 5–10.

44 Taylor, *A Secular Age*, p. 6.

45 Christopher Lasch, *The Culture of Narcissism: American Life in an Age of Diminishing Expectations* (New York: W. W. Norton, 1991), p. 4.

46 John Schumaker, 'The Demoralized Mind', *New Internationalist*, 1 April 2016, https://newint.org/columns/essays/2016/04/01/psycho-spiritual-crisis.

47 Catholicos Aram, 'An Ecumenical Ethic for a Responsible Society in a Sustainable Creation', in *Orthodox Perspectives on Mission: 17 (Regnum Edinburgh Centenary)*, ed. Petros Vassiliadis (Oxford: Regnum Books International, 2013), pp. 151–2.

48 Thomas Merton, *Conjectures of a Guilty Bystander* (New York: Doubleday, 1966), p. 83.

49 Elaine A. Heath, *The Mystic Way of Evangelism: A Contemplative Vision for Christian Outreach* (Grand Rapids, MI: Baker Academic, 2008), p. 101.

50 Taylor, *A Secular Age*, pp. 6–7.

51 Taylor, *A Secular Age*, pp. 6–7.

52 Taylor, *A Secular Age*, p. 5.

53 Taylor, *A Secular Age*, p. 7.

54 Taylor, *A Secular Age*, p. 10.

55 Taylor, *A Secular Age*, p. 10.

56 Heath, *The Mystic Way of Evangelism*, p. 48.

57 Mark Vernon, *A Secret History of Christianity: Jesus, the Last Inkling, and the Evolution of Consciousness* (Winchester: Christian Alternative, 2018), pp. 164–5.

58 Rupen Das, 'Becoming a Follower of Christ: Exploring Conversion through Historical and Missiological Lenses', *Perichoresis* 16, no. 1 (2018), p. 24.

59 Das, 'Becoming a Follower of Christ', p. 24.

60 Das, 'Becoming a Follower of Christ', p. 28.

61 Das, 'Becoming a Follower of Christ', p. 30.

62 Das, 'Becoming a Follower of Christ', pp. 31–2.

63 Walter Brueggemann, *The Psalms and the Life of Faith* (Minneapolis, MN: Fortress Press, 1995), pp. 4–7.

64 Brueggemann, *The Psalms*, pp. 4–6.

65 Brueggemann, *The Psalms*, pp. 5–7.

66 Brueggemann, *The Psalms*, pp. 5, 9–10.

67 Brueggemann, *The Psalms*, p. 18.

68 Tanner, *Christ the Key*, pp. 87–8.

69 Merton, *Conjectures of a Guilty Bystander*, p. 59.

70 Das, 'Becoming a Follower of Christ', p. 27.

71 Chung Hyun Kyung, 'Who is Jesus for Asian Women?', in *Liberation Theology: An Introductory Reader*, ed. Curt Cadorette, Marie Giblin, Marilyn J. Legge and Mary H. Snyder (Maryknoll, NY: Orbis Books, 1992), pp. 128–9.

72 Das, 'Becoming a Follower of Christ', pp. 31–2.

73 Merton, *New Seeds of Contemplation*, p. 3.

74 Thomas Merton, *He is Risen* (Niles, IL: Argus Communications, 1975), p. 8.

75 Anne Nasimiyu-Wasike, 'Christology and an African Woman's Experience', in *Liberation Theology: An Introductory Reader*, ed. Curt Cadorette, Marie Giblin, Marilyn J. Legge and Mary H. Snyder (Maryknoll, NY: Orbis Books, 1992), p. 101.

76 Hyun Kyung, 'Who is Jesus for Asian Women?', pp. 131–2.

77 Hyun Kyung, 'Who is Jesus for Asian Women?', p. 131.

78 Hyun Kyung, 'Who is Jesus for Asian Women?', pp. 131–2.

79 Hyun Kyung, 'Who is Jesus for Asian Women?', p. 136.

PART THREE

The Christian Contemplative Missional Journey

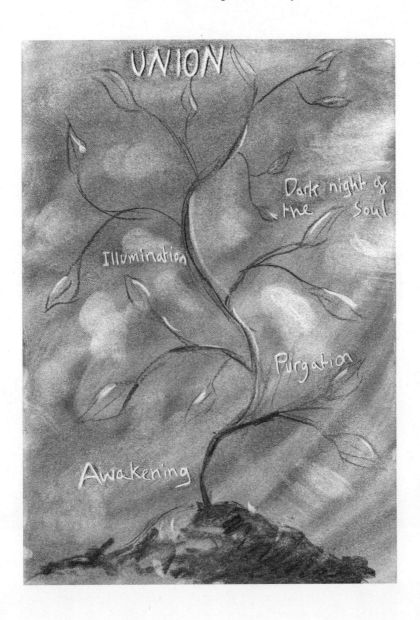

6

Awakening: The Beginning of the Spiritual Journey

It is not we who choose to awaken ourselves,
but God who chooses to awaken us.[1]

In this chapter, we begin an exploration of the first stage of the 'God's Kenosis, our Theosis' contemplative model of mission to consider the subject of awakening. I will explore the implications of this critical first step as the individual begins to become aware of the presence of God in their life. I will then explore the importance of using missional silent meditation groups as well as dialogue groups to help curate the opportunity to enhance an awareness of awakening, before suggesting an immersive set of missional activities to aid spiritual experience and reflection at this first stage.

Spiritual awakening can be an unexpected or unanticipated, dis-orientating new experience that begins with confusion as the individual is challenged by the conflict between rational opinions and trans-rational experience. Yet for others, awakening comes as a deep unanticipated experience of love, sensed as coming from within or transcendently, or in response to nature, which brings peace and happiness. This is particularly difficult for those who have been formed in contexts that are extremely rational and where spirituality and emotionality can be looked down upon, whereas such experiences require an ability to set aside rational disbelief in forms of trans-rational experience. For some, this is not a passing experience, but an encounter with God that awakens something in the depth of their being, something they did not know was there.[2] Here the inner self can awaken with sudden intensity, even as a momentary flash. For some, this becomes too painful to countenance and so they become avoidant about seeking spirituality. In time such experiences will cease as God respects the autonomy of the individual. However, where the individual says 'Yes' to the beginnings of an awareness of God, then the spiritual journey will continue on beyond awakening to the beginning of a path of ongoing transformative experiences.[3] This change in perception or knowing is immensely difficult to gain and maintain, and can take time. It requires an openness of the individual to the spiritual path, which is a messy one as they journey towards God in a 'centred-set' path heading from weak participation, towards strong participation. Immersion in relevant Christian contemplative practices, including meditation and dialogue, are important to resource such a spiritual pilgrimage. God initiates such experiences of inner awakening, but they require the participation of the individual to want to journey to and with God.

Mystical Christian traditions often teach that there are two pathways to contemplative spiritual awakening: the first is a dramatic, direct way and the second a slower, progressive way. The direct way is when the individual has a profound experience or realization leading to new knowing. Thomas Merton himself had a famous direct realization on the streets of Louisville, where he suddenly saw everyone blazing white. In such moments reality turns or opens up a new form of direct knowing in the now. Such a dramatic experience will need to bed down into ordinary life, which then switches from direct to progressive awakening. For most of us, it's more likely that we will have lots of small ongoing experiences of progressive awakening eureka moments, rather than a direct, dramatic awakening event. Both are important.[4]

This clash between the rational and trans-rational at the point of awakening was very evident in the spiritual journey of Jenny, as shown in Figure 20 below.

Jenny, ethnically Australasian and in her thirties, had completed graduate training and worked as a social researcher. She had little experience of Christianity. She described her spiritual journey as having

Figure 20: 'God's Kenosis, our Theosis': The Spiritual Journey of Jenny

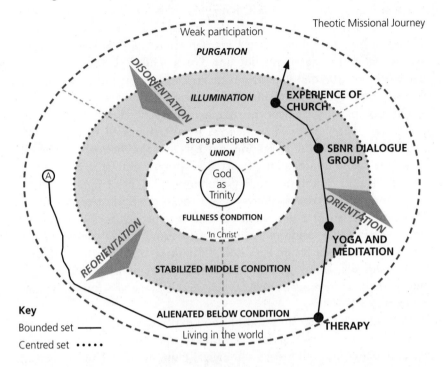

Key
Bounded set ——
Centred set •••••

been kindled by a difficult relationship with her father and resultant emotional pain. Therapy opened up spirituality for her, which led to her participation in meditation and yoga, and she joined the dialogue group after finding it through Meetup. From this she took up a job in a church institution, seeking to be open to Christian spirituality and applying her vocational skills, but she had a bad experience of working in this setting, which discouraged her from exploring spirituality further. She was married, her husband also being Australasian, and was on an above-average wage. As with others in the PhD study, pain and relational difficulties catalysed her spiritual seeking, and contemplative practices proved to be important media for this spiritual journeying. Interestingly, even though Jenny had grown up atheist in understanding, she described having childhood experiences of encountering a deep source of love through wildlife, nature and the seasons. Jenny came to the UK with her husband (starting from point 'A' in Figure 20). In the group dialogue, Jenny talked about how her life began to improve from feeling a deep ongoing trauma when she started to attend therapy (represented by the bottom dot). Her experience of counselling catalysed an interest in spirituality as a point of awakening, so she described beginning to attend yoga and forms of meditation that improved her life as the next step on her spiritual journey (marked by second dot up). For Jenny, attending the SBNR dialogue group was the next step in her spiritual journey. She then continued to explore Christian spirituality when she began working for a Christian churched-based organization as a social researcher (next dot up). For a while the combination of her work and the dialogue group opened up opportunities to explore Christian spirituality more comprehensively.

Through participation in the dialogue group, meditation group and immersive contemplative experiences, Jenny progressed from the state of awakening to that of purgation. Further, through therapy and the use of online audio-contemplative surrender-prayer practices, she moved from the stage of purgation to that of illumination, describing the whole process as deeply transformative. As a social scientist, Jenny found it difficult to let go of a dominant rationalist approach to knowing, and had to actively lay aside this reasoning to allow trans-rational experience, something she found very difficult to do in practice. But with one-to-one support, Jenny continued to make progress in encountering a 'higher power' beyond herself, which at this stage she found exciting and a new adventure.

Unfortunately, after a period of good experience of working for her church-based employer, Jenny's workplace ended up not being supportive and caused her a lot of psychological pain, not only putting her off Christianity, but taking her into a space of renewed pain and alienation akin to the 'alienated below condition' and purgation. As a result, Jenny withdrew from the dialogue group, disengaged from the research and left her job. However, from her responses it was clear that Jenny's story had passed from purgation into illumination and looked to be a positive experience with dialogue and meditation, until unfortunately her negative experience of the church ended her spiritual seeking and participation in the SBNR dialogue group. Again, a negative experience of church ended a time of positive missional engagement.

The place of mission curation

As demonstrated in the story of Jenny, how the various elements of contemplative mission were facilitated really mattered, ensuring an open-endedness and the autonomy of the individual. The role is therefore more akin to that of curating an event, as in an art or photography gallery, rather than being a teacher. This requires an ability to provide opportunities for spiritual experience and reflection, but otherwise to get out of the way of God and the person. The curator must allow God to do what God wants to do, while being ready to share their own spiritual experiences and wisdom. This approach to engaging in mission in a post-secular spiritual context, helps us, as I have expressed it elsewhere, to experience the Christian God as 'radically subjective. God's immanence as hyper-present, so that we can encounter God through the subjective experience of the presence of God in the ordinariness of our lives.'[5]

As Richard Sudworth has stated: 'The concept of God's mission, not ours ... should be no surprise to us ... God is God and will move, by his Spirit, speaking to people, engineering encounters, listening to the cries and prayers of all sorts of odd outsiders in ways that God is completely at liberty to.'[6]

The place of group dialogue as missional activity

All six of the dialogue groups of the PhD study proved to be important opportunities for spiritual seeking and exploration through shared conversations, where participants responded with attentive listening and considerate speaking along with times of silence, often with honesty and vulnerability. Only in one group did it get heated! This commitment to availability and vulnerability seemed to be critical and valued by group members. There was a tangible spiritual interest and at times thirst for encounter and exploration, reflecting the experiential centred-set approach to mission as spiritual encounter that I outlined in the previous chapter. Stephen Bevans and Roger Schroeder reiterate how important this form of dialogue is in the context of mission: 'There is a real need today to recognize that mission should be done in vulnerability, in humility, with a sense of being open to be evangelized by those who we are evangelizing.'[7]

In the group dialogues, I was struck by how many participants were surprised that I as a researcher and group facilitator was a Christian, because I was 'open' in this way, when many had experienced Christians to be judgemental, reserved and not open-minded, often in a controlling or 'fundamentalist' way. As demonstrated by Philip the Evangelist (as reflected in the previous chapter), the need for an open-ended approach, trusting in the power of the kenotic love of God, is critical to this form of mission activity. As Merton has said:

that is the spirit of the Gospel ... in the New Testament ... [this] means not only the willingness to discuss, but the readiness to meet one's adversary *as an equal and as a brother* ... They [the Church] forget that if we meet the non-Christian *as a brother* we meet him on ground that is Christian. If we fear to meet him on what is really our own ground, is this not perhaps because we ourselves are not sufficiently Christian?[8]

There is something profoundly important in the contemplative tradition taken to this dialogical form of mission, which is about letting go of being in control and about a quiet confidence in God. This underlines the need not to seek to control the result but to value shared space that is not overly programmed in order for true dialogue and authentic exploration to take place in this God's Kenosis, our Theosis model. As Merton reminds us: 'It is awakening, enlightenment and the amazing intuitive grasp by which love gains certitude of God's creative and dynamic intervention in our daily life.'[9]

Such an approach allows God to do what God will do. This raises questions for the church about how it engages in mission and evangelism with this more non-directive contemplative approach. As Merton says: 'Contemplation is also the response to a call: a call from Him who has no voice, and yet who speaks in everything that is, and who, most of all, speaks in the depths of our own being.'[10]

Dialogue is a key form of mission if we believe in God's kenotic centrifugal love and how this can be transformational through spiritual encounter. Dialogue, when it has space and silence incorporated into it, can be an important form of contemplative practice, an experience of God from within gained through inner searching, discussion and the insights of others. By implication, as Athanasios Despotis, an Orthodox theologian, writes, as people explore spirituality, this can be understood as a form of pilgrimage with three stages of existential change: 'meeting, dialogue and conversion (transformation)' where each of these stages reflects a reconstruction of 'one's own biography and a different view of the world ... a new ontology'.[11]

There is something wonderfully freeing and powerful about true dialogue, as it creates space for people to speak from their depths, fostering a mystical encounter from within. This ontology of dialogue often unfolds as an ongoing process of transformation.[12] Such dialogue holds profound significance, as it reflects the very nature of God. Bevans and Schroeder articulate this beautifully: 'Mission must be lived out in dialogue because of the nature of God ... because mission is participation in that divine, dialogical nature.'[13]

Such dialogue, then, reflects a missional theosis understanding of a dynamic flow of openness and receiving as people encounter God through conversation with deep connections: 'God's very nature is to be in dialogue: Holy mystery (Father), Son (Word) and Spirit in an eternal movement or flow of openness and receiving ... Relationship, communion and dialogue, therefore, is the ultimate goal of all existence.'[14]

For Bevans and Schroeder, this approach to dialogue draws on a theology of mission as not only participation in the mission of the Triune God, but also participation in the 'liberating service of the Reign of God' and the 'proclamation of Jesus Christ as "universal savior"'.[15] In bringing these three theologies together, dialogue becomes a powerful medium for encounter with God 'from within'. As I explored in the previous chapter with the work of Elaine Heath and others, this understanding resonates deeply with the idea of mission as a chosen restorative process, the healing and awakening of the inner self. For Bevans and Schroeder, there is a connection between dialogue, as a form of contemplative spiritual practice, and prayer as a form of missional engagement: 'when we speak of "mission as dialogue" ... we are speaking of dialogue as a "spirituality," a sense of "contemplation".'[16]

For Bevans and Schroeder, 'prophetic dialogue' is an essential approach for Christians involved in mission, and accordingly needs to be gentle, with openness and respect for the other, 'recognizing that God was present before our arrival, that the Spirit has sown the seeds of the word among all peoples and all cultures'.[17] In other words, we remember that mission is God's not ours, and that it is the role of the Holy Spirit (as explored in centred-set approaches to mission) to unsettle people through God's kenotic love, to experience this love for themselves and respond in a desire for deeper participation in God (theosis). The role of the missioner, then, is one of missional curation, enabling conversations and dialogues for people to have insights and encounter with the source of all love in the context of their own lives. As Bevans and Schroeder state: 'Mission as dialogue is the ministry of presence ... It is a witness ... to the God who moves among us in dialogue ... and the communion in Godself who calls us.'[18]

Such a focus on mission as gentle dialogue, as a form of communion, is therefore also a form of sacramentalism. This approach, then, critically needs not only to be Trinitarian, but also Christocentric, opening up the reality of Jesus as redeemer and at the same time healer and lifegiver. As we identified in previous chapters, the awareness of Jesus as a significant figure in the stories of SBNR spiritual seekers was lacking, so this presents a practical challenge. How do we in missional dialogue open up the reality of Jesus in the context of people's experience of God in their own lives? If this whole approach to mission is authentic, then should we not expect the Spirit to point to Jesus in missional group dialogues? Later in this chapter, I will explore the need to combine group dialogues with experience of Christian prayer practices, which can then increase an awareness and encounter with Christ, including some Ignatian approaches that use Gospel stories and accounts of Jesus. This combined approach could assist encounter with Christ as an experience of prayer taken into dialogue. So group dialogue becomes one of 'the "hows" of mission, and in many ways the "what" of mission as well, because it is a sacrament of the way God is'.[19]

In such group dialogues, it is hoped that, through the promptings of the Holy Spirit, participants will encounter God and in time explore the significance of Jesus, and thus be enabled to enter into pilgrimage towards the Trinitarian God. This beckoning of participants into a freely chosen deeper relationship with God through the Spirit will enable them, as Tanner expressed it in the previous chapter, to become 'in Christ' as a strong form of participation with God and thereby choose to be followers of the way of Christ. Importantly, it is hoped, participants will enter into this missional pilgrimage through the medium of group conversations.

This understanding of mission as prophetic dialogue also resonates with David Tacey's understanding of the religious listener drawing on the wisdom tradition, to support people to explore the 'natural' experience of the Spirit from within. Facilitating such dialogue is difficult because, as we explored in the previous two chapters, people will be in contact with their own sense of woundedness as much as with restorative spiritual experience:

> I am hoping that religion will eventually see its role ... as a sympathetic listener that offers discernment ... to what is unfamiliar, strange or challenging ... The act of conversation is itself a prelude to a deeper spiritual experience, insofar as it sensitises us to the authenticity and difference of the sacred other. Dialogue and conversation brings healing, but it also has the effect of making us more aware of our woundedness.[20]

For Tacey, such dialogue is possible because of a democratization of 'the spirit': young people wanted to explore spirituality 'with the use of direct experience ... a new desire to observe, create theories, and test these against the facts of our experience'.[21] This was clearly the case for Henrick:

> Just over the last five to ten years, I have been thinking ... is this it to life? Is this really all there is? However, I have never ever wanted to go down the orthodox kind of religious route. So I have always been

questioning what is this all about? ... This is why I found this group as it related to my questions ... spirituality is something that's very unique to ourselves and how we understand why we are here? What is life all about? ... we are probably all on the same path ... that's what I understand spiritualty to be ... as a group, there is something more to life here. And for me that's spirituality ... That is what has drawn me to this group. (Henrick, Borough dialogue group, 25 July 2018)

Clearly this approach has been effective for some. Some participants in this study found the open-ended focus of the dialogue groups important not only for exploring essential questions of life, but also, through building up relationships with those in the groups and the group facilitators, for helping them to move from an interest in spiritual dialogue to exploring Christian spirituality, and then to self-identifying with open and hospitable forms of ecclesial community:

The SBNR dialogue group explorations of spirituality opened up an area of my life I had never explored and I found I enjoyed. I found the group and the questions open-ended and allowed for exploration rather than a search for the right answers. Following this ... I decided to take more interest in Moot. Moot allowed me to explore ... Christian spirituality very much at my own pace as it seemingly had no agenda of its own for me other than to be a space of exploration. (Calum, Additional Interview)

The place of prayer and meditation as missional activity

Four out of the six dialogue groups of the PhD study were standalone event activities. However, the dialogue group in the City of London, completed in partnership with Moot, followed a silent meditation group, which a few of those who came to the dialogue group attended after finding and developing their meditation practice as an important first step. This was certainly the case with Calum and Sam:

Initially I attended meditation groups simply because I wanted to develop my practice with others. (Calum, Additional Interview)

The community I am now part of, called Moot, has a strong contemplative and mystical focus. I realize that this contemplative Christian tradition is largely unknown to many in and outside of the church. (Sam, City dialogue group, 25 August 2018)

This meditation group practice drew on the John Main approach to silent meditation.[22] This uses a repeated anchor word as a point of focus.[23] It was clear that this form of meditation was valued by those who attended, who were a diverse set of SBNR or Christian participants. Because they experienced this meditation as working for them by reducing stress, some sought to go deeper with exploring spirituality. It seemed the combination of the SBNR dialogue group coupled with experience of the weekly meditation groups was important, and that the depth of insight and awareness was greater when compared with other groups, because of the rich mix of dialogue and exposure to Christian forms of contemplative prayer. Reflecting on it now, I recognize that the combination of dialogue and prayer allowed for greater spiritual questing and engagement with Christian forms of prayer practices, and therefore some attention to encounter with Jesus and God as Trinity. I have therefore been struck by the importance of combining dialogue and contemplative prayer, as was the case for those who took part in the City dialogue group. For Calum, Peter and others, meditation and contemplation were an open-ended catalyst for spiritual exploration, where it seems the Holy Spirit had awakened a desire to go deeper:[24]

It is about a yearning and a search for meaning, the sense that there is something beyond randomness ... when we are offered an opportunity of something like meditation ... we can suddenly wake up, we can suddenly realize that there is something, there is some quality of light in the universe that infuses us. (Peter, Borough dialogue group, 27 June 2018)

The stories of Calum and Peter underline the reality that many people are seeking communities of spiritual practice – of contemplative prayer and dialogue – as part of their spiritual seeking. Contemplative prayer, then, is important for a more open-ended approach to mission informed by a missional theosis. I was therefore surprised to find very little written up academically in the area of contemplative forms of prayer as media for mission and encounter with God. The assumption of much writing seemed to be that Christian prayer and meditation are the preserve of those who are already Christian, rather than a missional medium for those who do not identify as Christian to encounter God. However, for Adrian Chatfield, a contemplative Christian practitioner and teacher, there is a deep connection between mission and contemplative forms of prayer: 'The link between prayer and mission is a simple one. Prayer leads us deeper into an active relationship with the missional God.'[25]

At the same time (and this is an important corrective), we do not pray for what we or others may get out of it, we pray because of the deep connection we seek with God: 'Prayer in all its forms – including word-less ones – the expressing of a living … relationship which necessarily results in mission because God is a missionary God … We pray because of who we are, not because of what prayer might accomplish.'[26]

Critically for Chatfield, many SBNR are open to prayer and medita-tion. This offers a rare opportunity for authentic and accessible mission, where 'prayer is one of the few contexts within which meaningful spiritual engagement and evangelism remain possible. The offer of prayer is rarely refused by the unchurched.'[27] However, prayer as an approach to mission and formation cannot be used in a way that is directive; its open-endedness is important, as Chatfield says: 'I've learned yet again that prayer whose primary aim is to achieve results is of little worth. It has to be enough that I pray because of who God is.'[28]

For John V. Taylor, a British theologian of mission, the connection between prayer and direct encounter with God was key to his under-standing of mission. So strong is the connection that Taylor called prayer a form of communion:

Every form of prayer that is stirred by the Spirit, therefore, is in essence a repetition of the love-word Abba! … Each time of prayer is an attempt to open ourselves more fully to that direct communion with the Father which Jesus knew, and to realize more deeply our relationship to him as adult sons and daughters.[29]

For Taylor, this more missional understanding of prayer as communion is made possible through the Holy Spirit, which dynamically creates the connection between us and God as the means of a form of communication:

'Ground of our being' has always seemed to me too static a concept of God. 'Ground of our meeting' is nearer the mark, and I think of the Holy Spirit as the elemental energy of communion itself, within which all separate existences may be made present and personal to each other.[30]

Of particular focus for Taylor was what he called the 'prayer of stillness' as a vehicle of our communion, something that was extremely import-ant in a culture fed up with too many words.[31] This had a critical place as a form of contemplative prayer for those who seek God: 'It may come as a surprise to many seekers to learn that the prayer of stillness can be a shared, corporate experience, and that it can be directed towards none other than the pure being of God.'[32]

Phileena Heuertz, an American activist and contemplative theologian, reminds us of the importance of contemplative prayer not only for missional awakening, but for helping the seeker to face being their true self and to let go of the false self in order to be transformed: 'Contemplation is the space and presence-of-being that allows for the dismantling of our illusions that wreak havoc on the world and nurtures the growth and development of our true selves.'[33]

For Heath, this connection between mission, the true self and contemplative prayer is key as a form of transformation of the self through a radical healing and reorientation of life as part of the missional ongoing walk with God. Contemplative prayer then becomes a form of 'homing':

> Through contemplative prayer we can find the path towards healing. I have come to think of it as 'homing' prayer. This kind of prayer leads me home to God and to my true self, as it opens ways for me to welcome others into the home of my life. Ultimately, contemplative prayer leads to hospitality.[34]

For Heuertz, development of contemplative prayer practices is essential for an approach to Christian discipleship as a form of 'contemplative activism' as a corrective to the negative aspects of a market society: 'Freedom for everyone instead of power and control of the few, co-operation instead of selfish grasps for security and survival, divine love instead of lust for craving of ego.'[35] Such an approach aims to use contemplative prayer as a form of evangelism to enable both the inner journey of awakening and exterior transformation, reflecting the path of becoming Christian that I outlined in the previous chapter as a form of centred-set missional theosis: 'Contemplative practices reinforce a posture of regular abandonment and surrender to God – in our exterior as well as our interior lives. Surrendering to the immanent presence of God around and within us allows for greater transformation.'[36]

I am reminded again of a point I made in the previous chapter. A number of participants in this SBNR study did not believe in a sense of self, and one of them came to the same meditation group as Calum. However, for Cathy, the pursuit of a sense of interior self promoted by the John Main approach proved to be distressing, as she experienced herself as having a sense of a fragmented state of self. Rather than facing this, Cathy instead pursued Zen Buddhism, which affirmed that there was no sense of self.

For Heath, this focus on the fragmented sense of the interior self reflects the distinction made between the true and the false self, which does not heed the inner voice of the love of God that beckons us. Instead, the individual succumbs to 'the spiritual fragmentation of inauthentic being' as an expression of the false self as 'universal to the human experience, arising from wounds received in life'.[37] For Heath, only through prayer can the individual draw on a:

> Divine Center, calling the scattered self into an integrated whole ... When we come home to the love of God everything changes, beginning with how we pray. Prayer is now at its foundation a contemplative soaking in the infinite love of God ... the anxieties of the false self, become clear in the light of God's day ... We discover to our astonishment the truth of Jesus's words.[38]

By implication, if the SBNR spiritual seeker does not believe in a sense of the human self, and at the same time has a fragmented sense of self, then healing and mission from encounter with God through forms of dialogue and prayer will not be possible, because of an egoic form of rejection of the gift of God's love. However, if the SBNR seeker believes in a human self yet also carries the wounds of a fragmented sense of self, mission and healing are possible through contemplative encounter with God.

Turning to forms of Christian contemplative prayer practices that can start people off on their spiritual journey, Heuertz suggests the following:

- Using breath prayers promoting well-being;
- Using centering prayer meditation practices;
- Using labyrinth walking prayers;
- Using *Lectio Divina* with biblical texts for spiritual learning;
- Using the Examen prayer to discern God in the details of your life;
- Using the Welcoming Prayer, particularly when feeling overwhelmed emotionally.[39]

Using such practices in this way then brings reduction of life's tensions and the effects of the chaos of the world, which can 'breed violence and exploitation'. In so doing, this type of Christian formation creates the environment for the individual to be 'anchored in contemplative spirituality, the active, exterior expression of our life [becoming] more peaceful, purposeful, and effective'.[40]

Continuing on the theme of the power and importance of contemplative forms of prayer and spirituality as media for encounter with God as a form of God's Kenosis, our Theosis mission model, Nicola Slee, a

British lecturer, feminist and practical theologian, in an ethnographic study explored the use of an 'apophatic' approach to Christian mission and formation through contemplative approaches to prayer for a group of women whom she described as being in or 'on the edges of, Christian tradition'.[41] Her study makes many connections and resemblances with the spiritual questing of the SBNR of the PhD study:

> Some women used journey imagery in a striking way to speak of being on a quest or search for something ... but ... unable even to name or know what they were searching for. There is a sense of longing and hunger for something unnamed, elusive, always 'around the corner', 'somewhere else', out of reach; an aspiration towards the 'something missing', the 'something more'.[42]

I was struck by the connection between the language of the contemplative path of awakening – purgation, illumination and union – that I have used as part of this missional theosis approach, and the themes of 'paralysis, awakening and relationality' identified by Slee in her research study.[43] Further, Slee made connections between the language and stories of those who took part in her research, noticing the 'overwhelming sense of loneliness and struggle', dealing with a spirituality of paradoxes and apparent contradictions, and Christian apophatic spirituality.[44] Slee defines apophatic spirituality as: 'an agnostic, paradoxical and elusive kind of knowing which operates at the edge of rational and critical thinking'.[45]

She recognized that such an approach required careful support:

> ... the need to accompany women in silence, paradox and unknowing. It requires a willingness and ability to desist from the effort to name or give form to experience, and to inhabit the place of silence ... It requires the creation of spaces for waiting, for silence, for apparent nothingness ... without attempting to control what happens in that space[46]

Such an approach therefore needs great insight and sensitivity, and engagement in contemplative prayer practices, to assist participants to 'embrace this way as [a] more conscious choice arising out of an owned awareness of paradox at the heart of things ... to hold the mystery and transcendence of faith'.[47] Slee advocated that a creative approach can encourage participants to:

explore contemplative ways of praying, in which images and words are abandoned, and the prayer remains in silence and darkness waiting upon God who is mystery beyond ... reading and reflection on sacred texts from the contemplative tradition ... validated by saints throughout the centuries ... making use of the writings of *The Cloud of Unknowing*, Meister Eckhart, Saint John of the Cross, Simone Weil and Thomas Merton ... exploring through prayer, poetry or painting ... and the traditions of desert spirituality.[48]

Slee's research writing here on the place of the apophatic prayer traditions as an open-ended approach to spiritual formation resonates with some of the responses of the SBNR of the PhD study who were wanting to draw on Christian contemplative prayer practices and resources to use for their own spiritual questing. Engagement in these prayer practices becomes an opportunity for a contemplative approach to mission. In the City SBNR dialogue group, as I have said earlier, there was definite surprise and shock that there was an authentic Christian contemplative tradition, where many had written off Christianity as overly rational and fundamentalist. The story of Calum shows what is possible when missional Christian communities open up the combination of contemplation and dialogue.

The writings of Slee and Sarah Coakley deeply resonate: the apophatic, the contemplative, the prayerful all open up experience of God as a deep resource for mission, as God's kenotic love experienced through prayer and dialogue as a path of theosis and Christian becoming:

> ... a vision of God's trinitarian nature as both the source and goal of human desires, as God intends them. It indicates how the 'Father', in and through the Spirit, both stirs up, and progressively chastens and purges, the frailer and often misdirected desires of humans, and so forges them, by stages of sometimes painful growth, into the likeness of his Son.[49]

For Coakley, such a form of engagement with God requires a willingness, through prayer, to wait silently on God's presence; through this, however, 'true spiritual deepening can start to occur'.[50] Coakley's approach here is a radical reconnection with a Christian contemplative spirituality, which by implication becomes an essential medium of encounter with God through prayer practices. This ancient perspective finds itself deeply relevant in the post-secular spiritual context of the SBNR, acting as a corrective to a church and mission practices that have become far too rational. Such an approach privileges contemplation:

> The practice of contemplation ... is the primary ascetical submission to the divine demanded by revelation, and the link to the creative source of life to which it continually returns. This practice is neither an élitist nor an arcane act, as might be feared: it is an undertaking of radical attention to the Real which is open to all who seek to foster it.[51]

For Coakley, utilizing such forms of contemplative prayer encourages forms of 'surrender' to God, opening up the individual to be led by the Spirit into a spiritual adventure that can bring 'surprise, adventure, purgation and conviction'.[52]

The approach taken by both Slee and Coakley suggests that this focus on prayer as the medium for awakened missional encounter or communion with God through individual personal experience is very significant. Experiencing the combination of forms of dialogue and contemplative spiritual practices had been important for many of the PhD study participants. I was struck by how important it was for SBNR spiritual seekers to hold a positive experience of the self, and the shift from an egoic understanding to a truer non-egoic sense of an inner personhood. The analysis arising from the PhD study suggests that if an individual arrives at a position of not believing in the individual self, then they are in effect denying the possibility of *imago Dei*, of the self being made in the form of the divine image, and therefore the path to the awakening to God from within is not possible. This suggests that a contemplative God's Kenosis, our Theosis model approach to mission will not be effective until the individual is able to affirm the reality of an individual human self.

The continuing story of Calum is a good example of the potential of what can happen drawing on a contemplative approach to mission. What was interesting in his case and a number of others was the combination of attending group meditation using Christian prayer practices, and the dialogue group, as part of their path into a missional theosis.

Finally in this chapter, I turn to some suggested immersive contemplative activities that can be drawn on to help spiritual seekers deepen their experiences of awakening to the presence of God as the source of love.

Immersive activities for the awakening stage

Returning to the work of Slee and Das, I have proposed an approach to utilizing group dialogue alongside contemplative prayer as media for mission. In this section, I propose an expansion of this proposal, to offer an immersive contemplative and formational experience using discussion, contemplative prayer practices and shared wisdom to assist the individual SBNR seeker to navigate spiritually through the path of awakening, purgation, illumination and union. I am proposing within this immersive experience the use of the *Lectio Divina* contemplative prayer practice to explore the metaphorical 'I AM' Christological names that Jesus uses for himself in the Gospel of John to express his divinity. These resonate with the four stages of the spiritual path, the first of which is summarized in Table 1 below.

Table 1: Christian Spirituality Immersive Learning Experience

1. Stage of contemplative condition	2. *Lectio Divina* engagement with the 'I AM' statements of Jesus in the Gospel of John	3. Contemplative wisdom sharing	4. Associated contemplative prayer practices
Awakening	'I AM the door' (John 10.7, 9) Jesus as God as source.	1. Learning to meditate 2. Kindness to self	John Main meditation practice on own 2x a day for 20 minutes

Lectio Divina *exploration*

Regarding an opening up of connections with helpful Christological metaphors, I propose one *Lectio Divina* exploration using the statement 'I AM the door' (John 10.7, 9). This biblical metaphor could be linked to the term arising in the ethnographic fieldwork of 'God as source'. It could also be used for a group dialogue to explore this image from personal spiritual experience. Jesus as the door can open up either a direct or a progressive form of awakening; it names Jesus as the source of that experience as God, and affirms that the awakening experience is instigated by God.

Contemplative wisdom sharing

1 Learning to meditate

Learning to meditate is not easy, and it is suggested that given the missional focus where the individual is not Christian, an adaptation should be used of the approach founded by John Main. Participants of the PhD study who attended these John Main meditation sessions talked warmly of them.[53] The avoidance of specific Christian language in these meditation sessions was important. The final benediction used to close this group was particularly powerful, employing the language of 'the divine' instead of God. Two of these meditation groups used contents from John Main's book *Silence and Stillness*, which has a mixture of general spiritual language and at times very specifically Christian terminology, which for SBNR spiritual seekers might feel too overtly Christian and non-inclusive.[54] As relationships build and people experience such a form of meditation to work, this sensitivity about Christian language could reduce, but this needs careful facilitation by the person leading the group. The fact that one of the sites of the PhD study had run these adapted meditation groups for over ten years shows the importance of this activity.

Regarding practice, much of the John Main approach to meditation resonated with the contemplative centred-set approach to mission. For example:

> The meditative journey is one, therefore, that has to involve our total being … every aspect of our life, must be brought into this exercise … as we journey from the periphery to the centre … because in the process of meditation everything in our life is aligned on the centre.[55]

2 *Kindness to self*

As I have discussed in this chapter, it is important to stress that any form of awakening is disorientating and challenging, even when it involves experiencing a form of spiritual love. Sometimes spiritual seekers have discussed these experiences with friends, family or work colleagues and on occasion have felt ridiculed and shamed by their responses. Wisdom sharing should emphasize kindness and respect for oneself. Rather than merely absorbing criticism or shame, participants should be encouraged to cultivate self-respect, openness and spiritual exploration. This can be particularly challenging for those accustomed to the dominance of rationalism, which often dismisses trans-rational spiritual experiences. Adapting to this mindset takes time, and one practical step could involve noting or journaling personal experiences to share with those curating the immersion mission activities. Crucially, mission practice should encourage participants, especially those identifying as SBNR, to articulate their understanding of God from their lived experiences. This process nurtures a growing awareness of God as they perceive it, while fostering connections between their understanding and the Christian faith.

Contemplative prayer practice

Given the reality that the adapted John Main silent meditation practice is probably very new, it is recommended that the individual practise twice a day for 20 minutes each time to consolidate a contemplative practice into the rhythm of the day.

The great challenge of this first step of awakening, in either direct or progressive form, as disorientating challenge or as the overwhelming experience of the love of God, is that it is usually quickly followed by the painful experience of human frailty and brokenness. This stage in the spiritual journey, which is never an easy one, will be explored in the next chapter.

Notes

1 Thomas Merton, *New Seeds of Contemplation* (New York: New Directions Books, 1972), p. 10.

2 Thomas Merton, *He is Risen* (Niles, IL: Argus Communications, 1975), p. 14.

3 Merton, *New Seeds of Contemplation*, p. 42.

4 Mark Vernon, 'Barfield and the Evolution of Consciousness', transcription following Zoom interview, 18 December 2020, pp. 1–2.

5 Ian Mobsby, 'Engaging in Mission with the "Spiritual Not Religious", Drawing on a Trinitarian Dialogical Approach', *Anvil Journal of Theology and Mission* 35, no. 2 (July 2019), pp. 13–19, https://churchmissionsociety.org/anvil/engaging-in-mission-with-the-spiritual-not-religious-drawing-on-a-trinitarian-dialogical-approach-ian-mobsby-anvil-vol-35-issue-2/. Ian Mobsby, 'The Beginnings of a Non-Directive Approach to Mission and Evangelism', *Anvil Journal of Theology and Mission* 36, no. 2 (July 2020), pp. 40–3, https://churchmissionsociety.org/wp-content/uploads/2022/05/Church-Mission-Society-Anvil-Volume-36-Issue-2-July-2020.pdf.

6 Richard Sudworth, *Distinctly Welcoming: Christian Presence in a Multifaith Society* (Bletchley: Scripture Union, 2017), p. 29.

7 Stephen B. Bevans and Roger P. Schroeder, *Prophetic Dialogue: Reflections on Christian Mission Today* (Maryknoll, NY: Orbis Books, 2011), p. 22.

8 Thomas Merton, *Conjectures of a Guilty Bystander* (New York: Doubleday, 1966), p. 218; emphasis original.

9 Merton, *New Seeds of Contemplation*, p. 5.

10 Merton, *New Seeds of Contemplation*, p. 3.

11 Athanasios Despotis, 'From Conversion According to Paul and "John" to Theosis in the Greek Patristic Tradition', *Horizons in Biblical Theology* 38, no. 1 (2016), p. 101.

12 Despotis, 'From Conversion According to Paul', p. 100.

13 Bevans and Schroeder, *Prophetic Dialogue*, p. 24.

14 Bevans and Schroeder, *Prophetic Dialogue*, pp. 25–6.

15 Bevans and Schroeder, *Prophetic Dialogue*, p. 2.

16 Bevans and Schroeder, *Prophetic Dialogue*, p. 22.

17 Bevans and Schroeder, *Prophetic Dialogue*, pp. 2–3, 21, 38.

18 Bevans and Schroeder, *Prophetic Dialogue*, p. 59.

19 Bevans and Schroeder, *Prophetic Dialogue*, p. 60.

20 David Tacey, *The Spirituality Revolution: The Emergence of Contemporary Spirituality* (London: Routledge, 2004), p. 89.

21 Tacey, *The Spirituality Revolution*, pp. 4–5.

22 John Main was a Benedictine monk who through exploration of medieval Christian mystical texts and dialogue with Christian contemplative communities formed and promoted a silent meditation practice using an anchor word. From this approach he set up the World Christian Community of Meditation.

23 John Main, *Word Into Silence: A Manual for Christian Meditation*, ed. Laurence Freeman (Norwich: Canterbury Press, 1980).

24 Peter was not a member of the City group, but had experience of attending John Main-based meditation groups before attending the Borough dialogue group.

25 Adrian Chatfield, 'Prayer and Mission: Entering into the Ways of God', *Anvil Journal of Theology and Mission* 32, no. 1 (2016), p. 17.

26 Chatfield, 'Prayer and Mission', p. 11.

27 Chatfield, 'Prayer and Mission', p. 18.

28 Chatfield, 'Prayer and Mission', p. 18.

29 John V. Taylor, *The Go-between God: The Holy Spirit and the Christian Mission* (London: SCM Press, 1975), p. 234.

30 Taylor, *The Go-between God*, p. 18.

31 Taylor, *The Go-between God*, p. 238.

32 Taylor, *The Go-between God*, p. 240.

33 Phileena Heuertz, 'Contemplative Activism as a Model for Mission', *Lausanne World Pulse Archives* no. 12 (2011), pp. 1–7, http://www.lausanne-worldpulse.com/perspectives-php/1481/12-2011 (accessed 08.08.2024).

34 Elaine A. Heath, *The Mystic Way of Evangelism: A Contemplative Vision for Christian Outreach* (Grand Rapids, MI: Baker Academic, 2008), p. 140.

35 Heuertz, 'Contemplative Activism'.

36 Heuertz, 'Contemplative Activism'.

37 Heath, *The Mystic Way of Evangelism*, pp. 71–2.

38 Heath, *The Mystic Way of Evangelism*, pp. 71–2.

39 Heuertz, 'Contemplative Activism'.

40 Heuertz, 'Contemplative Activism'.

41 Although this study is not specifically of the SBNR, from the responses of the women involved it is clear that they are a mix of unchurched, dechurched and post-church as well as some being churched, so the findings have relevance.

42 Nicola Slee, 'Apophatic Faithing in Women's Spirituality', *British Journal of Theological Education* 11, no. 2 (2001), p. 28.

43 Slee, 'Apophatic Faithing in Women's Spirituality', p. 24.

44 Slee, 'Apophatic Faithing in Women's Spirituality', pp. 28, 31.

45 Slee, 'Apophatic Faithing in Women's Spirituality', p. 32.

46 Slee, 'Apophatic Faithing in Women's Spirituality', p. 33.

47 Slee, 'Apophatic Faithing in Women's Spirituality', p. 30.

48 Slee, 'Apophatic Faithing in Women's Spirituality', pp. 33–4.

49 Sarah Coakley, *God, Sexuality, and the Self: An Essay 'On the Trinity'* (Cambridge: Cambridge University Press, 2019), p. 6.

50 Coakley, *God, Sexuality, and the Self*, p. 19.

51 Coakley, *God, Sexuality, and the Self*, p. 88.

52 Coakley, *God, Sexuality, and the Self*, p. 331.

53 See Appendix 1 for the script for this meditation group.

54 John Main, *Silence and Stillness in Every Season: Daily Readings With John Main*, ed. Paul Harris (New York: Continuum, 2006).

55 Main, *Silence and Stillness*, p. 197.

7

Purgation: The Crisis Stage

The night is the time to surrender the ... old ways, thought
patterns, and activities that have been idolatrous substitutes for
God in and of themselves.[1]

In this second stage of 'God's Kenosis, our Theosis', the spiritual seeker
enters into a difficult time of self-awareness in what is sometimes called
'the dark night'. Here, after a form of awakening, the individual can feel
regret or deep pain from the consequences of life choices and the realization of personal brokenness. Entering this stage can be experienced as
a form of personal crisis, so support and encouragement of the spiritual
seeker is incredibly important, particularly to ensure that they do not
feel they are alone, but realize that purgation is a normal part of the
authentic spiritual journey.

As explored in earlier chapters, the purgation space of being is a dark
place of human suffering and wounding. As such, great care needs to be
taken to ensure that contemplative experiential content (meditations,
dialogue groups, wisdom sharing and prayer practices) affirms the SBNR

person's experience, ensures that they are listened to, and emphasizes hope even in difficult situations.

As Sarah Coakley reminds us, for those entering into the contemplative life, purgation is a time when 'one is forced to acknowledge the messy entanglements' of life mixed in with an awakening as a new spiritual yearning or 'desire for God':[2]

> It seems that to step intentionally into the realm of divine, trinitarian desire, and to seek some form of participation in it through a profound engagement with the Spirit, is both to risk having one's human desires intensified in some qualitatively distinct manner, and also to confront a searching and necessary purgation of those same human desires in order to be brought into conformity with the divine will ... it veritably magnetizes the soul towards God.[3]

While many Christian mystics and saints have described experiences of 'dark night', the term is associated primarily with John of the Cross, the sixteenth-century Spanish Carmelite whose stunning poem 'Dark Night of the Soul' continues to challenge and nourish people from many spiritual traditions.[4]

Elaine Heath reminds us that John of the Cross's writings focus on the dark night as a stage of purgation concerning the 'freeing the soul from attachments that hinder the ability to receive and give God's love'.[5] It is the clinging to attachments that can create deep emotional pain, and the spiritual process of 'letting go', surrender or making endings that releases the individual to spiritual freedom. Undertaking this spiritual journey alone can be challenging. It is important to encourage individuals to consider one-on-one guidance from a trained spiritual director. In some cases, therapy, counselling or participation in a 12-step programme may also be beneficial. Often these painful attachments are experienced as forms of addiction, which is why many of them have been known as deadly sins, a list that traditionally includes gluttony, lust, greed, despair, fear, rage, carelessness, vanity, pride and deceit. What is critical is that the individual does not get overwhelmed, but feels supported to be brave in facing all that this time of purgation and need for surrender brings, particularly in this early stage of the spiritual journey towards God.

To illustrate the model, I turn to the story of Philippe and his spiritual journey from the PhD study, as expressed in Figure 21 below.

Philippe, ethnically northern European with French as his first language, began his spiritual journey as a secular atheist. He had come to London to work as a chef and for adventure, after previously complet-

Figure 21: 'God's Kenosis, our Theosis': The Spiritual Journey of Philippe

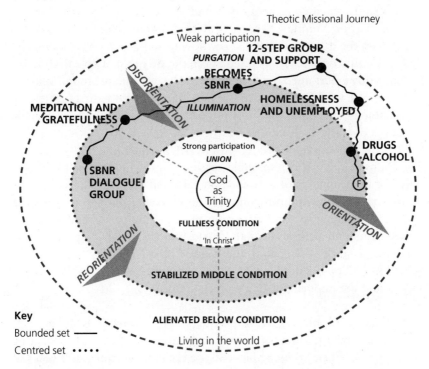

ing vocational training to the equivalent of A Levels, and was on an average wage. Unfortunately, the move resulted in the development of a serious addiction which, in time, left him homeless and unemployed, trying to survive on the streets:

> People miss the important things. I was homeless and had no job, it was very hard for me ... people take wrong turns. (Philippe, Borough dialogue group, 27 June 2018)

Fortunately, Philippe received support to get off the streets, and a 12-step fellowship helped him to get 'cleaned up' and to be in a place to be able to work again. Through this transformative experience and awakening moment, Philippe became interested in spirituality and began to self-identify as a SBNR seeker. The love received from a 'higher power', which helped in his restoration, continued in his focus on love rather than on the materialism and unhappiness of much of modern society:

> As I look around, many overvalue the attachment to materialism and things, and not to the importance of love and the infusion of love ...

Often on Fridays when I go to Sainsbury's there are people finishing work and you can see them say 'Thank God it is Friday', and I in response say on Monday, 'Thank God it is Monday'. Because they over-focus on the dark, and don't know how to see that we have so much, if they could only see it. You see this in the way that people need to be constantly entertained, and they miss the beauty and profound spirituality of the world, as they are not looking, obsessed with gadgets and technology, and miss the most important things. (Philippe, Borough dialogue group, 27 June 2018)

For Philippe, there was a tangible sense of a growing true self that has let go of the trappings of a more egoic false self. He clearly faced up to all the attachments and difficulties of his extended purgation and dark night through therapy and a 12-step programme, to surrender all the attachments and enmeshment that held him back. His responses give evidence of spiritual freedom and a gratefulness for life. Being SBNR was, for Philippe, centred around a reappreciation of the beauty of nature and the importance of a spirituality of life:

Spirituality, for me, is love, is reaching out to another human being by music or art or nature, the colour of the green of plants, the colour of the leaves. When I ride my bicycle, you see so many trees, and you say which colour is this, what type of green is this, but they are all different greens. So I often say I really enjoy my ride to work, and I don't sweat because I open my eyes, and I can see, and I can hear, and I do not rush, and am experiencing the world around you. (Philippe, Borough dialogue group, 27 June 2018)

However, for Philippe, negative experiences of the church – 'Religion which always tells people what to think and believe'[6] – resulted in a barrier at the time of the dialogue groups of this research. This then inhibited openness and exploration of the idea of a God; yet in its place Philippe described an awareness of the presence of a universal consciousness, which at times seemed to cross the line into a form of divine consciousness:

If we practise meditation, we can tap into that universal consciousness. So we take value in meditation and various forms of music meditation. And we can form art linking spirituality with meditation. It is open to anyone to receive it, and you wake up something inside yourself. (Philippe, Borough dialogue group, 27 June 2018)

Philippe remained in the sphere of illumination rather than purgation, and still had significant obstacles to face if he was going to be open to the source of the love he had discerned as spirituality, in the mystery of a loving God. This is not easy when having to deconstruct controlling and negative experiences of church and Christians. Again, we see the harm that church and Christians can do towards God's mission, when either are not immersed in the love of God.

Considerations concerning the external self and inner self in the stage of purgation in the God's Kenosis, our Theosis contemplative mission model

As I discussed earlier, the spiritual seeker must attend to the needs of their inner and outer selves, where the external is focused on survival and salvation in a constantly changing world, and the inner self on the spiritual path of encounter with God thorough the true self. It should be remembered that this approach is not without criticism. For Thomas Merton, the external self is that part of us that colludes with the egoic and false self; it is not able to engage with contemplation or encounter of God and therefore should not be a consideration.[7] Yet when we consider Walter Brueggemann's analysis of the pressures of the outside world regarding the constant flow of human experience as 'orientation, disorientation, reorientation', I am concerned that a dualism of 'internal = good' and 'external = bad' is created.[8] This is particularly true, and important, when the spiritual seeker enters into the difficult stage of purgation or a dark night of the soul. Yet after saying all that, and taking into account the needs of the internal and external self, I do suggest that a model of mission based on contemplation as a process should privilege the internal self, as that part of us where God reveals our 'real self' and as the place where we engage with contemplation and encounter with God from within. So what are the practical implications of this?

When thinking about the external self we do need to be serious about healthiness and well-being: eating well, exercising, keeping fit and healthy are important, particularly when the individual is feeling the pain of attachments and the costs of life. To work through these issues contemplatively, letting go of attachments, will require energy and focus, and we are able to do this by taking the needs of our bodies seriously. In much that I read on Christian spirituality there is sometimes a neglect of bodies and physicality, and at its worst an unhealthy dualism that can see bodies, being matter, as inherently sinful. This is the danger of forms of Gnosticism that we must avoid as the first Christian heresy. So attending to the self-care needs of the external self is important, if only to assist with the resilience and stability needed to face the inner contemplative journey.

It is therefore critical that the dialogue groups avoid an overfocus on the egoic that would then privilege the external over the inner self. To ensure the dialogues are a learning space where all are open to learning, they must avoid being a space for an argument where individuals just recite strong views, holding on to their deeply held convictions unquestioningly with a focus on winning. If this were to occur, it would undermine the whole open-ended approach of this particular model of mission. How dialogue groups are structured, then, matters.

Considerations for the dialogue group

Discussions in this stage of purgation could include themes such as refinding love, facing unhealthy attachments, mutuality and hope. Given the intensity of emotional pain, it is really important to ensure the dialogue group is well structured and boundaried. From the PhD research, it is suggested that the structure of the group should be consistent and include the following elements:

1. The facilitator briefly welcomes people to the group, explaining how it works and the process, and introduces the theme for discussion. Before beginning, the facilitator reiterates the ground rules (listed below).
2. Each person is invited to express what they want about the theme in five minutes without interruption, with a timer appointed who gives a one-minute warning to keep to time. If the group is larger than eight it is suggested this time be reduced to three minutes. After each person has initially shared, there should be a one-minute silence or, if the group is over eight, a 30-second timed silence.
3. At the end of initial sharing, people can ask clarification questions concerning what was shared, respecting the ground rules listed below.
4. Time for open discussion.
5. Once discussion has come to a halt, or has come to the end of a set period of time, the facilitator ends the open discussion.
6. The facilitator then asks each person to share, in a maximum of two to three minutes, what they are going away with at the end of this discussion, again without interruption.
7. Finally, agree what theme to discuss at the next meeting and confirm place, time and date for this next dialogue group.

It is extremely important to have clear ground rules to maintain good interpersonal communication and praxis in SBNR dialogue groups. From the experiences of the six groups in the PhD research study, the following ground rules were adapted and recommended:[9]

1. In this SBNR dialogue group, we all come to listen, think and learn. We are all here to explore the path of spirituality; there is no winning or losing, only reflection for our own spiritual path and growth.
2. All who participate in these dialogues speak as humble individuals and from their own experience; no one in the group is an expert, represents special interests or is a representative of anything other than themselves.
3. Everyone in these dialogues is equal and there should not be any overspeaking unless one of the facilitators intervenes to assert these ground rules or to de-escalate things if a dialogue is becoming an argument.
4. All are expected to be open and to listen to others in an attitude of mutual learning, even when you do not agree with an expressed point of view. It is OK to disagree from your own experience, as long as this is done respectfully.
5. All are expected to maintain empathic listening to others, and to do this with humility, acknowledging you have heard what has been said even if you disagree.
6. It is good to explore where you agree with other people's perspectives before you point out differences.
7. It is vital to maintain good 'adult–adult' dialogue, ensuring you manage your emotions and prevent a dialogue becoming an argument.
8. Disagreement is natural, but it should be ensured that this is around ideas and not about denigrating people's experiences and personalities. People should not feel disrespected about who they are and what is important to them.
9. Times of silence should be respected as pauses for reflection.
10. Be careful not to overtalk. The facilitators will make sure that all who come and want to share have the opportunity of doing so.

Considerations for the ongoing immersive experience for the stage of purgation as the crisis stage

As with the awakening stage of the God's Kenosis, our Theosis contemplative model of mission, it is critical that participants engage not only in meditation and dialogue groups, but also in the ongoing immersive experience, particularly as purgation and dark nights of the soul are never easy. Again, it is critical that facilitators practise an open-ended approach to mission curation: they should wait for individuals to approach them for wisdom, to ensure the process remains 'adult–adult'. The church at times has a terrible habit of infantilizing people by overbearing forms of pastoral and missional leadership, which must be avoided in this missional context.

The summary of recommended content for the immersive experience is listed in Table 2 below.

Table 2: Immersive Experience for the Stage of Purgation

1. Stage of contemplative condition	2. *Lectio Divina* engagement with the 'I AM' statements of Jesus in the Gospel of John	3. Contemplative wisdom sharing	4. Associated contemplative prayer practices
Purgation Alienated below condition Withdrawn from participation Crisis stage	'I AM the light of the world' (John 8.12; 9.5) 'I AM the good shepherd' (John 10.11, 14) Resonances with ethnographic responses: God as Life Force God is love	Starting out on our spiritual journey: 1. Facing attachments and things that harm you 2. Immersing ourselves in divine love through nature 3. Reducing our exposure to technology 4. Loving kindness 5. Rhythm and rest	The Well-being Welcoming Prayer Well-being Breath Prayers Loving-kindness prayer practice Serenity Prayer Serenity Prayer reflection Reflective Prayer seeking the presence of God in a painful childhood experience Walking Prayer Hand–Heart Prayer Ignatian prayers for anxiety, depression, grief, loneliness, insomnia

Lectio Divina *explorations*

Regarding an opening up of connections with helpful Christological metaphors, I propose two *Lectio Divina* explorations using the terms 'I AM the light of the world' (John 8.12, 9.5) and 'I AM the good shepherd' (John 10.11, 14). These biblical metaphors could be linked to the terms arising in the ethnographic fieldwork of 'God is Love' and 'God as Life Force'. These last two terms could also be explored in group dialogues from personal spiritual experience.

Contemplative wisdom sharing and prayer practices

Under the title of 'Continuing the spiritual journey when the rubber hits the road', I propose five elements for the sharing of wisdom at this stage. These seek to face the pain and trauma of living in this situation, promoting hope and the possibility of change and healing through the love of God.

1 Facing things that harm

Prayer is an essential medium not only for encounter with God, but also for the discipline of facing unhealthy attachment to people, emotions, roles, life experiences and trauma. Most addictions are identified with forms of unhealthy attachment. Jesus' teaching in the New Testament is clear: forms of attachment can come close to forms of idolatry, where we make people or things our 'higher power' rather than God. Such forms of attachment will bring pain and trauma, which can often be associated with family and childhood negative experiences. Jesus speaks to the need of facing destructive attachment through letting go, the discipline of walking away and taking this in prayer to God:

> 'Come to me, all you that are weary and are carrying heavy burdens, and I will give you rest. Take my yoke upon you, and learn from me; for I am gentle and humble in heart, and you will find rest for your souls. For my yoke is easy, and my burden is light.' (Matthew 11.28–30)

The writer of the First Letter of Peter encourages us: 'Cast all your anxiety on him, because he cares for you' (1 Peter 5.7). This perspective fosters a deeper connection with God and offers healing through the practice of disentangling ourselves from the complexities of life. Apophatic prayer, as highlighted by Phileena Heuertz (see the previous

chapter) and Cynthia Bourgeault (an ordained Anglican minister, theologian and contemplative practitioner), serves as a powerful medium
for surrendering various aspects of life to God's care. Such practices
can significantly aid in healing trauma and managing overwhelming
emotions.[10]

The Breath, Welcoming and Serenity Prayers are helpful when in a state
of pain and distress, to assist with well-being. There are also a number
of Ignatian prayer practices aimed at those feeling anxiety, depression,
grief, loneliness or insomnia.[11] Such powerful prayer practices can begin
people's journeys away from a sense of alienation through moments of
encountering the love of God. This approach can assist with three of the
modes of SBNR seeking that I identified in Chapter 3, of 'seeking integration, unity and connection'; 'seeking mystical truth that lies within'
and 'seeking mystical truth that lies outside of the self'.

2 Immersing ourselves in divine love through nature

'But ask the animals, and they will teach you; the birds of the air, and
they will tell you; ask the plants of the earth, and they will teach you;
and the fish of the sea will declare to you. Who among all these does
not know that the hand of the LORD has done this? In his hand is the
life of every living thing and the breath of every human being.' (Job
12.7–10)

Engaging in prayer in nature is a powerful contemplative practice that
creates a sense of connection and gratitude. Encounter with nature can
be deeply restorative, reminding us of the goodness of the world that
heals, revives and renews us. Nature reminds us that, even if we are
encountering harm and difficulty, goodness prevails and makes connection with the God of abundant love. There are many prayer practices
that are critical for the establishment and sustaining of hope and joy
in order to gain spiritual freedom from experiences of alienation and
wounding. Examples of such forms of practice include Ignatian 'walking in nature' prayer practices.[12] There are many forms of mindfulness
meditation that focus on restoring well-being by contemplation of a
leaf or flowers. Further, there are many Christian monastic practices
concerning the prayerful practice of gratitude.[13] This area of prayer
relates to two of the modes of SBNR seeking that I identified in Chapter
3: 'seeking transcendence in nature, spirituality and art' and 'seeking
authenticity through responsibility'.

3 Reducing our exposure to technology

One of the great stresses of our times is the need to be constantly 'plugged in' to the flows of various forms of information technology that includes social media, TV, internet and the like. We have a tendency to be addicted to our smartphones, email and social media, which can create the illusion of being connected yet at the same time be deeply harming. I suggest the need for times of technological abstinence. It can bring spiritual benefits and enhanced well-being if the individual takes a break from something, or has pauses, as forms of fasting and temporary abstinence. Temporary technological unplugging can be seen as a healthy form of temporary spiritual abstinence to re-establish balance. When taking such temporary technological abstinences, it is important for the individual not to flaunt them in any way – that would be a sign of egoic intent to show their spirituality almost as a form of status. As Jesus said: 'But when you fast, put oil on your head and wash your face, so that your fasting may be seen not by others but by your Father who is in secret; and your Father who sees in secret will reward you' (Matthew 6.17–18).

This form of technological abstinence addresses spiritual self-care, where a form of prayer could be used to take the individual away from patterns of self-neglect and alienation. By practising reduced technological exposure, the individual practises kindness to themselves, as often social media simply overwhelm us. This is extremely counter-cultural. There are examples of 'unplugging prayers' practices, some relating to the idea of 'sabbath' as the absence of work.[14]

4 Loving kindness

Love is patient; love is kind; love is not envious or boastful or arrogant or rude. It does not insist on its own way; it is not irritable or resentful; it does not rejoice in wrongdoing, but rejoices in the truth. It bears all things, believes all things, hopes all things, endures all things. (1 Corinthians 13.4–7)

Much has been written on the mindfulness movement, which is a more secular, individualistic form of spiritual practice. There are adaptations of the loving-kindness meditation as a daily practice, often around managing our inner sense of woundedness and pain. However, it can also be very individualistic. Some wording has become popular, including: 'May I be safe. May I be happy. May I be healthy. May I live with ease.'[15] Some Christians feel uncomfortable with this wording, concerned that it is too self-centred and too ego-focused. Irene Kraegel suggests an alternative wording: 'May I (you) know God's love. May I (you) know God's rest. May I (you) know God's peace.'[16]

Forms of self-neglect and unkindness to the self are commonplace in modern Western society because of the speed, uncertainty, materialism and consumerism of much of our culture which, as I have said, is unhealthy. Learning a loving disposition towards the self is part of a more affirming contemplative approach to prayer.

Such loving-kindness practices draw on an apophatic approach, which is not about effecting a result or making something happen, but rather adopting a gentler, a more open-ended approach to contemplative prayer as simply being.

Reflecting again on previous chapters, this focus on inner self-kindness reflects the SBNR mode of seeking as 'seeking integration, unity and connection' and 'seeking authenticity through responsibility'.

Regarding practice, not only are mindfulness practices possible, but also a number of reflective well-being prayers, such as the Examen prayer, which seeks to reflect on the day and the aspects of it that were either good or challenging, trying to notice where God has been present in the details of daily life.

5 Rhythm and rest

And after he had dismissed the crowds, he went up the mountain by himself to pray. When evening came, he was there alone. (Matthew 14.23)

This is the last of the contemplative prayer practices centred on the beginning (purgation) of the contemplative spiritual journey that I have called God's Kenosis, our Theosis, which at this stage is focused on well-being and addressing the pain, wounding and trauma associated with modern living. The contemplative life is marked by a focus on balance or living a rhythm of life that transitions through different spiritual and physical needs. Giving time for this is important so that the SBNR spiritual seeker does not attempt to live a machine-like existence. Practitioners of Centering Prayer meditation sometimes utilize transition exercises as part of their preparation for entering into a prayer practice.[17] John Main, in his writings on Christian meditation, recommends meditating for at least half an hour morning and evening to assist the individual to get into a healthy pattern of rhythm and rest.[18]

The potential for further experiences of a dark night of the soul in the missional journey

Unfortunately, in the contemplative spiritual journey towards God our awareness of attachments and things we have to face does not happen all at once. In fact, as we progress through the stages of purgation to illumination, and illumination to union, many experience further dark-night moments as they discover new layers of wounds and attachments. This is only to be expected.

Again, prayer practices will need to promote forms of coping and respond to the further wounding effects of our modern society. These contemplative prayer practices will need to include approaches to manage and dissipate intense emotional pain and anxiety. They will also need to include the practice of bravery to face further unhealthy attachments that bring suffering. These prayers will also need to promote forms of mindfulness and engagement with the natural world to promote healing through encounter with God's love.

In such times, when there are further dark nights of the soul beyond the stage of illumination, reference could be made to Jesus' Great Commandment:

> Jesus answered, 'The first is, "Hear, O Israel: the Lord our God, the Lord is one; you shall love the Lord your God with all your heart, and with all your soul, and with all your mind, and with all your strength." The second is this, "You shall love your neighbour as yourself." There is no other commandment greater than these.' (Mark 12.29–31)

In his book *Finding Sanctuary: Monastic Steps for Everyday Life*, written for unchurched spiritual seekers, the Roman Catholic Benedictine Abbot Christopher Jamison opened up a way to approach the Great Commandment of Jesus. He saw the Commandment not as some form of self-driven, egoic approach to Christian discipleship but, on the contrary, as an approach where we open ourselves up to God's love as the source of spiritual growth and transformation. He helpfully articulated a way of communicating this as: 'Learning to receive the love of God, to learn to love ourselves, to learn to love others.'[19]

This way of expressing the Christian contemplative and missional journey, particularly for those who are experiencing the emotional pain of a 'dark night', is extremely helpful. The awakening stage then becomes an increasing awareness of the presence of the love of God either transcendentally or immanently from within. The process of beginning the pilgrimage of the heart towards God comes with the openness to receive this love of God even when you are not sure what you think and believe, and to suspend any dominating rationalist approaches to life to experience this trans-rationally. The purgation and dark-night stages emphasize the importance of facing the attachments, pains and need for endings and surrender that arise by the immersion of the self in the love of God through meditation, dialogue, contemplative prayer practices, *Lectio Divina* and the sharing of wisdom. This then helps the individual learn to love and accept the self in this missional journey of self-discovery, which is ultimately centred on letting go of the false self or ego-self and encountering the true self through the love of God.

In the next chapter, I explore the step of moving from the stage of purgation into illumination with God.

Notes

1 Elaine A. Heath, *The Mystic Way of Evangelism: A Contemplative Vision for Christian Outreach* (Grand Rapids, MI: Baker Academic, 2008), p. 18.

2 Sarah Coakley, *God, Sexuality, and the Self: An Essay 'On the Trinity'* (Cambridge: Cambridge University Press, 2019), p. 13.

3 Coakley, *God, Sexuality, and the Self*, p. 13.

4 Heath, *The Mystic Way of Evangelism*, p. 18.

5 Heath, *The Mystic Way of Evangelism*, p. 18.

6 Quoted from the transcript for Philippe, Borough dialogue group, 27/06/2018.

7 Thomas Merton, *New Seeds of Contemplation* (New York: New Directions Books, 1972), p. 7.

8 Walter Brueggemann, *The Psalms and the Life of Faith* (Minneapolis, MN: Fortress Press, 1995), p. 18.

9 These ground rules were discussed and amended following feedback from the co-facilitators focus group conducted after the completion of all the dialogues, as a form of reflexivity.

10 Cynthia Bourgeault, *Centering Prayer and Inner Awakening* (Plymouth, MA: Cowley Publications, 2004), pp. 135–52.

11 See https://pray-as-you-go.org/prayer%20tools/.

12 See https://pray-as-you-go.org/retreat/walking-prayer.

13 For example, the Community of St John the Evangelist have created a prayer practice for focusing on gratefulness: see https://ssje.org/ssje/wp-content/uploads/2016/05/Contentment_Exercise.pdf.

14 An example of unplugging prayer to help reinforce punctuating the day with unplugging can be found here: https://www.creativecommonsprayer.com/occasion/prayer-for-unplugging/.

15 Irene Kraegel, 'Lovingkindness', *The Mindful Christian* (blog), 1 December 2018, https://www.themindfulchristian.com/blog/lovingkindness (accessed 08.08.2024).

16 Kraegel, 'Lovingkindness'.

17 A good example of this is found on the Insight Timer Meditation Application led by Marc Thomas Shaw, which can be found at: https://insighttimer.com/marcthomasshaw/guided-meditations/20-minute-centering-prayer-with-transition-exercise (accessed 08.08.2024).

18 https://johnmaincenter.org/about-meditation/.

19 Christopher Jamison, *Finding Sanctuary: Monastic Steps for Everyday Life* (London: Weidenfeld & Nicolson, 2010). This book resulted from Jamison's experiences at Worth Abbey, for the 2005 TV reality series *The Monastery*.

8

Illumination: The Insight Stage

For with you is the fountain of life; in your light we see light.
(Psalm 36.9)

In this stage of the contemplative model 'God's Kenosis, our Theosis'
we turn from the deep challenges of purgation and the dark night of the
soul to illumination, or what I want to call the 'insight' stage. The focus
therefore shifts, from facing up to painful attachments and difficulties
and surrendering these to God, to an openness to God the Holy Spirit
through the reception of God's love to develop an encountering relationship to and with God. As I explored in the last chapter, this does not
mean that there will not be the need to face the pain of further attachments and human frailty in the future as new layers of attachments
come to light. Nevertheless, in this stage of insight and illumination the
spiritual seeker is able to continue on their missional journey in their
desire or longing for further encounter with God beyond the spiritual
experience of awakening through the Holy Spirit.

Sarah Coakley reminds us: 'This practice is neither an élitist nor an
arcane act, as might be feared: it is an undertaking of radical attention

to the Real which is open to all who seek to foster it'.[1] Such radical contemplative attention is core to the Holy Spirit, which at this stage of illumination enables spiritual experience and encounter of the Trinitarian God by 'catching up the created realm into the life of God'.[2]

This missional journey, then, proceeds from a sense of weak participation or theosis through progressive experience, heading towards strong participation or theosis as a form of contemplative pilgrimage. However, to experience the Holy Spirit in contemplation is not something the individual seeker can control or domesticate. The Spirit after all is encountered trans-rationally, an experience that is unpredictable and wild: 'the Spirit always blows afresh to ... enlighten ... and it blows where it wills ... there is always also the deep propulsion to find in God, through the Spirit, the way to the true goal of human longing.'[3]

These spiritual encounters with the Trinitarian God through the Holy Spirit as source of the love of God enable further experience of the true self rather than the false self. This true self is that part of us which we can only encounter authentically through the love of God, which in turn emboldens the spiritual seeker to desire to encounter God more.

In so doing, and quite naturally, often without conscious awareness, a growing relational connection is beginning to be established between the seeker and God, in what some have called the 'I–Thou' relationship. As Coakley has said:

> When humans come ... into *authentic* relation with God as Trinity through the Spirit, their values and orders of 'hierarchy' change; they are not *imitating* God thereby, but rather being radically transformed by ecstatic participation in the Spirit.[4]

Participation into this stage of illumination then becomes an opportunity for a surprising and unpredictable spiritual adventure, which still requires the individual spiritual seeker to be brave, but where experiences of peace, transformation and encounters with God become part of the continuing missional journey.

In traditional understandings of the contemplative path, experience of the love of God through the Holy Spirit created the desire to want to live differently: to shift from a life dominated by the egoic false-self and attachments to the deadly sins that had to be faced in the crisis stage of purgation, to a God-led desire to live out the true self. This requires a contemplative discipline of practising the virtues, including: sobriety, innocence, generosity, patience/serenity, gladness, courage, awareness, magnanimity, humility and honesty. Again, living this way cannot be driven by the self-will, but by a life immersed in the love of God. This connects with the motivation of the SBNR in their spiritual seeking that I explored in Chapter 3 of 'seeking authenticity through responsibility'.

This connection between receiving the love of God and spiritual liberation is traditionally seen as core to this stage of illumination. For example, St Cyprian, a bishop in the early Christian church of North Africa, is reported to have said:

> When I had drunk the spirit from Heaven, and the second birth had restored me so as to make me a new man then immediately in a marvel-ous manner doubts began to be resolved, closed doors to be opened, dark places to be light; what before was difficult now seemed easy.[5]

Prayer practices therefore become key for this connection with God as the medium of encounter with God, when God reveals the divine presence in the experience of the individual. Such revelation is often with a still, small voice that needs discernment against the cacophony of competing sounds and distractions; through the use of contemplative prayer practices, however, it becomes possible to discern and experience God in the context of ordinary life.

For an example from the PhD study of the stage of illumination, I turn to the story of Jane.

For Jane, who was brought up in a strongly conservative church in Ireland, starting out at point 'A' in Figure 22 below, with an unstable family life, early experiences of Christianity were deeply formative. These led at an early age to the formation of faith and deep spirituality that took her from a space of pain and purgation to a form of union with God. However, coming to terms with her sexuality against the conservative teachings of the church, and a sense of God 'not being there for her in times of great need', led her to doubt her Christian faith and experience a sense of disconnection from conservative Christianity. This in turn led not only to a loss of faith, but also to deep pain and anguish and a concern not to be too open to any form of spirituality, as it could be further wounding.

Despite this, Jane acknowledged a sense of paradox, believing in the existence of something more spiritual but not religious, but also fearing it in equal measure. However, positive experience of some less conservative Christians, and a developing interest in spirituality through spiritual practices and participation in the dialogue group, led to a shift away from purgation into a space of illumination. For Jane, the stage of illumination was a time of openness, reconstruction and engagement with various forms of contemplative prayer practice. Yet she continued to struggle with issues of feeling overwhelmed, particularly because of

Figure 22: 'God's Kenosis, our Theosis': The Spiritual Journey of Jane

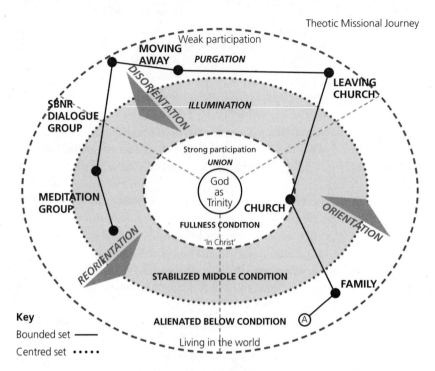

her vocation. Her work in an acute hospital unit in the NHS in London was a mixed blessing. Being a tough vocation with a cost, it meant that she had to manage her exposure to spirituality, and at times she found the unpredictability and wildness of trans-rational experience overwhelming. However, the combination of life, spiritual practices, dialogue and relationships with some Christians had resulted in an openness to more contemplative forms of Christian spirituality. Jane remains on a spiritual quest, continuing in the space of illumination and reconstructing a contemplative Christian faith while deconstructing her wounding experiences of more conservative forms of Christianity and the church. Jane's story reminds us how important it is that spiritual seekers like her are made to feel welcome: all curated contemplative missional events need to be a balance of being deeply hospitable while maintaining an open-endedness so that no one feels pressure to attend or not attend.

Immersive spiritual activities for the illumination stage

I return now to the considerations required for the immersive contemplative experience to support the spiritual seeker in the insight stage of illumination.

Table 3: Immersive Spiritual Elements for the Stage of Illumination

1. Stage of contemplative condition	2. *Lectio Divina* engagement with the 'I AM' statements of Jesus in the Gospel of John	3. Contemplative wisdom sharing	4. Associated contemplative prayer practices
Illumination Stabilized middle position Insight stage	'I AM the bread of life' (John 6.35, 41, 48, 51) 'I AM the way, the truth, and the life' (John 14.6) Resonances with ethnographic responses: God as ground of our being; God as divine consciousness	Going deeper in our spiritual journey: 1. Immersing ourselves in divine love for us 2. Loving surrender of the false self 3. Our becoming and pilgrimage 4. Experiencing God from within 5. Ebb and flow	Centering Prayer practice The Welcoming Prayer Waking well-being prayer End-of-Day well-being prayer Ignatian Contemplation on God's Love The Jesus Prayer in adapted form

Lectio Divina *explorations*

Continuing to develop the metaphorical approach to opening up a Christology in *Lectio Divina* reflections, I suggest using two of the 'I AM' statements in the Gospel of John: 'I AM the bread of life' (John 6.35, 41, 48, 51) and 'I AM the way, the truth, and the life' (John 14.6). These can be linked to the ethnographic fieldwork responses of 'God as ground of our being' and 'God as divine consciousness'.

Contemplative wisdom sharing

For this stage, there are five areas of shared wisdom that relate to going deeper with God in developing a Christian contemplative prayer practice under the heading of 'Going deeper in our spiritual journey'.

1 *Immersing ourselves in divine love for us*

Moving into the Illumination phase or the stabilized middle condition of the missional journey, the spiritual seeker will have a greater ability to encounter and receive the love of God not blunted by the consequences of trauma, pain, wounding or delusion. Elaine Heath's view of mission as 'healing from original woundedness' is essential to this process of contemplative mission: 'God the Father, Son, and Holy Spirit are all working together to bring about the healing of the cosmos. Their almightiness is revealed through kenosis.'[6]

This form of contemplative prayer requires a disposition of openness to the reception of God's love. This is not easy, but a focus on gratitude creates such an open disposition. To remember and think about someone we love, or something we enjoy or appreciate, all helps to create such a disposition of openness. The John Main 'anchor word' silent meditation practice helps establish the inner environment and focus for creating such a disposition of openness and the reception of the love of God, as does the Thomas Keating Centering Prayer practice.[7]

2 *Loving surrender of the false self*

In previous chapters, I explored the writings of Owen Barfield, Thomas Merton and others to explore how the egoic false self was promoted in a consumerist and materialistic culture, and how toxic and unhealthy this false self was to the individual. If the false self is not faced, then it is difficult to progress on the spiritual journey. Many of the deadly sins are about the negative consequences from forms of attachment to the egoic self. As demonstrated by those seeking to recover from forms of addiction, surrender of this way of living is an essential if healing and restoration are to follow. As Merton states:

> The obstacle is in our 'self' … the need to maintain our separate … egotistic will. It is when we refer all things to this outward and false 'self' that we alienate ourselves from reality and from God. It is then the false self that is our god, and we love everything for the sake of this self.[8]

Practising a form of surrender with prayers such as the full Serenity Prayer or the Welcoming Prayer that I referred to earlier is essential to maintain this sense of surrender of the false self, and requires consistent practice.[9] This is not about taking a punitive approach to the self, but rather a seeking to be the true self, to get away from defining the self through the false or fantasy self: 'Our inner self awakens, with a momentary flash, in the instant of recognition when we say "Yes!" to the indwelling Divine Persons.'[10]

3 Our becoming and pilgrimage

Continuing in this phase of illumination, the individual seeker might now begin to explore spiritual questions. This is where a Christian spiritual immersion group creates the opportunity for deeper reflection, using forms of *Lectio Divina* with Gospel texts concerned with the person of Jesus, mixed in with silence and prayerful contemplation. This can be a powerful opportunity for an open-ended Spirit-led activity using the stories of Jesus in an experiential way. For an example of good practice, I recommend the recent book on *Lectio Divina* and life as prayer by David Benner, a Canadian psychologist, spiritual director and writer.[11] Prayer practices at this stage, in addition to *Lectio Divina*, could include forms that embody pilgrimage and movement, such as labyrinth walking prayers, and prayers that take a spiritual journey, such as Ignatian forms of the contemplation of God's love.[12]

4 Experiencing God from within

This is the last element in the illumination stage, and important for the transition between illumination and seeking mystical union with God. As explored in the previous two chapters, utilizing the writing of Kathryn Tanner and Michael Gorman, this step is crucial for entering into full participation with God: the individual needs to become 'in Christ' as the shift from exploring Christian spirituality to a commitment to following the way of Christ. Drawing again on the 'God's Kenosis, our Theosis' model, this is a key stage for the inner awakening to the reality of God as Trinity through the unsettling of the Spirit from within, as Merton states: 'There exists some point at which I can meet God in a real and experimental contact with His infinite actuality. This is the "place" of God, His sanctuary – it is the point where my contingent being depends upon His love.'[13]

Contemplative prayers in this stage are about the discernment of the Spirit that speaks from within. They include the use of the ancient Jesus Prayer in the full version, which the Orthodox Church practises as the 'Prayer of the Heart': 'Lord Jesus Christ, Son of the living God, have mercy on me a sinner.'[14] The problem with this prayer for SBNR seekers is the concept of sin and sinners. If the SBNR seeker becomes aware of the problem of the egoic false self, as we explored with the 'loving surrender of the false self', and how this wounds the self, a connection might be possible with the concept of 'sin'. Rightly, however, some SBNR (including those quoted in this study) point out how the concept of sin has been used as a tool of power over people, leading to controlling and shaming abuse by the church:

> I really do get angry about the idea of sin as I find it very negative and very controlling ... so abusive to people who are made to feel guilty ... We know we are broken: what people need to hear is hope and love. (Sam, Life History Interview)

Accordingly, in a missional context the prayer has been adapted to the form: 'Lord Jesus Christ, Son of the living God, have mercy on me.' Or as I have been playing with it in my own context: 'Lord Jesus Christ, Son of God, have mercy on me a seeker.' This form seems to be easier for SBNR to use as it is not shaming, more a matter of fact.

Ultimately it is important not to live the Christian spiritual life out of any sense of self-will, self-determination or shame. Only when the individual is immersed in the love of God can we live this way of love. As Merton puts it: 'We must learn to realize that the love of God seeks us in every situation, and seeks our good. His inscrutable love seeks our awakening.'[15] Thinking again of the modes of SBNR seeking, this stage reflects the 'seeking mystical truth that lies within' and 'seeking meaning to guide one's life'.

5 Ebb and flow

The movement between purgation, illumination and union is rarely a linear one, but rather a cyclical pattern that ebbs and flows. Usually awakening has definite origin, but then the spiritual life becomes a flow between these three different stages; they are never a once-and-for-all set of experiences. In the next chapter, we will explore the significance of entering into a 'union' space as a moment of becoming 'in Christ' and crossing into strong participation; however, as we have seen in the missional stories of participants in the PhD study, people can choose not to be 'in Christ' as an expression of being dechurched. So this means that there are two oscillating realities in the spiritual journey of the Christian faith: the external self and the reality of 'orientation, disorientation and reorientation', and the internal self and the reality of purgation/dark night of the soul, illumination and union.

This does make the Christian contemplative missional journey messy and unpredictable, and hence the importance of daily prayer and meditation practices that seek to immerse the self in the love of God. In this way the contemplative missional journey is not unlike working the steps in the 12-step movements, where individuals oscillate between steps, having to go back to working previous steps when new unforeseen issues arise, and where they need to immerse the self in the 'higher power'. Those in the PhD study who had experience of 12-step fellowships responded positively to the God's Kenosis, our Theosis missional model.

Considerations for those who have a fragmented sense of self

Continuing further with the issue of the fragmented self identified in previous chapters, and the rejection of the human self promoted by some who come from the 'non-duality' spiritual tradition or Zen Buddhism, I suggest that great care should be taken when thinking of those who carry deep wounds from life experiences that have resulted in a fragmented sense of self into adulthood. As we have noted, for one participant of this study, meditation became a deeply distressing experience, indicating that meditation in their situation may be counter-indicated. For Graham Cray, the therapeutic needs of the individual might be masked by their desire for spirituality:

> There are a larger number of 'seekers', on a therapeutic quest, looking for healing more than spirituality. The contemporary climate is therapeutic not religious. People hunger not for personal salvation ... but for the feeling, the momentary illusion, of personal well-being, health and psychic security.[16]

It seems to me that, as we have discovered in previous chapters, many SBNR seekers are spiritually wounded and seek spiritual freedom from these wounds that are commonly experienced as pain. While I agree with Cray that many do need therapeutic intervention to address mental health issues, particularly in the purgation/dark night stage, to say that these are not at the same time spiritual issues is for me too dualistic. I would suggest that, for many, the combination of both therapy and the pursuit of spirituality can be a restorative process of healing. As I have explored previously, drawing on the work of Elaine Heath, this is also a missional journey of healing from original wounds, hence the need for this to be non-directive and led by individuals themselves. As I have argued, this approach to mission emphasizes the restorative, kenotic love of God, and God's desire for our restoration and human flourishing as the mission of God. I argue that this is the main motivation for running the dialogue, meditation and immersive contemplative groups.

However, research does suggest that around 8 per cent of people might experience adverse effects from some forms of meditation that can trigger anxiety and other mental health issues.[17] For individuals who have experienced forms of psychosis, research suggests that care should be taken to warn that, for a small minority of people, meditation may not work, and may not assist a participant to develop a more integrated sense of self. I would suggest that in this situation the individual may need the support and skills of a spiritual director – if possible, one who is also a trained psychotherapist skilled in Cognitive Behavioural Therapy (CBT). With this in mind, I have suggested the inclusion of the following sentences into the meditation script in Appendix 1:

> For the majority of people, research has shown that forms of meditation help reduce stress, and promote integration, health and well-being. For a small minority, meditation might not help, particularly those who have experienced psychosis. If this is you then please do discuss meditation with your doctor or therapist. For all those who are spiritually searching on the path of inner awakening, we always recommend the need for a trained spiritual director or mentor to accompany you.[18]

Regarding the rejection of the self as promoted by the non-duality movement, some forms of Buddhism and Eastern esoteric religions, I suggest that such an approach can be dangerous and harmful and not consonant with Christianity. As Vernon stated when I interviewed him:

> People can get very hooked on the idea of the 'no-self'. I mean I think it's partly a reaction against the individualism of modern times ... take them to the Maudsley Hospital, then they will see people with no sense of self and it is a complete disaster, it is an absolutely hideous experience.[19]

I affirm that in the missional practice of the dialogue, meditation and immersive contemplative groups, a growing and strengthened sense of the human self is an essential aspect of this approach to noticing the presence of God. In previous chapters I have emphasized how *missio Dei*, *imago Dei*, *missio in Dei* as participation in God is the basis for a growing focus on a greater, or restored and healed, sense of the divinely loved human self. This has the practical implication that facilitators of the proposed mission activities with the SBNR need to be upfront about believing in the centrality of the human self as a gift of God.

In the next chapter, we turn to the last stage of the God's Kenosis, our Theosis contemplative model, that of 'union'.

Notes

1 Sarah Coakley, *God, Sexuality, and the Self: An Essay 'On the Trinity'* (Cambridge: Cambridge University Press, 2019), p. 88.

2 Coakley, *God, Sexuality, and the Self*, p. 113.

3 Coakley, *God, Sexuality, and the Self*, p. 267.

4 Coakley, *God, Sexuality, and the Self*, pp. 321–2; emphasis original.

5 Anon, 'Purgative and Illuminative Stages', Societas Ignatianorum, IGNATIANS, 2023, https://societyofignatians.com/how-we-are-equipped/ignatian-asceto-mystical-equipping/ascending-the-triple-storey-mountain/purgative-and-illuminative-stages/ (accessed 08.08.2024).

6 Elaine A. Heath, *The Mystic Way of Evangelism: A Contemplative Vision for Christian Outreach* (Grand Rapids, MI: Baker Academic, 2008), p. 42.

7 See https://contemplativeoutreach.org.uk/centering-prayer/.

8 Thomas Merton, *New Seeds of Contemplation* (New York: New Directions Books, 1972), p. 21.

9 See the original full version of the Serenity Prayer: https://www.prayerfoundation.org/dailyoffice/serenity_prayer_full_version.htm.

10 Merton, *New Seeds of Contemplation*, p. 42.

11 David G. Benner, *Opening to God: Lectio Divina and Life as Prayer* (London: IVP, 2021).

12 See https://labyrinth.org.uk/index.html and https://www.ignatianspirituality.com/ignatian-prayer/the-spiritual-exercises/contemplation-on-the-love-of-god/.

13 Merton, *New Seeds of Contemplation*, p. 37.

14 Father Lazarus, trans., *On the Prayer of Jesus: From the Ascetic Essays of Bishop Ignatius Brianchaninov* (Boston, MA: New Seeds, 2005), pp. 2–4.

15 Merton, *New Seeds of Contemplation*, pp. 15–16.

16 Graham Cray, 'Doors to the Sacred through Fresh Expressions of Church', in *Doorways to the Sacred: Developing Sacramentality in Fresh Expressions of Church*, ed. Phil Potter and Ian Mobsby (London: Canterbury Press, 2017), p. 6.

17 M. Farias, E. Maraldi, K. C. Wallenkampf and G. Lucchetti, 'Adverse Events in Meditation Practices and Meditation-Based Therapies: A Systematic Review', *Acta Psychiatrica Scandinavica* 142, no. 5 (2020), pp. 374–93.

18 See Appendix 1 where this passage has been inserted.

19 Mark Vernon, 'Barfield and the Evolution of Consciousness', transcription following Zoom interview, 18 December 2020.

9

Union: The Transformation Stage

Humanity was created for union with God, capable of being made
one with God, called to be the place of God's indwelling.[1]

Finally, we come to the last and critical stage of union, where the spiritual
seeker comes to a significant threshold between Kathryn Tanner's weak
and strong participation, passing from Charles Taylor's stable middle
condition to the fullness condition. Regarding mission, this threshold
marks the decision of the individual to become Christian and 'in Christ'
and therefore also has deep sacramental transformative significance.

As I have explored in previous chapters, this end stage is particularly
focused on the fulfilment of the mission model and of a deep theology of
theosis. As Michael Austin has stated:

At its heart, *theosis* is best understood as a transformative union with
Christ, made possible by God's grace and power in the life of the
cooperative believer. In other words, *theosis* is *a progressively transformational and loving union between the believer and Christ*. This
relationship includes a shared mind and heart, but it is also an em-

powering union that is grounded in God's love and its transformative effects on the heart and mind of the believer who seeks him via a variety of spiritual disciplines.[2]

Traditionally, the shift from the stage of illumination to that of union also marks a shift from cataphatic to apophatic spirituality. In all the previous stages, emphasis has been on the cataphatic and an array of spiritual experience that Elaine Heath has defined as 'a path of spiritual advancement in which images, forms, subjective spiritual experience, creation, incarnation, and discursive thought all lead to union with God'.[3] Continuing into the apophatic, the emphasis is on 'unknowing' or the limits of knowing, and the need for encounter of God beyond words as we seek to 'see through a glass darkly', where the new Christian seeks to encounter God beyond an approach solely based on God's self-revelation.[4]

For example, Heath distinguishes the cataphatic from the apophatic by the biblical use of the metaphorical language for the Trinity, Father, Son and Spirit, as God's self-revelation. This allows the spiritual seeker to experience God through these terms. Although they are true, there is for the apophatic more to the three persons of the Trinity than these terms, and there are many other biblical images and metaphors that God has given us. The apophatic seeks to get beyond the need to 'fixate on specific aspects of God's self-revelation as if they were exhaustive ... when God is actually much more than Father and the many other images God has given us ... we cannot know God exhaustively.'[5] God cannot be known or described as just one more term or metaphor; all language and terminology for God ultimately fails. The apophatic emphasizes the need to let go of our understandings and allow God to approach us autonomously beyond our fixed understandings and projections.

Rather than the individual seeking to construct an understanding of God through various ongoing 'I–Thou' spiritual experiences, the apophatic tradition suggests surrendering this self-directed need, and instead allowing God to do the constructing from within the inner self. This then draws on wordless surrender-based forms of contemplative prayer to a God you cannot see or know. Although it sounds abstract, such an approach is deeply and 'awesomely intimate', where the Christian is 'truly called to share not only in what God has, but in what God is'.[6]

In the immersive contemplative resources below are three apophatic prayer resources, but this does not mean that the spiritual seeker and new Christian should suddenly abandon all the cataphatic prayer resources that have been helpful so far in their contemplative spiritual journey. It is important not to be too purist here. I would want to argue that a healthy contemplative life should include both the cataphatic and the apophatic. At any meal, overeating one form of nutrient to the detriment of others is not balanced or healthy – the same with prayer. Developing an apophatic contemplative prayer life can be frustrating, so having a balanced diet of both/and cataphatic and apophatic prayer practices will be essential to help the spiritual seeker become a new or returning Christian.

To illustrate this important stage of transformation and union, I turn to the missional journey of Calum, as illustrated in Figure 23.

Figure 23: 'God's Kenosis, our Theosis': The Spiritual Journey of Calum

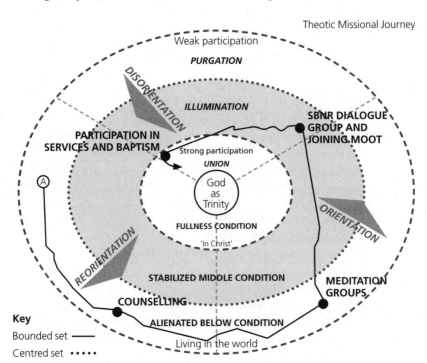

At the time of the PhD research, Calum was in his fifties and lived with his partner in north London. He had previously completed graduate studies but was now an unemployed sales manager on a low income. His spiritual journey began through an emerging interest in spirituality following therapy after a period of depression.

For Calum, there was a strong sense that there had to be more to life. He found the missional dialogue group after attending a well-being meditation group hosted by a missional community in central London. The combination of attending meditation and the dialogue group created the environment for Calum to have a number of progressive awakening experiences. These began in a sense of disorientation, but as he allowed himself to suspend his disbelief in trans-rational experience and effectively say 'Yes' to God to open up direct experience of God, Calum progressed in his spiritual journey.

Calum had grown up in a strictly atheistic family with a focus on scientific rationalism as the conveyor of truth. Spirituality was a totally new quest for him. Significant in Calum's spiritual journey is the place of pain and depression as a catalyst for spiritual explorations, and the importance of reaching beyond scientific rationalism as the only trust-worthy container of 'truth' and recognizing the place of spirituality as a means of knowing and exploring.

Turning to Calum's spiritual journey as expressed in Figure 23, Calum began his spiritual questing, at point 'A', after experiencing depression and attending counselling, signified by the bottom-left black dot. At that point he understood himself as an atheist drawing on scientific rationalism as a way of life, particularly regarding his valuing of what is important. Counselling opened the path of a form of spirituality as a profound moment of awakening. At this stage of life, Calum was not OK and voiced several times that he knew his life was impoverished. He turned to searching on the internet, exploring forms of spirituality and spiritual resources, which resulted in his coming and joining the medi-tation group with Moot at St Mary Aldermary Church in the City of London, which was one of the six sites of the PhD research.

Interestingly in Calum's story, the place of meditation was key to keeping healthy. Like many spiritual seekers, Calum moved from inner awakening to the stage of purgation quite quickly, as the reality of his brokenness and dysfunctionality became a painful and dark experience of life. However, the practice of dialogue and meditation allowed for an extended time of awakening and purgation in Calum's case.

This meditation practice, together with the experience of other forms of meditation in other religions, resulted in Calum's moving from the internal space of purgation or alienated below condition, to the internal space of illumination or stabilized middle condition, where life was not quite so wounding. Calum began to get to know some of the people in the meditation group, and from this began to attend the SBNR dialogue group of the PhD study, marked by the top-right black dot. This was a significant time for Calum, although not straightforward because of problems over the need to disassociate himself from Christian forms of fundamentalism and thus overcome the negatives concerning church and Christianity. However, being part of Moot, an inclusive and con-templative form of missional ecclesial community where the meditation and dialogue were hosted, provided the basis for an ongoing progressive experience of God's revelation as a spiritual pilgrimage. In this way Calum was enabled to explore both church and Christianity by experiencing them relationally. In time this led him to a desire to be baptized as a Christian, which took him into the decision of becoming 'in Christ' and into the mysteries of following the way of Jesus, and therefore the Trinity, into greater union. Calum had experienced many awakening moments on his own unique spiritual journey resulting in the establishment of a Christian faith, where he had responded in theosis or desire for deep relationship with God in response to the kenosis and deep love of God in a 'centred-set' form of mission. This internal journey of experiencing meditation and dialogue, as well as other contemplative events hosted by Moot, was clearly significant. However, the external journey is still uncomfortable for Calum: the tension of owning being a Christian, which is at odds with his whole previous way of life, together with the discomfort of fundamentalist and unhealthy forms of Christianity and church, are clearly external sources of concern for his continuing spiritual journey.

Immersive spiritual activities for the union stage

I turn now to the immersive spiritual contemplative resources to support the spiritual seeker at this point of transformation in the stage of union, as illustrated below in Table 4.

Table 4: Immersive Contemplative Content for Transformation and Union Stage

1. Stage of contemplative condition	2. *Lectio Divina* engagement with the 'I AM' statements of Jesus in the Gospel of John	3. Contemplative wisdom sharing	4. Associated contemplative prayer practices
Mystical union with God Fullness condition Transformation stage	'I AM the resurrection and the life' (John 11.25) 'I AM the true vine' (John 15.1, 5) Resonances with ethnographic responses: God as multifaceted God, as Creator, Redeemer and Spirit Jesus as God-human: mystic liberator and teacher	Encountering the divine source and threshold in our spiritual journey: 1. Choosing to follow 2. Communion and mystical union 3. Resilience and endurance	The three-doorways contemplative prayer using the words 'I no longer live but Christ lives in me'. Jesus Prayer in original form The Examen

Lectio Divina *explorations*

This stage is critical: not only to have a strong sense of the significance of Jesus, but to be willing to become 'in Christ'. The following 'I AM' metaphors from Jesus as recorded in the Gospel of John are suggested: 'I AM the resurrection and the life' (John 11.25), 'I AM the true vine' (John 15.1, 5). Regarding connection with terminology from the ethnographic fieldwork, this could include references to the Holy Trinity, such as God as multifaceted, God as Creator, Redeemer and Spirit, and Jesus as the God-human: mystic liberator and teacher.

Contemplative wisdom sharing

There are three critical stages correlating to becoming Christian. It is hoped that the content of this stage will assist the SBNR seeker to commit to a contemplative form of Christian discipleship.

1 Choosing to follow

The first step into this stage of becoming 'in Christ' is the choice to seek to follow Jesus as an act of free will to respond to the kenotic love of God. It is critical in the sharing of wisdom that this is not manipulated but a freely chosen next step. There are a number of contemplative prayers that can be used at this stage. A good example is the contemplative 'three-doorways' prayer using the words 'I no longer live but Christ lives in me' as a prayer focus;[7] or the use of Taizé prayer chants as contemplative practice, such as 'Bless the Lord my soul, bless God's holy name, bless the Lord my soul, who leads me into life.'[8] Such an approach needs to be made, as Chatfield says:

> with the tools of prayer. It turns us inward, in the primary act of obedience, to relationship restored by God in Christ. This is the true worship demanded of the disciple: 'Follow me' means first of all, 'return to me'. Prayer is a converting action.[9]

2 Communion and mystical union

Using the 'God's Kenosis, our Theosis' model and its centred-set understanding of the missional journey, mystical union crosses over into what Tanner identifies as 'strong participation' in God, where the individual not only recognizes Christ, but becomes a committed follower of Jesus, which will involve some sacramental form of baptism or confirmation. As we have explored in previous chapters, this is about the mystical path of experiencing and being drawn into the relationality of God through forms of prayer and meditation. This form of deeper mystical union is where our being and God's become deeply connected as a form of theosis, as Michael Gama states: 'Theosis was assumed as the ultimate destiny of the believer, and it was on the foundation of this assumption that the fathers built their theological systems of the incarnation and Christology.'[10]

At this stage, one further connection could be made to the original form of the Jesus Prayer. Gama reminds us that this prayer became extremely important to the ancient desert monastics because it was deeply transformative as a converting prayer practice:

> The Jesus prayer ... 'Lord Jesus Christ, Son of God, have mercy on me, a Sinner.' The hesychastic prayer rule often included the repetition of this prayer, at times accompanied by particular bodily posture and rhythmic breathing ... monks, then, were essentially claiming to have experienced God ... claiming to have experienced 'true initiation in this lifetime into the deifying grace of God.' ... 'direct and personal knowledge of God ... through a mystical communion with Him'.[11]

There are a number of contemplative prayer resources that can encourage this form of mystical union. Examples are the Carmelite prayer practices of Elizabeth of the Trinity, and Ignatian Imaginative Prayer, in which you place yourself creatively into a Gospel story of encounter with Jesus.[12] This form of contemplation relates to the modes of SBNR spiritual journeying as desire for mystical union with God both by 'seeking mystical truth that lies within' and also by 'seeking mystical truth that lies outside of the self', as external transformation and the motivation to be saved from the ravages of existing in the complexity of the modern world.

3 Resilience and endurance

Finally in this process of God's Kenosis, our Theosis is the support of new Christians to develop resilience and endurance. As I raised in previous chapters, for many religious communities the central teaching they draw on is Jesus' Great Commandment, which can be summarized as, 'Hear, O Israel: the Lord our God, the Lord is one; you shall love the Lord your God with all your heart, and with all your soul, and with all your mind, and with all your strength', and 'You shall love your neighbour as yourself' (Mark 12.29–31). A central application of this text is to focus on the essential desire of the *Via Positiva* form of contemplation, that of 'receiving the love of God, to be able to love yourself, to be able to love others'. One example of this form of prayer is the Examen which seeks to discern God's presence as love in the details of your life on a daily basis. Knowing that we continue in cycles of experiences of blessing and testing/suffering, it is critical that the new Christian should have the opportunity to deepen their contemplative path, drawing on the prayer practices I have identified in the table above, to assist with endurance.

Designing a potential phone application and supporting writings

There is an important and complex issue here concerning how to promote healthy spiritual practices and how to be 'in but not of' contemporary culture. Earlier in this immersive experience I promoted the need for technological abstinence in a culture addicted to smartphones and being online. However, at the same time, this technology provides an opportunity for prayer and meditation applications that could be used by an SBNR seeker having a spiritual pause or break at work, or when commuting or travelling in the rhythm of their day. I believe it is possible to promote a spiritual rhythm that balances times of technological abstinence with careful use of the phone and applications to promote exploration and experience of Christian spirituality. Therefore, drawing on this immersive contemplative experience of Christian spirituality, an ongoing learning event using contemplative prayer practices in a non-directive way could be further developed into a phone application.

This could include powerful images from nature with relaxing music and a number of different reflections. These could also include audio and written versions of various prayer practices that could be used by spiritual seekers when they are on their own, as well as links to opportunities for people to join in groups that could meet in person. Further, these could link in with the John Main adapted silent meditation groups, or with the dialogue groups, as well as promote immersive Christian spirituality experiences. A potential book could hold source materials for the three sections of this contemplative spiritual journey, with a compilation of prayer practices written in a language appropriate for the SBNR.

The practical considerations for churches hosting SBNR missional activities using the proposed God's Kenosis, our Theosis model

The greatest challenge concerning the proposed approach of this book to missional engagement with the SBNR and the church is the separation in traditional forms of evangelism between mission practice and pastoral practice. I am advocating an approach to mission that draws on both gentle non-directive evangelism and healing. In my experience of working as a missioner in the Church of England, mission and evangelism are largely focused on providing courses such as Alpha and forms of apologetics that assume a modernist culture by using forms of rational argument, focused on thinking rather than on spiritual experience and the heart. By the same token, pastoral care becomes the preserve of priests and other licensed ministers to support those who are largely Christian. The present book, by contrast, focuses on the healing approach to mission, seeking restoration from 'original wounding'. This more contemplative approach to mission with the SBNR requires a radical and non-dualistic relationship between mission and pastoral care through the medium of prayer, meditation and dialogue. It requires the joining up of mission, evangelism and spirituality.

The work of the Blackfriars Community in London, pioneer/mission-ers and other missional communities engaging with spiritual seekers, including the SBNR, demonstrates what is possible when there is posi-tive engagement from Christians and the church with this more holistic understanding.[13] The Blackfriars Community, as a contemplative Fresh Expression of church inspired by new monasticism, practised the sensi-tivity, openness and availability necessary for engagement with the SBNR. Unfortunately, as we have heard in the stories of the SBNR of this study, Christians and the church have more generally left the SBNR feeling judged, shamed and ridiculed. Forms of the church that feel their tradition and interests fit well with contemplative prayer, meditation, dialogue, hospitality and generosity to SBNR spiritual seekers could easily be involved in this practice and model of mission as God's Kenosis, our Theosis. I believe there is the potential to do this well with individ-ual churches of the liberal Catholic and open evangelical traditions, or where they are specifically contemplative in practice and ethos. With these traditions in mind, it should be possible for some form of engage-ment in this mission practice in the mixed ecology of many Anglican and Roman Catholic parishes, Methodist circuits and local free churches. I am reminded of the prophetic words of David Tacey:

What if it [the church] ignores the present challenge or does not care enough to take up a dialogue with the world? The yearning for sacredness, spiritual meaning, security, and personal engagement with the spirit are the primary needs and longings of the contemporary world. What is happening if the institutions of faith are so bound up in themselves and resistant to change that they cannot make some contribution to these needs? Our contemporary situation is full of ironies and paradoxes. Chief among these is that our secular society has given birth to sense of the sacred, and yet our sacred traditions are failing to recognise the spiritual potential.[14]

Drawing briefly on the work of Avery Dulles, a Roman Catholic ecclesiologist, I am struck by the connection between forms of missional church like the Blackfriars Community and Dulles' 'Church as mystical communion' and 'Church as sacrament'.[15] It seems to me that if a local church wanted to explore an appropriate form of contemplative SBNR mission practice, the resulting ecclesial form would need to model a combination of 'Church as sacrament' and 'Church as spiritual fraternity'. Church as spiritual fraternity emphasizes an ecclesial form that is deeply relational and participative, a communion of relationships with a high regard of the church as the mystical body of Christ.[16]

Dulles emphasizes that this relates to the biblical writing of St Paul concerning 'mutual union, mutual concern, and mutual dependence of the members of the local community upon one another'.[17] This resonates with what Tanner has written and I have explored in previous chapters about those who are 'in Christ': it is the gathering of all those who have committed themselves to the way of Christ and to seeking ever stronger participation in God in theosis. As Dulles states: 'The Church is made up of all who are brought into union with God by supernatural grace flowing from Christ as head ... The Church is seen as a community of persons each of whom is individually free.'[18]

Church as mystical communion therefore sees mission as aiming to 'lead men into communion with the divine'. This resonates with the biblical notion of koinonia, a relational union found in the book of Acts and in Pauline descriptions of the church as the body of Christ. The concept of church as sacrament builds on the idea of church as mystical communion, presenting it as 'a kind of sacrament of intimate union with God and of the unity of all mankind; that is, she is a sign and instrument of such union and unity'.[19]

By implication this does mean that this missional model of God's Kenosis, our Theosis will not fit well with ecclesiological forms that have more conservative theological bases. As Dulles has said, Church as sacrament does not fit easily with expressions of the church based on more conservative Protestant ecclesiology.[20] In short, this approach makes two assumptions: that people need to know that they are loved by God, to experience God's unconditional love as grace, in order to then be able to face their own brokenness and selfishness, transformed by the love of God; and that the path to faith, of being 'in Christ', the path of theosis, is open to all who seek to respond to this kenotic love of God.

This is important, as one of the great concerns of the SBNR of this study is to avoid encountering or being identified with what they call 'fundamentalist' Christians. For example, Calum was extremely concerned about this when considering joining a church and becoming Christian:

> I wanted to continue with others, specifically Moot. I'm still not sure that I'm hearing the same message as fundamentalist Christians but that has ceased to bother me. (Calum, Interview, 14 June 2021)

Teressa voiced great concern about the manipulation and control of 'fundamentalist religion and Christianity':

> Fundamentalism is rule-book religion ... It's a complete perversion of spirituality ... People are offered a very easy identity, and plug people into a group and belong and are unfortunately manipulated by these very real spiritual needs. But it is a complete perversion and abuse. (Teressa, City dialogue group, 31 May 2018)

For Caleb, there was a strong concern to avoid religions that expected conformity:

> Religions have created resentment which is why so many people think that religions have no truths or resources in them ... This is the danger of religious cultures, you end up with too many rules, and too much just thinking. The danger of fundamentalism causing fundamentalist conformity. (Caleb, Borough dialogue group, 30 January 2019)

Taking these responses together, it is extremely important that the ethos of this approach to mission should be reflected in the DNA of the church tradition. Otherwise there is the great danger not only that SBNR seekers might be put off joining a particular group and missional initiative, but also that their encounters with Christians associated with different types of churches might actually put them off Christianity entirely and create dechurched people. I suggest that good practice requires the church tradition to be fully accepting of contemplative Christianity and practices, as well as being able to be generous with SBNR spiritual seekers. In the Anglican tradition, I suggest that church traditions that are liberal Catholic, middle of the road, or open evangelical and committed to contemplative prayer and meditation, are best placed to support this form of mission activity.

Further considerations regarding a contemplative worship service that relates to the content of the God's Kenosis, our Theosis missional model

The point of entering the union stage of the model is a critical and difficult time for spiritual seekers when they have reached the place of feeling ready to become a Christian. Largely this is because of the prevalent negative stereotype (which is sometimes true) of Christians and the church as being antithetical to spirituality, or sometimes it can be a reaction to fundamentalism as the antithesis of spirituality and spiritual seekers. For example, only yesterday a colleague was criticized by a Church of England archdeacon for using the word 'divine' rather than 'God': the word was regarded as being too New Age whereas it was, rightly, intended to be contextual.

We need to remember that some of our churches are still dominated by the immanent cultural frame sustaining a very rationalist modernist world view and language, when our culture has firmly shifted into post-modernity and post-secularism. Many of our worship services and gatherings are therefore predominantly rationalist and full of words: they allow for no silence and are often the opposite of contemplative. I therefore recommend adopting a new service format tailored for those with a contemplative focus. I have implemented a Sunday evening service in three New Monastic Communities and two mixed-ecology parish churches, specifically designed to host contemplative gatherings. This was critical to help new Christian spiritual seekers to engage in a Christian worship service that is spacious, uses silence, is careful about language and uses familiar prayer practices. I include an example of this type of liturgy in Appendix 2. The leap from the God's Kenosis, our Theosis approach to formation to a traditional Anglican liturgical service is, in my opinion, a bridge too far. Finding a home in a contemplative service helps new Christians to land and contextualize themselves into this situation.

Those facilitating this contemplative approach to mission should remember that individuals at this stage will be fragile and a bit anxious.

They will ebb and flow between the stages of purgation, illumination and union triggered by encounters with Christians and life situations. Spiritual seekers will need a lot of encouragement and support, particularly when it comes to forms of baptism and confirmation to mark their becoming 'in Christ'. Often this will be seen as a negative decision by family, friends and work colleagues, as if they had been brainwashed by a cult. I know this as it was my own personal experience when I became a Christian as a 19-year-old atheist spiritual seeker. With this in mind it would be good to encourage the new Christian to develop an independent relationship with a properly trained spiritual director with a proven record of supporting those who are coming from a more spiritual contemplative perspective. I can happily recommend, for example, the London Centre for Spiritual Direction and their online register, and would avoid any spiritual director who has not completed training and does not have supervised practice.

Regarding further content for the new Christian and the forming of contemplative Christian community, I would recommend consideration of the following questions:

- What is a spiritual retreat, and where is good to go (with a daily spiritual meeting)?
- How do I begin to approach the Bible as a new Christian from a more contemplative perspective?
- What is church? How do I relate to it and healthily participate in it?
- What happens at Christian spirituality centres and what is available near me?
- How do I cope with interacting with Christians who are different from me, those I find very difficult?
- What are some of the good and the challenging things about the Anglican Church and tradition?
- How do I cope with the ongoing challenge of faith and doubt?
- How do I build resilience when my family, friends and colleagues see Christianity negatively?

Further suggested training

I now run regular online training events through my website (ianmobsby. net) that include training in running SBNR adapted John Main missional meditation groups, running SBNR missional dialogue groups, an introduction to missional New Monastic Communities and much more. Do get in touch if I can be of assistance.

Notes

1 A. M. Allchin, *Participation in God: A Forgotten Strand in Anglican Tradition* (London: DLT, 1988), p. 6.

2 Michael W. Austin, 'The Doctrine of Theosis: A Transformational Union with Christ', *Journal of Spiritual Formation & Soul Care* 8, no. 2 (2015), p. 186, https://dallaswillardcenter.com/wp-content/uploads/2016/03/Finalist_Doctrine-of-Theosis_Austin.pdf; italics and emphasis original.

3 Elaine A. Heath, *The Mystic Way of Evangelism: A Contemplative Vision for Christian Outreach* (Grand Rapids, MI: Baker Academic, 2008), p. 8.

4 Heath, *The Mystic Way of Evangelism*, p. 17.

5 Heath, *The Mystic Way of Evangelism*, p. 17.

6 Allchin, *Participation in God*, p. 31.

7 See https://rodwhite.net/three-doorways-contemplative-prayer/.

8 See https://www.taize.fr/spip.php?page=chant&song=256&lang=en.

9 Adrian Chatfield, 'Prayer and Mission: Entering into the Ways of God', *Anvil Journal* 32, no. 1 (2016), p. 11.

10 Michael P. Gama, *Theosis: Patristic Remedy for Evangelical Yearning at the Close of the Modern Age* (Eugene, OR: Wipf & Stock, 2017), p. 106.

11 Gama, *Theosis*, p. 123.

12 Jennifer Moorcroft, *He is My Heaven: The Life of Elizabeth of the Trinity* (Washington DC: ICS Publications, 2015), pp. 103–12; David L. Fleming, *What is Ignatian Spirituality?* (Chicago, IL: Loyola Press, 2008), pp. 55–60.

13 See http://www.blackfriarscommunity.org including 'Hamilton's Well' in Hamilton, Ontario, Canada. See https://www.meetup.com/hamiltons-well-community-wellness-and-exploration/.

14 David Tacey, *The Spirituality Revolution: The Emergence of Contemporary Spirituality* (London: Routledge, 2004), p. 20.

15 Avery Dulles, *Models of the Church*, expanded edn (New York: Doubleday, 2002), pp. 39–54, 55–67.

16 Dulles, *Models of the Church*, pp. 40–1.

17 Dulles, *Models of the Church*, p. 43.

18 Dulles, *Models of the Church*, pp. 43, 36.

19 Dulles, *Models of the Church*, p. 56.

20 Dulles, *Models of the Church*, p. 67.

10

Afterword

> [T]he devout Christian of the future will either be a 'mystic',
> one who has 'experienced' something, or he will cease
> to be anything at all.[1]

Imagine for a moment what it would be like to have more contemplative-focused Christians involved in the church, and for my context, more contemplative Anglican Churches. How would it affect synods? Dioceses? Deaneries? Spiritual wisdom? A deeper discipleship, kindness and generosity? There would be a profound difference, I would hope.

One of the continuing consequences of the declining presence and influence of Anglican religious orders and communities of the various traditions has been the loss of these mitochondrial powerhouses to the wider church. For nearly 200 years, beginning with the Oxford Movement (some 500 years after Henry VIII closed them), they have lived and breathed mystical and contemplative prayer, spirituality and practice, contributing to parishes and dioceses alike not just in the Church of England, but around the Anglican Communion.

Now, these communities are far from perfect, and some that exist today can be very conservative and as hard and disconnected as other elements of the dysfunctional church. Nevertheless, over the years, monks, nuns and friars in traditional communities, alongside some of the newer acknowledged religious communities, contribute and keep the flame for contemplative Christianity alive.

Ironically, at a time when contemporary culture is increasingly focusing on spirituality and spiritual seeking, and we see an increasing cultural context of spiritual hunger outside the churches that resonates so deeply with a contemplative mission approach, we find the Church increasingly weakened to the point that it is not able to respond to this new opportunity because of a lack of those who have the wisdom and experience to lead. Further, until recently most dioceses had spirituality advisors on their staff, but this too has gone out of fashion as roles have shifted more to business advisor-type roles rather than core specialists reflecting the Christian faith. This is therefore a double bind. For a very long time the church has struggled to communicate the faith in a culture of modernity dictated by the dominance of rationalism, and now in a time of post-secularism, where people are again interested in prayer, meditation and spirituality, the church is unable or at times unwilling to engage.

However, even though the church seems so disconnected from these opportunities of enabling post-secular spiritual seekers to enter into the 'God's Kenosis, our Theosis' model, I remain hopeful. I do believe that God the Holy Spirit is prompting the church to dig deep, to engage with post-secular spiritual tourists to enable them to encounter God through contemplative prayer resources, to become co-travelling Christian pilgrims. This is the central purpose of the model, to enable spiritual tourists to become contemplative Christian pilgrims.

In the middle of a declining church and church traditions that are increasingly in conflict, clinging on to the vestiges of Christendom expressed as broken communion, some still continue to seek to exclude those who are generally marginalized in the churches anyway. People, their lives and identities, are reduced down to 'issues' of homophobia, misogyny, racism and classism, which does so much harm to these affected groupings and damages the church and God's mission. Yet in this complete mess there are still Christians who get the contemplative traditions and God's love mission to the world, who grasp the potential for real engagement with a more open-ended Christopraxis and a contemplative approach to mission and pioneering.

Would it not be amazing if, from these little seeds, a small but significant contemplative movement for mission was to grow? For me personally it has taken a lifetime to have the spiritual maturity to appreciate, understand and see how important the neglected Christian contemplative traditions are, with their deep resources forged out of forms of religious community going right back to the desert mothers and fathers. The potential for significant impact using a contemplative model and approach to mission remains great.

But there are, as I see it, three significant threats. First, so many older Christians whose framework remains rational modernity would rather see the church die than change. This just reveals a lack of discipleship and focus on Jesus. The second, as I have said earlier, is the malignant effect of the immanent cultural frame that holds back so much. The third, and more troubling for me personally, is that so many Christians I meet are negative about meditation, prayer and the contemplative traditions because they challenge the whole attractional, commodified church as social product, and the overprivileging of worship services to the detriment of community and mission. In my experience, too many churchgoing Christians think that meditation and silence are dodgy and New Age!

Close friends I made when I became a Christian in my late teens are no longer Christian or attend church; they experience it as controlling and unresourcing, which continues to break my heart and at the same time makes me angry. The Christianity they experienced was conceptually rationalist and if there was anything experiential around God and Jesus then it tended to be at best a charismatic group worship service. The contemplative was never opened up to them, and they now have little interest.

Yet I do believe that a church with a prayerful and deep contemplative heart can override these debilitating realities of today's market society.

In a small way, I hope the vision of the God's Kenosis, our Theosis conceptual framework, theology and practices will seem sustainable and not too threatening for many churches who get contemplation and want to be involved in this form of missional endeavour. I know from practical experience that exposure to the resources of the contemplative traditions can be transformative for everyone when practised deeply, with a willingness to let go of our contemporary culture's desire for control and dominance of the ego-self.

New Monasticism and new forms of contemplative ecclesial communities are still small in number, but they have already contributed so much, in and outside the parish and diocesan structures. Yes, many have remained fragile and small, but they nevertheless still continue to contribute a great deal. I continue to be really excited to see the potential of these communities growing as a response to contemplative forms of mission, which I think will not only transform the individual spiritual seekers but, potentially, transform the church and wider society. The alternative – and it is a very real danger – is of even more religious fundamentalism or dumbed-down commodified church. I do believe that Karl Rahner was right: if the Christian of the future is not a contemplative, then there will be very little left of a deep authentic Christianity. I remain hopeful, because the church has had many critical epoch crises in the past, and I trust God that this is just another one of these, and that contemplative Christianity can contribute to the renewal of the church with a deeper discipleship and mission practice.

I hope in collaboration with others to develop more resources and learning opportunities to advance this contemplative approach to mission, and I have seen how amazing it is when these new communities come together around contemplative practice – people who were formerly dechurched or unchurched and would never have gone near Christians or the church. The potential is great if we are willing to try out this approach.[2]

If you have been moved and challenged by this more contemplative approach to mission, then I hope you will have gained some insight and confidence to begin on this path. I have seen it work and continue to work in the lives of SBNR spiritual seekers, and as an exciting and effective form of missional pioneering in very different contexts in the world. I finish with an excerpt from a profound prayer of Thomas Merton, which is pertinent for this contemplative missional journey.[3]

My Lord God,
I have no idea where I am going.
I do not see the road ahead of me.
I cannot know for certain where it will end.
Nor do I really know myself,
and the fact that I think I am following your will
does not mean that I am actually doing so.
But I believe that the desire to please you
does in fact please you.
And I hope I have that desire in all that I am doing.
I hope that I will never do anything apart from that desire.
And I know that if I do this you will lead me by the right road ...
I will not fear, for you are ever with me,
and you will never leave me to face my perils alone.
Amen.

Notes

1 Karl Rahner, 'Christian Living Formerly and Today', *Further Theology of the Spiritual Life I* (Theological Investigations, Vol. VII), trans. David Bourke (New York: Herder & Herder, 1971), p. 15.

2 If you want to keep up to date with what's happening or want to get in touch, please do see my website, ianmobsby.net, where these and other resources are listed.

3 Thomas Merton, *Thoughts in Solitude* (New York: Farrar, Straus & Giroux, 1958), p. 83.

Appendix 1

Script for the Meditation Group using an adapted John Main Approach

Suggested resources needed

InsightTimer for bell (app)
Book: *Silence and Stillness in Every Season: Daily Readings with John Main.*

Note on the recommended book

You need to be careful with some of the wording as it can be very Christian and religious. Vary the language by using 'Higher Power' or 'the divine' in place of 'God' or 'Jesus'. Sometimes I use 'Multifaceted God' instead of the Trinity. Sometimes the readings of the day cannot be adapted, so in these instances I will find a reading in the book that is more conducive to unchurched and dechurched SBNR spiritual seekers.

Suggested format

1. Music and welcome with candle lit
2. Welcome and introduction
3. Short relaxation (optional)
4. Reminder of adapted John Main meditation
5. Reading
6. Ending and benediction

Setting up

What is required? If starting at 6 p.m.
Be at venue for 5.30 p.m.
Put out chairs in circle, leaving two chairs outside circle for latecomers.
Put candle in middle and light when ready.
Put a ready-prepared card on each chair with a summary of the meditation method on it, something like: 'Welcome to meditation. Take some deep breaths and focus in on the anchor word "Ma-Ra-Na-Tha". There will be bells to start and end the meditation practice.'

At 5.45 p.m., set the atmosphere
Put on music and sit so that people feel you are ready for them when they come in.
Be visible as facilitator; sit centrally. Welcome people with eye contact, a smile and a verbal greeting and perhaps a handshake.
If they are new or feel new, explain that you're using the waiting time to dial down until the start at 6 p.m. Explanations help people feel at ease.

Start group sharp at 6 p.m., be online at 5.59 p.m.
Use InsightTimer app
Settings: Starting Bell: Basu
Duration: 20 Minutes
Interval bells: 3 single
Ambient Sound: Off
Ending Bell: Basu
Candle/matches

End of group: Remind people when group will meet again.

What to say!

(This is a guideline for leading the group.)

Welcome to this meditation group hosted by XXX, whether you come regularly or occasionally.
My name is XX and I am facilitating this evening's meditation.
Remember to switch off your phone.

In a few moments we will have a short relaxation exercise to help us prepare for meditation.

When it comes to the meditation, we will start with three bells and end with three bells. Every five minutes there will be a single intention bell to remind you to return to the anchor word practice.

Find a body posture where you are comfortable, yet not prone to nod off, keeping your back straight and your shoulders relaxed. The key to meditation is sitting still.

We use an anchor word-based meditation, which involves repeating a word to yourself in silence, using it as an anchor to hold your attention. The method we use was developed by the Benedictine Monk John Main, and we use it as our approach as it is a straightforward method.

The anchor word we suggest is 'Ma-Ra-Na-Tha', four equal syllables. It's suggested because it does not have an immediate meaning to distract our minds, although it literally means the presence of the divine.

(You could choose another word like 'Peace', or 'One', or whatever your current meditation practice word is.)

If you are a very visual person, or if your stress level is very high and closing eyes is difficult, then focus in on the candle flame, and, if you relax enough, close your eyes and hold an image of the flame in your mind as an anchor.

Meditation is a way of stilling a restless mind and allowing for spiritual connection beyond ourselves. But you can't stop the mind thinking. So your mind will almost certainly wander! When you notice this has happened, gently, without beating yourself up, bring your attention back to the anchor word.

For the majority of people, research has shown that forms of meditation help reduce stress, and promote integration, health and well-being. For a small minority, meditation might not help, particularly those who have experienced psychosis. If this is you then please do discuss meditation with your doctor or therapist. For all those who are spiritually searching on the path of inner awakening, we always recommend the need for a trained spiritual director or mentor to accompany you.

So let's form the group now.

If we could just go round and say our first name and how we are feeling in a few short sentences in this moment.

So now we go into a period of meditation.

If you wish to take your shoes off, please do.

You will hear lots of different noises from inside and outside this space. If your attention wanders, just bring it back to your anchor word.

(I think it beneficial to stand and stretch just before getting into the sitting position.) Please do use the green cards to help you to use the anchor word 'Ma-Ra-Na-Tha'.

Meditation Time

Meditation time 20 minutes

After ending, three bells

After Meditation Time

Reading/reflection – see workbook and choose a reading
Feedback time; any questions or comments?

Closing prayer in the tradition of John Main

May this group be a true spiritual home for the seeker,
a friend for the lonely, a guide for the confused.
May those who meditate here be strengthened by the divine Spirit
to serve all who come and to receive from the divine.
In the silence of this room may all the suffering,
violence and confusion of the world
encounter the power that will console,
renew and uplift the human spirit.
May this silence be a power to open the hearts of women and men
to the vision of the divine, and so to each other, in love and peace,
justice and human dignity.
May the beauty of divine life fill this group and the hearts of all who
meditate here with joyful hope.
May all who come here weighed down by the problems of humanity,
leave giving thanks for the wonder of human life.

Thank you and see you next week.

Appendix 2

Contemplative Worship Service Liturgy (adapted Anglican Version of the Service of the Word)

This service includes meditations and other spiritual practices. It begins with two minutes of silence. The gathering should last for approximately an hour, allowing time to explore either a particular spiritual practice or a text. Words in bold type are for the singing or saying of all. The mark '+' denotes points in the liturgy when participants cross themselves as an embodied devotional response to naming the presence of the Trinitarian God as an act of faith. You are completely free to cross yourself or not.

INVOCATION

Single-note chant said slowly with long breath at the end, sung three times

Be still and know that I am God
Be still and know that I am
Be still and know
Be still
be

We name the Triune God + who brings hope and centredness to our world:
God the Source, the Creator, the Father, who brings all existence into being.

Light candle

God the liberator, the Redeemer, the Son who brings us salvation showing us a better way to live, and who calls us to follow.

Light candle

God the Sustainer, the Guide, the Spirit, who sustains all life and enables us to grow and find peace and wisdom.

Light candle

God who is present to us now and always.
**+We meet in the name of God the Creator, God the Redeemer, and
God the Sustainer. Amen.**

WELCOME

We welcome all to this place and this time to worship God.
All are welcome.
Find here acceptance, love and peace.
Encounter the divine.
Relax, God is here.

*Five minutes of disciplined silence using bell
We recommend using the John Main approach of using an anchor
word – 'Ma-ra-na-tha' – to bring centredness to still us.
As thoughts and feelings arise, lay them aside and come back to the
anchor word. In time not only do we find stillness, but we are then free
to encounter God as our true selves free from distractions.*

INTRODUCTION

Who is it that we worship?
We gather to worship the Lord our God.
How do we worship?
**We worship you God
with the whole of our minds
with all of our strength
and with all our being,
and to love our neighbour as ourselves.**
May the prayers of our mouths and the meditations of our hearts be
acceptable in your sight, O Lord.

CONFESSION

Let us pause and remember the week that is just ending, and the week
that lies before us; as we do so, offering it back to God, both the good
and the challenging.

Three minutes of disciplined silence

As we sit before you, God, as a community seeking to model you, the divine and perfect body, we are aware of our own individual brokenness and delusions.

So easily we put ourselves before others. Too easily we allow our emotions and pains to overtake us and hurt others. We use our mouths and tongues given to build people up, to push people too high or knock people too low.

We have poisoned our planet, our souls and our nations.

Lord, forgive us our selfishness,

Lord forgive us.

Lord, forgive us for our false delusions,

Lord forgive us.

Lord, heal us from our brokenness,

Lord heal us.

Lord, free us to be the human 'becomings' you call us to be,

Lord restore us.

In a moment of silence, we commit to you the things that we know hold us back, which we bring into contemplative prayer as we seek to grow in depth and your love.

Silent pause for minimum of three minutes

Let us affirm our faith trusting in God's love for us:

May our attitude be as that of Christ,

who, being in very nature God, did not consider equality with God something to be grasped, but made himself nothing, being in the very nature of a servant,

and became obedient to death, even death on a tree. Amen.

Scripture or other readings with response activity if appropriate
Meditation/Contemplative prayer practice

THE PRAYERS

Let us pray for our community, and for the world. Feel free to pray aloud or silently.

At the end of each prayer let us say

Lord, in your mercy, hear our prayer.

A pause for silent prayer. Participants are invited to share petitions out loud or in the silence of their hearts.

We pray for all those known to us,
those for whom life is difficult and those who have difficult tasks to face,

those who find it difficult being themselves,
those who have difficult people to work with or difficult situations to
work in,
those who live in fear, in loneliness or in pain,
those who are ill, oppressed or poor.
Lord, in your mercy, hear the prayers of your people. Amen.

CONCLUSION

In this God, we find hope to envision us
today and tomorrow.
In this God, we find life, sustenance and a future.
In this God, we join in with the whole of creation giving thanks for all
that is good.
In this God, we may struggle in life, but we will not be overcome.
As we leave this place and this time,
teach us to care for all that is entrusted to us.
Motivate us to devote times of silence to encounter you.
Help us to share with others that which you have abundantly given us.
Lead us to see what is possible
when all seems impossible.
Enable us to stand up for justice
when all seems to oppress.
Help us to love generously and to give unconditionally.
Give us hope and joy so that we can keep walking this Christian road
less travelled.
Teach us, help us, lead us, enable us, give us, love us.

BLESSING

May we see and know God in the world that's around us.
May God take us through desert and take us through storms.
May God guide us,
protect us,
and give us a purpose.
Lord, give us your peace wherever you take us.
Bring us joyfully home.
Bring us joyfully home.
+In the name of God, Source, Liberator and Sustainer. Amen.

References

Allchin, A. M., *Participation in God: A Forgotten Strand in Anglican Tradition*, London: DLT, 1988.

Ammerman, Nancy Tatom, *Sacred Stories, Spiritual Tribes: Finding Religion in Everyday Life*, New York: Oxford University Press, 2014.

Anon, 'Consciousness', *Lexico.com*, https://www.lexico.com/definition/conscious ness, accessed 3.12.2020.

Anon, 'Purgative and Illuminative Stages', Societas Ignatianorum, IGNATIANS, 2023, https://societyofignatians.com/how-we-are-equipped/ignatian-asceto-mys tical-equipping/ascending-the-triple-storey-mountain/purgative-and-illumina tive-stages/, accessed 08.08.2024.

Aram, Catholicos, 'An Ecumenical Ethic for a Responsible Society in a Sustain-able Creation', in *Orthodox Perspectives on Mission: 17 (Regnum Edinburgh Centenary)*, ed. Petros Vassiliadis, Oxford: Regnum Books International, 2013.

Ashworth, Jacintha and Ian Farthing, 'Church Going in the UK: A Research Report from Tearfund on Church Attendance in the UK', Tearfund, April 2007, http://news.bbc.co.uk/1/shared/bsp/hi/pdfs/03_04_07_tearfundchurch.pdf.

Austin, Michael W., 'The Doctrine of Theosis: A Transformational Union with Christ', *Journal of Spiritual Formation & Soul Care* 8, no. 2 (2015), p. 186, https://dallaswillardcenter.com/wp-content/uploads/2016/03/Finalist_Doc trine-of-Theosis_Austin.pdf.

Barfield, Owen, *Saving the Appearances: A Study in Idolatry*, Oxford: Barfield Press, 2011.

———, *The Rediscovery of Meaning and Other Essays*, 2nd edn, Oxford: Barfield Press, 2013.

Bauman, Zygmunt, *Consuming Life*, Cambridge: Polity Press, 2007.

Benner, David G., *Opening to God: Lectio Divina and Life as Prayer*, London: IVP, 2021.

Bevans, Stephen B. and Roger P. Schroeder, *Constants in Context: A Theology of Mission for Today*, New York: Orbis Books, 2004.

Bevans, Stephen B. and Roger P. Schroeder, *Prophetic Dialogue: Reflections on Christian Mission Today*, New York: Orbis Books, 2011.

Boeve, Lieven, 'Religion after Detraditionalization: Christian Faith in a Post-Secu-lar Europe', *Irish Theological Quarterly* 70, no. 2 (2005), pp. 99–122.

———, 'Religion after Detraditionalization: Christian Faith in a Postsecular Europe', in *The New Visibility of Religion*, ed. Michael Hoelzl and Graham Ward, London: Continuum, 2008.

Boff, Leonardo and Frei Betto, *Mistica y Espiritualidad*, Madrid: Trotta, 1996.

Bourgeault, Cynthia, *Centering Prayer and Inner Awakening*, Plymouth, MA: Cowley Publications, 2004.

Bria, Ion, ed., *Go Forth in Peace: Orthodox Perspectives on Mission*, Geneva: WCC Mission Series, 1986.

Brueggemann, Walter, *The Psalms and the Life of Faith*, Minneapolis, MN: Fortress Press, 1995.

Campbell, Colin, 'I Shop Therefore I Know That I Am: The Metaphysical Basis of Modern Consumerism', in *Elusive Consumption*, ed. Karim M. Ekstrom and Helene Brembeck, Oxford: Berg, 2004, pp. 27–44.

Chatfield, Adrian, 'Prayer and Mission: Entering into the Ways of God', *Anvil Journal* 32, no. 1 (2016), pp. 11–18.

Coakley, Sarah, *God, Sexuality, and the Self: An Essay 'On the Trinity'*, Cambridge: Cambridge University Press, 2019.

Cray, Graham, 'Doors to the Sacred through Fresh Expressions of Church', in *Doorways to the Sacred: Developing Sacramentality in Fresh Expressions of Church*, ed. Phil Potter and Ian Mobsby, London: Canterbury Press, 2017, pp. 3–15.

Croft, Steven, Rob Frost, Mark Ireland, Anne Richards, Yvonne Richmond and Nick Spencer, *Evangelism in a Spiritual Age: Communicating Faith in a Changing Culture*, London: Church House Publishing, 2005.

Das, Rupen, 'Becoming a Follower of Christ: Exploring Conversion through Historical and Missiological Lenses', *Perichoresis* 16, no. 1 (2018), pp. 21–40.

David, Nicola, 'Developing the Community Habit', *Church Times*, 22 March 2011, https://www.churchtimes.co.uk/articles/2011/25-march/features/developing-the-community-habit, accessed 07.08.2024.

Davie, Grace, 'Believing without Belonging: Is This the Future of Religion in Britain?', *Social Compass* 37, no. 4 (1990), pp. 455–69.

Day, Abby, 'Non-Religious Christians', in *Post-secular Religious Practices*, ed. Tore Ahlbäck and Björn Dahla, Åbo/Turku, Finland: Donner Institute for Research in Religious and Cultural History, 2011, pp. 35–47.

Despotis, Athanasios, 'From Conversion According to Paul and "John" to Theosis in the Greek Patristic Tradition', *Horizons in Biblical Theology* 38, no. 1 (2016), pp. 88–109.

Dittmar, Helga, 'The Costs of Consumer Culture and the "Cage Within": The Impact of the Material "Good Life" and "Body Perfect" Ideals on Individuals' Identity and Well-Being', *Psychological Inquiry* 18, no. 1 (2007), pp. 23–31.

Dulles, Avery, *Models of the Church*, expanded edn, New York: Doubleday, 2002.

Dyer, Wayne, *Change Your Thoughts, Change Your Life: Living the Wisdom of the Tao*, London: Hay House, 2007.

Farias, M., E. Maraldi, K. C. Wallenkampf and G. Lucchetti, 'Adverse Events in Meditation Practices and Meditation-Based Therapies: A Systematic Review', *Acta Psychiatrica Scandinavica*, 142, no. 5 (2020), pp. 374–93.

Fiddes, Paul, *Participation in God: A Pastoral Doctrine of the Trinity*, Louisville, KY: Westminster John Knox Press, 2000.

Fleming, David L., *What is Ignatian Spirituality?*, Chicago, IL: Loyola Press, 2008.

Gama, Michael P., *Theosis: Patristic Remedy for Evangelical Yearning at the Close of the Modern Age*, Eugene, OR: Wipf & Stock, 2017.

Gorman, Michael J., *Abide and Go: Missional Theosis in the Gospel of John*, Didsbury Lectures Series, Eugene, OR: Cascade Books, 2018.

———, *Becoming the Gospel: Paul, Participation, and Mission*, Grand Rapids, MI: Eerdmans Publishing Co., 2015.

Graham, Matthew D., Marvin J. McDonald and Derrick W. Klaassen, 'A Phenomenological Analysis of Spiritual Seeking: Listening to Quester Voices', *The International Journal for the Psychology of Religion* 18, no. 2 (2008), pp. 146–63.

Greggs, Tom, 'Religionless Christianity and the Political Implications of Theological Speech: What Bonhoeffer's Theology Yields to a World of Fundamentalisms', *International Journal of Systematic Theology* 11, no. 3 (July 2009), pp. 293–308.

Habermas, Jürgen, 'Notes on Post-Secular Society', *New Perspectives Quarterly* 25, no. 4 (September 2008), pp. 17–29.

Heath, Elaine A., *The Mystic Way of Evangelism: A Contemplative Vision for Christian Outreach*, Grand Rapids, MI: Baker Academic, 2008.

Heelas, Paul and Linda Woodhead, *The Spiritual Revolution: Why Religion is Giving Way to Spirituality*, Oxford: Blackwell, 2005.

Heuertz, Phileena, 'Contemplative Activism as a Model for Mission', *Lausanne World Pulse Archives*, no. 12 (2011), pp. 1–7, http://www.lausanneworldpulse.com/perspectives-php/1481/12-2011, accessed 08.08.2024.

Hiebert, Paul G., 'Conversion, Culture, and Cognitive Categories', *Gospel in Context* 1, no. 4 (1978), pp. 24–9.

———, 'Sets and Structures: A Study of Church Patterns', in *New Horizons in World Mission: Evangelicals and the Christian Mission in the 1980s*, ed. David J. Hesselgrave, Grand Rapids, MI: Baker Book House, 1979, pp. 217–27.

———, 'The Category "Christian" in the Mission Task', *International Review of Mission* 72, no. 287 (1983), pp. 421–7.

Hobbs, Thomas, 'UK Ad Spend Hits Record £21.4bn as Digital Dominates Again', *Marketing Week*, 25 April 2017, https://www.marketingweek.com/2017/04/25/uk-ad-spend-digital/, accessed 07.08.2024.

Hornborg, Anne-Christine, '"Are You Content with Being Just Ordinary? Or Do You Wish to Make Progress and Be Outstanding?" New Ritual Practices in Contemporary Sweden', in *Post Secular Religious Practices*, ed. Tore Ahlbäck and Björn Dahla, Åbo/Turku, Finland: Donner Institute for Research in Religious and Cultural History, 2012, pp. 111–28.

Hyun Kyung, Chung, 'Who is Jesus for Asian Women?', in *Liberation Theology: An Introductory Reader*, ed. Curt Cadorette, Marie Giblin, Marilyn J. Legge and Mary H. Snyder, Maryknoll, NY: Orbis Books, 1992.

James, Oliver, *Affluenza*, London: Vermilion, 2007.

Jamison, Christopher, *Finding Sanctuary: Monastic Steps for Everyday Life*, London: Weidenfeld & Nicolson, 2010.

Johnson, Sheree, 'New Research Sheds Light on Daily Ad Exposures', SJ Insights, 29 September 2014, https://sjinsights.net/2014/09/29/new-research-sheds-light-on-daily-ad-exposures/, accessed 07.08.2024.

Kapolyo, Joe, 'The Conversion of Ubuntu – an African Vision of Human Nature', Cambridge Centre for Christianity Worldwide, 2010, www.cccw.cam.ac.uk.

Kim, Chong, 'From Imago Dei to Missio Dei', *Frontier Ventures* (blog), 21 September 2015, https://www.frontierventures.org/blog/imago-dei-2, accessed 08.08.2024.

Kraegel, Irene, 'Lovingkindness', *The Mindful Christian* (blog), 1 December 2018, https://www.themindfulchristian.com/blog/lovingkindness, accessed 08.08.2024.

Lambert, Yves, 'A Turning Point in Religious Evolution in Europe', *Journal of Contemporary Religion* 19, no. 1 (29 June 2006), pp. 29–45.

Lasch, Christopher, *The Culture of Narcissism: American Life in an Age of Diminishing Expectations*, New York: W. W. Norton, 1991.

Lazarus, Father, trans., *On the Prayer of Jesus: From the Ascetic Essays of Bishop Ignatius Brianchaninov*, Boston, MA: New Seeds, 2005.

Lyon, David, 'Being Post-Secular in the Social Sciences: Taylor's Social Imaginaries', *New Blackfriars* 91, no. 1036 (November 2010), pp. 648–64.

———, 'Memory and the Millennium', in *Grace and Truth in the Secular Age*, ed. Timothy Bradshaw, Grand Rapids, MI: Eerdmans Publishing Co., 1998, p. 248.

Main, John, *Silence and Stillness in Every Season: Daily Readings with John Main*, ed. Paul Harris, New York: Continuum, 2006.

——, *Word Into Silence: A Manual for Christian Meditation*, ed. Laurence Freeman, Norwich: Canterbury Press, 1980.

McCarthy, Marie, 'Spirituality in a Postmodern Era', in *The Blackwell Reader in Pastoral and Practical Theology*, ed. James Woodward and Stephen Pattison, Oxford: Blackwell, 2000.

McGuire, Meredith B., *Lived Religion: Faith and Practice in Everyday Life*, Oxford: Oxford University Press, 2008.

Mercadante, Linda A., *Belief without Borders: Inside the Minds of the Spiritual but not Religious*, Oxford: Oxford University Press, 2014.

Merton, Thomas, 'A New Christian Consciousness?', Essay for Monastic Novices, February 1967, https://conversi.org/wp-content/uploads/2018/03/A-New-Christian-Consciousness-TMerton.pdf.

——, *Conjectures of a Guilty Bystander*, New York: Doubleday, 1966.

——, *He is Risen*, Niles, IL: Argus Communications, 1975.

——, *New Seeds of Contemplation*, New York: New Directions Books, 1972.

——, *The Inner Experience: Notes on Contemplation*, ed. William H. Shannon, London: SPCK, 2003.

——, *The Wisdom of the Desert: Sayings from the Desert Fathers of the Fourth Century*, New York: New Directions, 1970.

——, *Thoughts in Solitude*, New York: Farrar, Straus & Giroux, 1958.

Mobsby, Ian, *Emerging and Fresh Expressions of Church: How are They Authentically Church and Anglican?*, London: Moot Community Publishing, 2007.

——, *God Unknown: The Trinity in Contemporary Spirituality and Mission*, London: Canterbury Press, 2012.

——, 'Engaging in Mission with the "Spiritual Not Religious", Drawing on a Trinitarian Dialogical Approach', *Anvil Journal of Theology and Mission* 35, no. 2 (July 2019), pp. 13–19, https://churchmissionsociety.org/anvil/engaging-in-mission-with-the-spiritual-not-religious-drawing-on-a-trinitarian-dialogical-approach-ian-mobsby-anvil-vol-35-issue-2/

——, 'The Beginnings of a Non-Directive Approach to Mission and Evangelism', *Anvil Journal of Theology and Mission* 36, no. 2 (July 2020), pp. 39–43, https://churchmissionsociety.org/wp-content/uploads/2022/05/Church-Mission-Society-Anvil-Volume-36-Issue-2-July-2020.pdf.

Moorcroft, Jennifer, *He is My Heaven: The Life of Elizabeth of the Trinity*, Washington DC: ICS Publications, 2015.

Nasimiyu-Wasike, Anne, 'Christology and an African Woman's Experience', in *Liberation Theology: An Introductory Reader*, ed. Curt Cadorette, Marrie Giblin, Marilyn J. Legge and Mary H. Snyder, Maryknoll, NY: Orbis Books, 1992, pp. 92–103.

Rahner, Karl, 'Christian Living Formerly and Today', *Further Theology of the Spiritual Life I* (Theological Investigations, Vol. VII), trans. David Bourke (New York: Herder & Herder, 1971.

Raja, Joshva, 'Mission in Theological Education: Review and Prospects', London: USPG, https://d3hgrlq6yacptf.cloudfront.net/uspg/content/pages/documents/1596795184.pdf.

Reith, Gerda, 'Consumption and its Discontents: Addiction, Identity and the Problems of Freedom', *The British Journal of Sociology* 44, no. 2 (2004), pp. 283–300.

Ricard, Matthieu, Christophe André and Alexandre Jollien, *In Search of Wisdom: A Monk, a Philosopher, and a Psychiatrist on What Matters Most*, 1st Eng. edn, Boulder, CO: Sounds True, 2018.

Root, Andrew, *Churches and the Crisis of Decline: A Hopeful, Practical Ecclesiology for a Secular Age*, Grand Rapids, MI: Baker Academic, 2022.

Schumaker, John, 'The Demoralised Mind', *New Internationalist*, 1 April 2016, https://newint.org/columns/essays/2016/04/01/psycho-spiritual-crisis.

Slee, Nicola, 'Apophatic Faithing in Women's Spirituality', *British Journal of Theological Education* 11, no. 2 (2001), pp. 23–7.

Smith, James K. A., *How (Not) To Be Secular: Reading Charles Taylor*, Grand Rapids, MI: Eerdmans Publishing Co., 2014.

Sudworth, Richard, *Distinctly Welcoming: Christian Presence in a Multifaith Society*, Bletchley: Scripture Union, 2017.

Tacey, David, *The Spirituality Revolution: The Emergence of Contemporary Spirituality*, London: Routledge, 2004.

Tanner, Kathryn, *Christ the Key*, Cambridge: Cambridge University Press, 2009.

Taylor, Barry, *Entertainment Theology*, Grand Rapids, MI: Baker Academic, 2008.

Taylor, Charles, *A Secular Age*, Cambridge, MA: Belknap Press of Harvard University Press, 2007.

Taylor, John V., *The Go-between God: The Holy Spirit and the Christian Mission*, London: SCM Press, 1975.

Turner, Bryan S., 'Post-Secular Society: Consumerism and the Democratization of Religion', in *The Post-Secular in Question: Religion in Contemporary Society*, ed. Philip Gorski, David Kyuman Kim, John Torpey, Jonathan VanAntwerpen, London: New York University Press, 2012, pp. 135–58.

Vernon, Mark, *A Secret History of Christianity: Jesus, the Last Inkling, and the Evolution of Consciousness*, Winchester: Christian Alternative, 2018.

——, 'Barfield and the Evolution of Consciousness', transcription following Zoom interview, 18 December 2020, https://docs.google.com/document/d/10 GVFCxYXj_MGzf3X3uMMuUqBWOToX7l3/.

Michael L. Yoder, Michael H. Lee, Jonathan Ro and Robert J. Priest, 'Understanding Christian Identity in Terms of Bounded and Centered Set Theory in the Writings of Paul G. Hiebert', *Trinity Journal* 30, no. 2, 2009, http://hiebertglobalcenter.org/wp-content/uploads/2014/04/199_Chang_Critical-Contextualisation.pdf, pp. 177–88.

Zahl, Simeon, *The Holy Spirit and Christian Experience*, Oxford: Oxford University Press, 2020.

Zizioulas, John D., *Lectures in Christian Dogmatics*, ed. Douglas H. Knight, London: T&T Clark, 2008.